PRAISE FOR
*The Girlfriends' Guide to Surviving
the First Year of Motherhood:*

"Invaluable. . .[a] funny, honest new volume."

—*L.A. Parent*

"If humor is the best medicine, Vicki Iovine has all the tonic a new mother should need. Her information comes from experience and her humor from the heart. An invaluable dialogue with a girlfriend who's been there, and got the most from her adventure."

—*Rocky Mountain News*

PRAISE FOR
The Girlfriends' Guide to Pregnancy:

"A chatty, candid, laugh-out-loud primer for unseasoned moms-to-be."

—*People*

"Iovine and her gaggle of Girlfriends are ready with reassuring and frequently irreverent advice."

—*Newsweek*

continued on next page . . .

Also by Vicki Iovine

THE GIRLFRIENDS' GUIDE TO PREGNANCY
THE GIRLFRIENDS' GUIDE TO PREGNANCY DAILY DIARY
THE GIRLFRIENDS' GUIDE TO SURVIVING THE FIRST YEAR OF MOTHERHOOD
THE GIRLFRIENDS' GUIDE TO TODDLERS

The Girlfriends' Guide to Getting Your Groove Back

Loving Your Family Without Losing Your Mind

VICKI IOVINE

A Perigee Book

Most Perigee Books are available at special quantity discounts for bulk purchases for sales promotions, premiums, fund-raising, or educational use. Special books, or book excerpts, can also be created to fit specific needs.

For details, write: Special Markets, The Berkley Publishing Group, 375 Hudson Street, New York, New York 10014.

Some of the Girlfriends' names have been changed to protect their privacy . . .
but Girlfriends, you know who you are.

Perigee Books
Published by The Berkley Publishing Group
A division of Penguin Putnam Inc.
375 Hudson Street
New York, New York 10014

First edition: April 2001

Published simultaneously in Canada.

The Penguin Putnam Inc. World Wide Web site address is
http://www.penguinputnam.com

Library of Congress Cataloging-in-Publication Data

Iovine, Vicki.
    The girlfriends' guide to getting your groove back : loving your family without losing your mind / Vicki Iovine.
        p. cm.
    ISBN 0-399-52630-7
    1. Motherhood. 2. Mothers—Psychology. 3. Mothers—Conduct of life. I. Title.

HQ759 .I67 2001
306.874'3–dc21

00-065793

Printed in the United States of America

10   9   8   7   6   5   4   3

I dedicate this book to my baby brother,

GREGG VANCE MCCARTY.

Thank you, my childhood partner and ally, for astonishing me with
your courage, enlightening me with your transcendent wisdom, and
allowing me to be in your life forever. You are my history, my perspective,
and my confidence. You are the repository of all our private jokes
that tickle me every single day.

Thanks, too, for sharing your love with our babies and for helping me
to teach them to love and care for each other and to do it with gratitude.

I love you to the ends of the universe and to the ends of my days.

Love,
"Anna"

Contents

Contents

A Note of Thanks

My gratitude to my family, friends and the world at large is so gigantic that describing it here would sound like a bad speech at the Academy Awards. Rather than list everyone specifically, let me just say that I can't face a day without the love, guidance and support of my husband, my children and my growing treasury of friends.

Here's what I have learned: humility. I know I am always safe in the knowledge that someone who loves me is standing nearby, just in case I start to totter.

Here's the other thing I learned, again: Having Girlfriends is as essential to my being as oxygen, and just as refreshing.

I pray that I live my life in a way that gives some of this magic back.

—Vicki Iovine

Why I Wrote This Book

I'm so confused. My kids are all in school, the little crises like allergies and sleep disorders are under control—my youngest has even memorized at least twenty of her friends' phone numbers and makes her own playdates. I've finally reached the oasis after ten years of crawling across the burning sands of colic, projectile vomiting, mastitis, Terrible Twos, and separation anxiety, and you'd think I'd finally hung my hammock between a couple of shady palms.

This is the stage in my mothering life when I would have thought I'd get my groove back, if I'd been able to even conceive of such a day. Pregnancy, new motherhood, and surviving toddlers were so all-consuming that I don't think I was ever really able to think far enough ahead to envision being the mother of four self-sufficient little humans. Perhaps I just assumed that the next step after teaching my kids to talk was teaching them how to do their own laundry before they went off to college.

You know how in any good chick flick, the romance is built up and detailed for nearly two hours and the story ends with the two stars getting married, or committed or "hooked up" or whatever, and then the credits roll? That's it, end of story. No one ever starts a movie with the wedding day and then dramatizes the actual marriage, unless of course, one of the partners becomes an alcoholic or dies. That's how I felt about having kids. First of all, it took more than three years of fertility treatments for me even to conceive our first baby. When the miracle finally occurred, I devoted my entire consciousness to pregnancy and babies. It was rather like joining a cult, I suppose; I looked at the entire universe through "Mommy-colored" glasses. And since I then proceeded to have four babies in six years, I guess you could say that my "prescription" was adjusted for the nearsightedness of little tiny kids. Not a day passed that I didn't talk myself down from a suicide leap (usually during those "mommy witching hours" between dinner prep and bed) by repeating my mantra, "This, too, shall pass"—I just never knew what it would pass into.

Now that I think about it, part of the problem was that I never tried to imagine the future by looking ahead; my future plans revolved around the past. I never pictured my life moving steadily from the frenzy and urgency of mothering babies and toddlers to starting a new career from scratch or retiring to Miami Beach to await the visits from my grandchildren. Someday I would wearily dream, I would go *back* to being the gal I was before I ever had kids. There were times when I was so overwhelmed by the demands of young motherhood that most of my fantasies involved moving back to the crummy studio apartment I shared with three people in college. Sure, it may have smelled like a kitty litter box, but it wasn't my mess and I couldn't have cared less who scooped it out.

Occasionally I would read something in the newspaper about a woman I went to school with being appointed Superior Court judge or running her own Silicon Valley venture capital firm and have daydreams about what it used to feel like when my biggest project was, well, ME. Or whenever we returned from a vacation and I was even more exhausted than before we left, I'd feel a yearning for the old days when vacation actually meant rest, sex, and mindless reading; not choreographed activities, repeated applications of sunblock, and arguing with the kids about hotel mini bar privileges.

The Epiphany

It seemed to happen overnight: one day I yelled up the stairs, "Everybody get in the car!" and they did it! No carseat installation required, no diaper bags to pack—heck, I didn't even need to fasten any seat belt but my own. I was so stunned that I couldn't get the key into the ignition. *It was so easy*; four kids old enough to understand verbal instructions, well-behaved enough to carry them out, and with the fine motor skills necessary to accomplish the task at hand. It was like the mommy version of the Emancipation Proclamation. By the time I had reversed out of the driveway, my moment of euphoria had settled into a couple of months of a minor depression. The format of my life remained the same, but the story was totally unfamiliar.

For a full decade my kids, in ever-increasing numbers, had depended on me to personally handle their most rudimentary needs—picking them up and tossing them into their carseats, stocking bottles and juice boxes for parching emergencies or nervous breakdowns, adjusting shoulder harnesses, and making sure to put on the driver's lock to prohibit them from opening their windows or doors without my permission. I'd been dreaming of this lighthearted liberty for eons, and it had finally arrived. In itself, it was truly a thing of beauty. In the bigger picture that is my life, it was like being orphaned in reverse.

Hot on the heels of this epiphany was my youngest child's entrance to a full-day kindergarten program. At that precise moment I seemed to be rendered obsolete; a dinosaur holdover from a dead era. Sure, they still needed me for a multitude of mommy services; everything from straight-ahead chauffeuring to the construction of geometry mobiles to signing notes excusing my nonathletes from P.E. when it was time for national fitness testing, but still, I knew deep in my heart that I had closed a chapter of my life. I had successfully launched my kids, and, theoretically at least, they could survive and thrive without me.

You're thinking to yourself, this is the time that we mothers dream of: that time when we are reasonably sure that we are out of maternity wear and no longer subscribing to The Right Start Catalog, no longer eating to maintain the quality of our breastmilk, and even free (with strategic planning) to carve out a couple of hours a week for fitness, meditation, or even reading that requires more time than that devoted during a visit to the toilet. Reproduction is no longer our hobby, nor is standing guard against such threats against life as choking on puzzle pieces, having reactions to vaccinations, growing an incurable diaper rash, or falling out of the crib headfirst.

In other words, there was nothing standing between me, the mother of kids, now ages six to twelve, and the spontaneous, flirtatious, and lighthearted me that thrived pre-children. Without really thinking about it in any earnest manner, I realized that my subconscious plan had been something to this effect: I would marry, launch my career, get pregnant, adjust my career plans a bit, get pregnant again, bolster up my tattered marriage, readjust my career to allow for working at home or not at all, getting pregnant AGAIN, recovering from postpartum depression, forget what my career was in the first place, get pregnant yet again, patch up the marriage here and there as my need for sleep lessened, and then move back into my college dorm, rejoin the intramural water polo team, read for hours every afternoon, and skip school occasionally for a gang drive to the coast or a visit to the Renaissance Fair.

Foolish as it may sound to you, I subconsciously believed that once I completed my tour of duty as the gestator and monster killer of my family, I would morph back into the spirited, carefree, semi-irresponsible gal I had been when my biggest concerns were scheduling finals early enough to get to Mexico or Hawaii as early as possible to guarantee the maximum Spring Break. What I learned instead is something I suspected but denied on some level:

The Road to Maternity is a One-Way Street

This may sound self-evident to some of you, but I suspect that I'm not the only delusional woman in my neighborhood. I simply had no pictures or frame of reference for what a woman who'd moved beyond childbearing, nursing, and fading stretchmarks was supposed to look and act like. Sure, I had my own mother and her friends to draw upon, but I didn't see any correlation. I'd been raised with the Pill, I'd had a career that partly defined me (if only in my hazy recollection), and I was a much younger and hipper "mature" woman than they were. I planned to live to be at least 100 and reaching the age of forty put me on the safe side of middle age. I still loved rock and roll (and now hip hop), I still wanted to seduce my mate with more than Viagra and a couple of stiff drinks, and I sincerely yearned (although was loathe to admit it) to get a catcall whenever I passed a construction site. I still looked more to Cameron Diaz for hairdressing advice than to Hillary Clinton.

What the Girlfriends Had to Say

If you've read any of my other books, you already know that I'm convinced that 99 percent of everything I'd ever need to know to survive marriage and motherhood can be learned from my Girlfriends. The problem was, I wasn't seeing nearly as much of my Girlfriends as I had in the first couple of years. In fact, if it weren't for birthday parties, trick-or-treating, and playdate drop-offs and pickups, we'd rarely see each other. When we were all pregnant or running after toddlers, we were still the bosses of our own social lives. Our friends' kids were our own kids' friends. They went where we went and hung with the people we wanted to hang with.

A by-product of having schoolage children, however, is that they drag all manner of strangers into your life. Fortunately for me, the first pal my oldest son foisted on me was Bennett. I still recall the day Bennett's mom, my now-cherished Girlfriend Shirley, and I introduced ourselves to each other in the preschool office with the words, "I guess we'd better be friends, since our sons already are." Now, of course, I'd hang on to Shirley even if our boys stopped talking, but at the time it was kind of scary and foreign territory.

The older kids get, the more obvious their talents, interests, and tastes become. If you happen to have a little jock, you'd better be prepared to spend a lot of time with the mothers of other jocks. If you have a dancer, you're going to have to be friendly with the other moms standing in the wings with tutus, hairbrushes, and face glitter. If you have a child who has to be forcibly restrained to read a chapter book, get ready to make friends in the parking lot as you wait for after-school tutorials to end. The Girlfriends who saw you through water retention and anal retentiveness might not be part of this new social circle. That often means that what you and your new friends have in common is a lot more about what your kids share than what you do. Therefore, you might find yourself feeling a little adrift while trying to get your groove back.

Another thing that happens as we pass out of the stage when our pregnancy hemorrhoids are still acting up and we can't get a mammogram without expressing milk: We begin to settle back into our careers outside the home. I'm not suggesting that this is a smooth transition, but, hey, maternity leave can only last so long. Unless you work as a Mary Kay cosmetics salesperson, being back at work seriously cramps a woman's social life with her Girlfriends.

I hate to admit it, but as your Girlfriend, it's my job to speak the unspeakable: Sometimes we're so overextended with our husbands, kids, careers, and domestic business that making time for a beloved Girlfriend can seem like just one more chore. It breaks my heart to say so, and I honestly believe that getting back into the groove is only fun if you do it with your Girlfriends, but I don't know a mother of active kids who doesn't feel like she's bobbing in a sea of unreturned phone calls, belated birthday cards, and conversations cut short by the need to pick the kids up from water polo practice. The love is still there in full force, but the intimacy gets significantly diluted by other demands that tug harder on our apron strings; especially because a great Girlfriend never guilts you into sharing yourself with her . . . while your mate, your kids, and your career all use guilt as their weapon of choice.

What the Experts Say

The bottom line here is that there are no experts to guide us through this transition into this new world of Mommydom. Believe me, I've checked. There are books on what your first grader needs to know to be culturally literate, books on sibling rivalry, books on time management for working moms (try looking in the Mythology section of your local bookstore), books on learning disabilities, books on raising geniuses, and books on picking the right college for your second grader. Nowhere, however, is there a book telling mothers how to define and enrich their lives once they move on to being parents of "middlers"—no longer babies and not yet teenagers. Not a single book, at least that I could find, charting a navigational course from mothers who have looked their marriages in the face and seen divorce or redoubled their efforts to live out their lives together. And nary a word has been published about helping us discover who we become once we emerge from the underground maze in which most new mothers live.

When Does it Get to Be About Me?

Theoretically, this middle time of motherhood is when we should be revving up at work, rediscovering long-abandoned hobbies and interests, and reacquainting ourselves with the person who has been in the trenches with us as we learned to become moms. Aside from a growing trend encouraging women to discover the "goddess" within them, I can't find anything that helps me know when my figure no longer belongs in hip-hugging pants, how to make the transition from fireman-mom (in which you spend your days running around looking for flare-ups and extinguishing them) to manager/counselor mom (when the parenting problems are a lot trickier and can't always be put out with a good squirt of water) or when to start wearing shoes with heels again.

More critically, my bookstore browsing left me feeling pretty alone to deal with the life changes that strike me as catastrophic but are actually statistically normal. For example, who gets custody of me when a couple within our group gets divorced? How do my husband and I reassign the parenting responsibilities when my career takes a surge? How do I respond to a sad child who says she wishes I would never leave the house to go the office because "she misses me deep in her heart"? And how do I deal with the pain of learning that my own child is moving down a life path that I never intended and, frankly, would have preferred to avoid altogether? And how do I ever figure out what fun and fulfillment feel like now?

Here's the Book We've Been Waiting For

Right from the get-go, I want to make it clear to you, Girlfriends, that I didn't appoint myself to write this book because I have figured out what our groove is and how to get it back. I may have a few good ideas that I've gleaned along the way, but between you and me, it's been a whole hell of a lot easier stating the problems than finding the answers. I'm still on this journey and I'm only groovy about fifty percent of the time.

What I can promise you, however, is that I've devoted two years to living in the question and stalking any woman who even looks like she might have some insight. Therein lies the value of this book. *The Girlfriends' Guide to Getting Your Groove Back* is a collection of anecdotal information and wisdom from women who have already begun this wild ride. At the very least, you'll find tremendous reassurance in the fact that, no matter how out of kilter you may feel, one of us Girlfriends will share stories about the times when she wanted to pull the blankets up over her head and never get out of bed again. And, if I've done my best job, you'll also find tried-and-true tools for getting bits and pieces of your groove back—it's up to you to put all the pieces together, my friend. If we're lucky, you'll get a chuckle right when you're considering putting everyone in boarding school and moving back in with your parents.

These really are the golden years of motherhood, of that I am certain. My kids are my companions, my inspirations, my moral compasses. Whether my daughter is telling me that I have lipstick on my teeth out in public or my son is reminding me that it wouldn't kill me to get out of bed an hour earlier to help feed the homeless before school, they make me better for knowing them. The fact that they actually *love* me is frosting on the cake. They give me a front-row seat from which to witness history being made, if only I can muster the energy to keep up with all the historical events they can squeeze into a day. No matter how blasé I might have become about the thrill of touching a sea anemone or keeping a kite in the air, I'm infected by their wonder. Looking at the world through Mommy-colored glasses may seem limiting at first, but ultimately, those lenses make everything look unique, exquisite, and miraculous. I'd much rather look at a T-Rex through the eyes of an eight-year-old than the museum curator's. I missed so much my first trip through this life, and it's a blessing to get another run-through.

It's also a blessing to be able to reinvent myself, yet again. Just as I stopped being a lawyer by the time my third child came along, I can consider grooming myself for yet another career change. I can find a deeper romance and friendship with my mate (or in some Girlfriends' cases, NOT!), I'm still youngish, I'm still optimistic, and there's still a lot of living to do. Remember, the teen years are right around the corner, and all hell could break loose then.

Top Ten Goals of Getting
Your Groove Back

10. Finding a personal style that is as good as that of someone you admire.

9. Believing that you can seduce anyone, even your mate, if you really want to, even if you are experiencing premenstrual bloat.

8. Learning to embrace as a sign that you are fulfilling your destiny a constant sense of guilt over someone's needs not being fully met.

7. Rediscovering the Girlfriends who brought you this far and reaching out to the ones who will help you the rest of the way.

6. Waking up each morning and overcoming the impulse to hunker back down into the bed, pulling the covers up over your head.

5. Accepting that you may not be perfect, but you are more than good enough.

4. Remembering what your hobbies and interests used to be and recommitting to them.

3. Learning to "triage" your responsibilities: dealing with the most critical first; dealing with the serious, not life-threatening or scarring, either physically or emotionally, second; and ignoring everything that falls into the third category.

2. Saying a gracious goodbye to the girl you used to be and hello to the woman you have become since sacrificing your body and mind to motherhood.

1. Stop waiting for your mate to wake up and smell the coffee so that he might relieve you of the care for your in-laws, of knowing the children's innoculation schedules, and remembering when the tooth fairy owes someone a visit.

It's a Marathon,
Not a Sprint

Grooving, Now and Forever

Not too long ago, I emerged from my writing cocoon to have coffee with my Girlfriend Sally, the mother of two terrific grown children. I told her the occasion for celebration was that I'd finally discovered the key to getting my groove back, just in the nick of time, since I happened to be writing a book about it. As I vaguely recall, my epiphany consisted of something about wearing higher heels to look taller and thinner and subscribing to Oprah's magazine. Sally tapped her latte cup against mine and congratulated me, but still, she seemed to be holding something back. Not in the mood to hear that I was delusional about my "eureka" moment, I pretended not to notice how hard she had to purse her lips to keep her own perspective from pouring out. Still, as a journalist of sorts, I could never deliver a book to you, my Girlfriends, that failed to take in another valid point of view.

"Have you realized yet that the real truth about getting your groove back is that you have to do it over and over again for the rest of your life?" Sally sweetly inquired while I was busying myself with the half-Equal, half-Sweet 'n Low mixture I use in my coffee to spread out my chances of getting rat cancer from all the chemicals.

"Huh?" I replied, nearly spilling the latte over both of us and suddenly feeling that panicky sweat that humidifies the hair surrounding my face. "What do you mean, 'over and over'?" What was she telling me? I'd spent months and months on this book just framing the problem of what it means to lose our groove, then even more time struggling with gathering some solutions, no matter how feeble, for all of us in search of our grooves.

It seems to me that our grooves are like towers made by a deck of cards. Each card represents a single issue including everything from our sex lives to our acceptance of our children's true natures to what we wear to whether we attend to our physical wellness to trying to find that magical balance between work and family. Take one card out, and the groove tower tumbles. That alone seemed like a tremendous epiphany to me, and I guess I believed that just dealing with these issues once and restoring our towers would be an incredible feat. I sort of trusted that this one gargantuan effort would finally bring me the satisfaction, fulfillment, and balance that I yearn for in my life. Can you blame me for hoping the high heels were my trump card?

Well, according to my Guru Girlfriend Sally, the most we can expect from this great endeavor to recapture our grooves is the experience and strength to do it again, and again and again. Like a ship that has a hole in it, you can bail out most of the water and enjoy a patch of smooth sailing for a while, but sooner or later you're going to find yourself knee-deep in the tide of change. You either stand still and whine that you've already bailed out the water once or you remember where you placed the bucket and bend over to start bailing again.

"But once your kids are somewhat independent and your marriage rescued," I asked frantically, "what else do you have to worry about?"

"Let's see, where do I start?" asked Sally, trying hard not to sound too patronizing. "How about after you've managed to reestablish your career and your husband's work requires that you move the family across the country? Or how about when one of the grandparents moves in with you because he's alone and sick? Then again, we could talk about the predictable trials that even a 'good' teenager will put you and your co-parent through. And what if you find a lump? What if one of your children has a learning disorder? What about what happens when your children leave the nest and your reason for existence flies away with them? There's always the prospect of menopause, of course, and what about your plans for retirement? Will your children marry appropriately? Will they get good jobs in a nearby town or start their families two airplane connections away? When one gets a divorce, will you still be able to see your beloved grandchildren? And, speaking of grandchildren, can you even imagine a passel of little kids calling you 'Granny' right out there in public?"

Although the prospect of redefining myself and coming to terms with unexpected (hell, even the pretty *predictable*) sea changes in my life as a mother and woman had, up till Sally, seemed like a onetime proposition, the truth of what she said rang in my head like the Liberty Bell before it cracked. Some little voice inside my head had been placating me for the last thirteen years by insisting that all the changes and upheavals and loss of control that I'd experienced since I first joined the Sorority of Moms would be put to rest as soon as I'd found the most efficient and expedient way to return to the glory and balance of my prepregnancy life.

Like you, my Girlfriend, I couldn't envision, nor did I want, a life that didn't include my beautiful babies. I had no doubt that they were the greatest, most amazingly significant achievement of my humble existence. I guess what I pictured was a kind of circle; a journey in which I picked up a few fabulous souvenirs from other universes I'd visited along the way, be they little people or just more wisdom or examples of how much larger my heart had grown, but a journey that ended back where I started. I'd be this fabulous mother, but I'd have the body of a bride, the style of a starlet, the wisdom of Job, the professional accomplishment expected of a Phi Beta Kappa, and the sexual appetite of that girl who could spend an entire flight from Los Angeles to New York thinking of tantalizing games and positions to try out on her beloved. Like Dorothy, I assumed that once I'd clicked my ruby slippers together a couple of times, I'd be back in Kansas for business as usual. That was what getting my groove back meant to me.

What Sally told me changed my entire plan. She was telling me that the journey was a line, not a circle. Most terrifying, she was telling me that the finish line was nowhere in sight, but that the race had to continue. Whether I felt up to it or not really didn't matter, because that's just the way it was. I could either keep running, adjusting, and reevaluating, or I could fall out of the race and have my tarnished groove thrown out on top of me.

Setting the Pace

Shocking though Sally's insight was, I wasn't completely surprised. You will remember that it was I who told you in earlier Girlfriends' Guides that motherhood is a marathon, not a sprint, and not to waste all your energies on the breast-or-bottle controversy, or the proper age for potty training or whether your brilliant child should be reading by kindergarten. I knew to expect the rejection I'd feel when my daughter's best friend wanted to enlarge her social circle, the sense of ineptitude I'd know when my son couldn't put a project together for the science fair without the intervention of three engineers and a computer programmer from my office, and the shame I'd suffer when I waited patiently in the school parking lot to pick my child up after a three-day Astro Camp sleepaway *after he'd only been gone for two days.* Even though I suspected that making it through the long haul of my life as a mother required that I stay light on my feet about all matters pertaining to raising my children, I realized that when it came to my long haul as a woman who happened to have children, I was wearing a pair of cement sneakers.

I know there are lots of women out there achieving more and sweating much less than I, but I swear, I'm running as fast as I can. I am hustling every single day, just to meet the demands of running our house, turning in the unending medical history forms for my kids' schools, providing a comfortable and welcoming home for my husband (yeah, I have one of *those* kinds of marriages), keeping in touch with my mother and mother-in-law, faking my way through algebra (yet again), and meeting the deadlines of my writing career. I start thinking about summer camps for the kids in April, I prepare for their return to school in July and start thinking about how we'll celebrate Christmas by October, at the latest.

I do my best to keep true to those plans and commitments and end up feeling like one of those crazy dogs that chases cars to bite the tire. Then Mother Nature looks down from her place in the heavens and hits the brakes. One of my kids breaks a bone and needs surgery to fix it. Another one needs to be assessed to see if she has attention deficit disorder. My mother needs heart surgery, and I'm getting my period every two weeks. This is when the rubber hits the road, with my teeth lodged in it.

They Keep Moving the Finish Line

Raising children reminds me of roasting a turkey; it looks like it's done, all golden brown and crispy on the outside, then you take it out to carve it and realize it's not done cooking. And since the turkey is the most important part of a meal, no good cook begins making the salad or steaming the vegetables till it's done. I guess I just kept waiting for the turkey to "drip clear juices" before I could focus on all the aspects of my life that had been neglected. The day we removed all the babyproofing from the cupboards, stairs, and toilets and put away the last carseat seemed like a reasonable cooking time. My groove would come naturally to me and I would start focusing more on my job, getting fit, learning another language, and visiting art museums. And, of course, my darling life partner would be there beside me, sharing my new interests.

How does that old Yiddish proverb go: "If you want to make God laugh, tell Him your plans"? Well, God must be splitting a rib up there when he eavesdrops on me. It's been three years since we got around to removing all the safety latches and passing the carseats on to the local Head Start program, and by my calculations, I should be ready for a marathon, speak Spanish fluently, and volunteer as a docent at the Getty Museum. Instead, I find myself overwhelmed by a whole new set of responsibilities, crises, and agendas that actually make me yearn for the less complex time when my kids were babies.

When I was trying to get pregnant, I could imagine, sort of, a life of nursing, burping, changing, worrying about daycare, and avoiding all open pools and parking lots. What I never imagined was doing home-work every night till nine or ten P.M., watching my child strike out at every Little League game, comforting a little girl who wasn't included in a slumber party, or dealing with several little people who wanted to negotiate every rule I set. Even more shocking, I never imagined what it would feel like to fight with my husband and not be able to walk out the door and drive off into the sunset.

I may be slow, but I'm not stupid. It only stands to reason that these life surprises won't just disappear one day. If things keep going this way, I can safely expect to move right into another life phase where I have to explain what condoms are for, why I don't think *all* teenagers should get their driver's license at sixteen years of age, and why teen pregnancy only looks interesting in the movies. If I keep waiting till the day when I think my kids are fully baked, I will never get that salad made. That leads me to two conclusions:

First, if I'm going to keep pulling this family train, I should take better care of myself.

Second, if I want to do anything with my life besides raise my kids, I'd better get started because the race has already started.

In fact, it might have started several years ago, and I was just too distracted to notice.

We're the Locomotives Pulling This Train

I ran into one of my closest Girlfriends, Marty, recently at *yet another* school fund-raising function and immediately asked her whether she'd gotten the lump on her neck checked out by a doctor. She'd shared her lump discovery with me while we were wandering around the zoo as chaperones for our children's class, and I'd been fretting ever since. There's something awful happening to me these days; I no longer dismiss all physical ailments as temporary, insignificant lapses in our general robust health. I don't know if it's because I personally feel more fragile or if I always extrapolate from the simplest little clogged pore to the orphaning of children. It's so much more fun and interesting to be sick on your own, but when you might be unable to meet your motherly duties, it really sucks.

Anyway, she had, indeed, seen the doctor and been told she had a lymph infection and would be able to clear it right up with antibiotics. She was clearly relieved, but she jokingly said that she kind of wished that the doctor had insisted on putting her in the hospital for a few days of rest and recuperation. I knew exactly what she meant, only when I have those same secret wishes, there's not a jokey tone for miles.

I know this makes me sound like an idiot or a wussie, but I have had the deep desire more than once to just drop the kids off at school and keep going straight to the hospital to beg them to put me in a room with a TV and an intravenous drip of some mild sedative. You know as well as I do that just getting a cold or a migraine isn't nearly as much fun as it used to be. Instead of curling up on the couch with a pot of tea and the television remote, most of us have to live our regular lives with the added impediments of nausea, pounding headaches, and drippy noses. PLUS you might have to find time in an already frantic day to go to a doctor, and everyone knows you'd rather phone that in—after all, you just need the prescription for the antibiotic or the painkiller, and you're going to ignore the doctor's advice to rest in bed for a couple of days.

This is one of the most astonishing effects of looking at the world through Mommy-colored glasses: We become almost psychic in our ability to detect a fever in our kids at forty paces, and yet can live with walking pneumonia for two or three months, only pausing to wonder why we fall asleep standing up in the checkout line at the grocery store. If only my own mother still had the authority to keep me home from school and in bed, sipping chicken soup . . . I crave a world in which a note from my parent could insulate me from all responsibilities until I feel up to facing them again.

Who Sets This Pace, Anyway?

Most of my Girlfriends live like this, too. We create lives that run so fast on all cylinders that we haven't got an inch of tread left on our tires when we most need the traction. It's like motherhood abhors a vacuum. Hey, if you have time for a regular exercise routine or to read the newspaper from front to back, you really should be volunteering more in the kids' classrooms, heading up the neighborhood hospitality group, or cleaning your husband's drawers.

Where in the world does this insanity come from? I have my suspicions. First, I think the constant depictions in the media of other people's apparently perfect and significant lives is a big culprit. Martha Stewart alone has raised my blood pressure at least 10 percent. Then there's that nasty inclination so many women have that I call Competitive Mothering. These are the unGirlfriendly gals who show up completely groomed at school drop-off, drive cars that show no debris of spilled sunflower seed shells and empty diet Coke cans, who dash confidently off to work and mention how "terrific" they feel now that they get up at five A.M. every morning to do yoga and spinning classes. I don't know about anyone else, but after seven or eight years of sleeping around the schedules of my kids, I have turned into a bed hog. I awake each morning, no matter how close to eight hours of sleep I've gotten, thinking that I cannot possibly get up and face the music of another day. Psychiatrists call this depression, but I don't think that's it. I think it's entirely rational for me to be fearful about beginning a day that will have me running faster than a hysterical roadrunner until I collapse again into my beloved bed.

Take my Girlfriend Shirley, for example. She hasn't called me from anywhere other than her car in four years. I swear to God, she lives there. She has three teenagers who are, unfortunately for Shirley's groove, very athletic. They're so good, in fact, that she has to drive them miles away from home so that they can compete against the best athletes Southern California can offer. We all know this would be impossible in itself, if only for its tedium, but Shirley works, too, selling fine clothing and jewelry in trade shows and home parties. That means that in addition to loading her Suburban with everything from bats, mitts, and soccer balls to cleats and changes of clothes, she has three fifty-pound suitcases of fine fashion to hoist in, too.

Neither my Girlfriends, Marty, Shirley, or I would suggest for a moment that we dislike any single thing we do. In many ways, we are enjoying the most gratifying and stimulating times of our lives. It's the totality of it all that kicks us in the butt. We don't want to give up a single thing, but we all know that we're doing far more than we can enjoy or even endure.

So, even more potent than any television propaganda or pressure from our effervescent and in-control colleagues, I confess that I think we are our own worst enemies. I'm not saying that we all should sit back on the new chaise lounges we've just bought for the backyard and dig into Oprah's Book Club Selections till we've read them all. Hey, we have jobs to do, people who depend on us, and usually, money to be earned to support them. Why do we keep running ourselves down without staying in shape for a life that should, knock wood, last another fifty years?

It's because we are so blinded by motherhood that we lose sight of all the other parts of life that matter to us, that's what I think. Either because of wishful thinking or sheer shortsightedness, we can't see past the day when our children will be launched into their own independent lives. We want them to be great, we want them to have the opportunities we didn't have, and we want them to love us so much that they would never dare utter about us any of the crummy things that so easily roll off our tongues about our own parents. We want to be loved, admired, significant, and *never left in their dusty pasts.*

Were parents of generations past so neurotic and frantic? I don't think so, but I can't speak for the universe. First of all, the rules and behavior seemed more defined and easily followed than they do now. Some mothers had jobs outside the home, but not in the numbers they do now. Marriages tended to last longer, too. And, perhaps most important, the community provided a prop for parents trying to keep a protective tarp of concern and care over their kids' heads. In my neighborhood, if you smart-mouthed the lady next door or were discovered with a pack of matches by the father of your partner in pyromania, not only would you get a verbal lashing from the adult witness, but your parents were sure to hear about it sometime before dinner.

In our generation, we often get pregnant within the asexual environments of our jobs (well, I don't really mean the *act* actually happened right there, but the repercussions are experienced in that setting). As I mentioned in *The Girlfriends' Guide to Pregnancy*, many of us don't "grow in the garden in which we were planted," which means that the tribe of women we might naturally rely on to help us raise our kids has disappeared. A lot of good it does a mom when her sister has taken a teaching job in Auckland, New Zealand, her mother has retired to Florida, and her school friends haven't been heard from since that agonizing high school reunion you attended ten years ago! I believe that if we had stronger support groups around us, as in the form of a whole city block of blood relatives, we might be able to shoo the kids out the door and into Grandma's or Auntie Janet's so that we could really succumb to a case of cramps, the world would be a more hospitable place. It also wouldn't hurt to have several wiser women around to keep us in check when we were spinning like Tasmanian Mommies.

One is Silver and the Other Gold

In the early years of my pregnancies and new motherhood, I aggressively sought out other Girlfriends who were in the same boat. Lucky for me, I found several and we embraced each other with an affection and trust that I still have never again found in a friend. My Girlfriend Nikki maintains that there are only four windows of opportunity for making lifelong friends: high school, college, first job, and pregnancy/new motherhood. I suggested to her that I thought there was a fifth window, also known as widowhood, but she told me to bite my tongue and keep the evil eye at bay, so pretend I never mentioned it.

The Girlfriends I acquired during the pregnancy/early motherhood window often had nothing else in common with me besides a delivery date near mine, but the really golden ones were those who also shared my concerns about returning to work, my dilemma about whether to pump my milk at the office to keep nursing for six months to a year, and my constant ambivalence about being able to work, be a wife, and be a mother simultaneously. No matter how inconvenient, I was the first to call reunions of my Lamaze class or drive thirty miles to connect with a Girlfriend who had a baby my baby's age and crises my crises' ages. While much of my life seemed beyond my control, I was the boss of my friendships and those of my babies.

There came a day, however, when the babies began to have minds of their own. They had absurd ideas, like inviting strangers' kids to their birthday parties and joining Brownie troops with a bunch of girls from first grade. I confess, I fought it, but I knew I had to follow their lead and let them branch out from the protective boughs of the charter members of the Girlfriends' Family Tree.

By the time the new Girlfriends starting making their way into my heart, everything was different. Simply stated, I hadn't kept enough time and energy in reserve to nurture these unexpected blessings. We didn't have long leisurely afternoons watching our toddlers splashing in a blue plastic pool to bond sharing secrets about how our sex life was surviving the parental onslaughts, who had a secret crush on their Tae Bo trainer, or who worried that she was pregnant again, at least a year ahead of schedule. More to the point, these friendships were no longer about ME, they were determined to a large extent by my children.

The new Girlfriends were great, but they were already on the parenting conveyor belt and so much of our getting to know each other was punctuated by shared complaints about how hard the second-grade homework is, how devastating it is when your child is the only one who still doesn't understand phonics, and who would drive whom to the next weekend's dance competition or T-ball practice. Yes, we struggled to get to know each other in the bleachers, in the buses, or sitting in the waiting room of the orthodontist's office, but there was little time spent getting to know each other over a cup of coffee while we nursed at one or another of our houses. We were on kids' turf and usually introduced ourselves not by saying, "Hi, I'm Vicki Iovine," but rather, "I'm Jessica's mom." We could become quite intimate as "parents of" and never once discuss how we spent the rest of our life and dreams. I swear to you, I stood beside "Rosemary's mother" for two years on the local softball field before either of us discovered that her company and I were developing a T.V. show together. It just never came up once. The erosion of our groove was happening and we didn't even know it.

Public Opinion, Our Worst Enemy

After all this evidence (plus your own poignant recollections), it's obvious that we are selling ourselves short, both as mothers and as Girlfriends, by living our lives as though we are being graded for effort, not fulfillment. When we overextend ourselves, we get all sorts of societal applause. Our mothers-in-law begin to think that, perhaps, their darling boys have found a girl who doesn't just sit around in her gym clothes all day eating Power Bars. We match up to the Superwoman descriptions in *Cosmo* quizzes, and we feel entitled to our subscriptions to *Working Mother*. Most pathetically, those of us who live our lives as if they were one big itinerary, the bigger the better (hey, I thought that was the men's mantra!) are gratified, even if we're not particularly *grateful*.

It goes without saying, at least in my little world, that the Mommy Triage goes something like this: Meet all real and imagined needs of your children first. Career comes second. Any attention or caloric investment left goes to the home and its empty refrigerators and stopped-up toilets. After that, we devote our zombie-like bodies to our mates and hope that they don't notice that they're sleeping with a pod, not a real human being.

My Girlfriend Johanna reminds me that she is a clear exception to this rule because she finds time for herself and her spirit several times a week, even though she is the mother of four kids. When I've pressed her

13

on this point, however, her list of indulgences includes facials (to stay fresh and younger looking), waxes (because her husband happens to like that new Van Dyke–like beard cut for her pubic hair) and working out with a personal trainer (since, as she says, her husband Berry had a rule they refer to as NFCA; meaning No Fat Chicks Allowed). Maybe I'm just envious, since my butt is spreading while I write these words and my pubic hair threatens to encroach on my upper thighs if I don't invest in something like a Weedwacker really soon, but I don't think those "indulgences" do a damn thing to give Johanna an extra source of inner strength or resilience should a crisis be dumped on her head like a raw egg on Halloween.

Seize the Moment . . . Now

From the moment when it became clear that our helpless infants' needs would be replaced by our preschoolers' wants, we should have seen this job for what it was; as essential and unchangeable as our height and tendency to sunburn. If we were going to sit around waiting to grow, shrink, or stop freckling before we went out into the world, we were going to miss our day at the beach, Girlfriend.

Before you get defensive and hand me a laundry list with all the exceptional reasons for putting your life at the bottom, don't bother. Just because I may have one hand on this bull, it doesn't mean I have him by the horns. I wake up every day and hope that I'll be wiser and more able to allow me to be the mom I want to be, as well as the woman I always wanted to be when I grew up. I'm already pretty grown, and I don't have this philosophy fully integrated into my life yet. Let's just make a pact to carve out the fulfillment of our own precious dreams while helping the dreams of the people we adore to come true.

With the hindsight of a gal who still has several eggshells in her hair from Mother Nature's little cosmic pranks, I'm here to tell you that there are six things we Girlfriends must do to prepare for the unexpected curve balls that She is sure to pitch:

1. We Must Be Healthy. I hate to be an alarmist, Girlfriend, but as a general rule, women who are far enough along in their lives to consider working on their grooves are old enough to have to take their physical condition seriously. Even if we feel terrific, and who even has the time to notice, we are of an age where it's important to get enough sleep, get regular pap smears, get baseline mammograms and bone density tests, and swallow enough calcium to turn us into whalebone. Maybe it's just me, but I've noticed that a common cold now lays me flat on the couch for three days. Even just missing a couple hours of sleep has me so jittery and disoriented that I don't feel safe driving carpool, let alone capable of picking up a child with a suspected fracture.

2. We Must Be Fit. We all know that good health is only half the picture; if we wheeze just running up a flight of stairs, how can we ever expect to dash across a football field to see if one of the two kids making out under the bleachers belongs to us and needs to be pulled out by the hair? We have to think about our blood pressure, our cholesterol and fat ratios because when the time comes that the protective mantle of ovulation and menstruation disappears, we are as vulnerable to heart disease as our beloved men. This is the time, too, to commit to exercise that relieves stress (stress? What stress??!!) and adds weight resistance to our bones so that the hobgoblins of osteoporosis and bulging discs don't "bench" us during the most important plays of our family's game.

3. We Must Have Sex. Countless studies have documented the health benefits of an active sex life for adults, but there are so many other considerations. First of all, a woman who is desired by her mate is prettier, calmer, and more confident than one who has given up the sexual ghost. Second, a woman who has a great sex life with her mate stands a better chance of staying married to that particular fellow. Third, and most important, a woman who thinks she's sexy and desirable has a more youthful and vital self-image. In other words, if you think you're irresistible and have the sex life to prove it, you're in a position to draw more stamina and endurance from your sex life than a vampire can suck from a virgin's neck.

4. We Must Be Idle. Do you even remember what that means? It means that we must be willing to sit in a chair, daydreaming or whatever, so that we are ready and able to recognize a wonderful opportunity, like unexpected sex or your preteen's sudden willingness to share confidences. Who knows? Maybe nothing will happen and you'll sit alone in that chair till you fall asleep. That's even better, since a nap is one of Sophia Loren's greatest beauty secrets. But if you, like me, are too overamped to sit quietly in anticipation of a spectacular Mommy moment, try needlepoint, read a book, or file your nails until something more pressing presents itself. Just let go of the "completion complex" connected to the activity so that you don't miss some great conversation or an impromptu Ping-Pong game because your topcoat hasn't dried.

5. We Must Always Remember: We Are Not Steering This Ship. We moms don't ask for much, just CONTROL, CONTROL CONTROL over our families' lives. No Girlfriend is ever really able to say she has her groove back if it depends on life abiding by her plans. That's the kicker in life—we can prepare up to a point, and then Mother Nature will toss a monkey-wrench into them and our grooviness depends on how able we are to adjust and change tacks. Too often, we fight change and refuse to acknowledge it. We may have a family illness thrown at us, but we don't cut ourselves any slack for grief or disappointment, let alone for the fact that we don't seem to be able to remember to touch up the roots of our hair. We may experience a financial blow, but we don't let our kids in on the quandary, and instead, we kill ourselves trying to create an atmosphere of "business as usual." We frantically rush around, taking a second job, getting another mortgage on the house, and putting a moratorium on frivolous things like getting our teeth capped or keeping our gym membership.

Whatever your personal theology, you must at least understand that we are but humble passengers on this wild ride through the universe. Even though children crave the belief that Mommy and Daddy are strong enough and big enough to keep all danger at bay, there comes a time when they, too, must be let in on the secret that life is like surfing; you catch a wave and ride it as long as you can, then you may wipe out, but all you have to do is hold your breath, dive down as far as you can go until the white water passes you, and then you can come up in time to look for the next wave. It's really not fair for you to lead ten- and twelve-year-olds to believe that sheer will and determination can always rule the universe. True survival skills depend a lot on that breath-holding bit.

6. We Must Love Our Lives Today, And Today And Today. Sitting around and waiting for our grooves to find us is a losing proposition. Some aspects of our lives will have to be changed, no *ifs, ands*, or *buts*. Bedtimes must be enforced, children must learn to clean up after themselves, and you are entitled *not* to volunteer for four different committees each semester. At our jobs outside the home, we owe it to ourselves to at least express a schedule that works for us, even if we get turned down flat. With proper preparation, we may be able to show why job-sharing is better for the company and for you. Or you may be able to stay in touch with the office from your home computer one day a week. Remember, being a squeaky wheel may make you a pain in the corporate butt, but well-conceived suggestions for modifying your career life will have to come from you. They don't just land on your desk one morning, dropped by the Job Stork.

And those things that can't be changed can be made more acceptable by a subtle shift in your own attitude. When work/family conflicts seem insurmountable, it can't hurt to stop for a moment to rediscover the pride you should feel in your ability to make money to contribute to the family and the gratitude you should feel for the great good fortune of having another outlet for expression besides checking homework and chauffeuring people who still cannot even legally sit in the front seat of a car.

And speaking of breath, Girlfriends, our biggest challenge in getting our grooves back is in learning to stay steady and resist the temptation to pile more chores and responsibilities on our plates. As marvelous and generous of you as it is to view yourself as the sole source of oxygen for your family, you are useless unless your own lungs are full. We're talking about staying fully oxygenated for the next twenty, thirty, or forty years. That means you have to pace yourself and your breath accordingly. Take a sip of pure oxygen from a solitary walk on the beach, or from a needle-point class or from writing a long letter to you best friend from high school. Remember, always save a little air for yourself, Girlfriend—otherwise, you will never be able to keep up with this race. Or you may inadvertently find yourself approaching the elusive finish line with the realization that you've been breathing nothing but bus fumes for the entire run. If you haven't smelled as many flowers as you've smelled farts, it's no one's fault but your own.

"What Did I Do to Deserve This Body?"

People magazine recently published an issue that really got my dander up. It was devoted to showing women who were "still going strong," even though they'd looked middle age in the eye and hadn't fainted dead away. Sure, they'd blinked at thirty, stumbled at forty, and called their plastic surgeons by fifty, but there was page after page just brimming with still-incredibly beautiful and improbably thin women. What genius over there in the editorial department had the "eureka" moment when he or she thought that a lineup of women who were intimidatingly lovely to look at in their twenties and still were a couple of decades later offered hope and reassurance to Girlfriends like me? All I learned was that the media-inspired pressure to survive on microwave popcorn and diet soda was never ending. Oh, God, did that imply that I STILL had to hold in my tummy every time I was around people over the age of eight?

With sickening fascination, I pored over the magazine and read every single little blurb describing their diets, their fitness regimens, and the perfunctory sentence about how much they loved motherhood or grandmotherhood. Of course, most of the grannies they showed had their own babies while still in their teens, as did their own kids, so they were all about my age, except Joan Collins, and there just aren't enough hours in a day for me to put myself together with the obvious meticulousness of that diva. Every one of the women looked vibrant and happy in her picture and was quoted saying something like "I've never felt better if my life," or "I have never had any plastic surgery, but if I ever need it, I'll consider it." Could someone please pass me an airsickness bag?

I haven't had enough energy to stay awake through *Saturday Night Live* in thirteen years. My breasts are a living, breathing example of Newton's First Law of Gravity. I have enough loose skin around my waistline that I could have it removed and make a duffel bag out of it. And I've got this little line forming between my eyebrows that I am certain is a result of all the scowling I do as a mom. Would I trade my kids for my former appearance? Not in a million years. But I do have a full-length mirror, Girlfriend.

Somewhere, sometime, someone decreed that one of the most critical measurements of our success as women who have gotten their groove back is how well we have weathered the maternity storms and recaptured our romanticized ideals of what we looked like up until that moment when we officially crossed the line from being menstruating women to being baby-growing vessels. Even those of us who adopted, purchased, or found our babies in a basket floating among the reeds generally sustain the traditional beatings of new motherhood, if not pregnancy, and the first thing that is affected, well, at least second— after our sanity—is our appearance.

Pamela Lee comes to mind. She is the only maternal "repeat offender" I can think of offhand who recovered her former appearance in about three hours and was able to pierce her navel and have it hang straight about a week later. I don't hold her up as someone to be emulated, but simply to point out that once again, Mother Nature has given us a sublime example of a genetic miracle, much like a two-headed snake or an albino cat. Bless Mother Nature in her infinite abilities— but did she have to perform one of her biological feats right there in the pages of every tabloid and on a successful television show? But I digress . . .

Girlfriends as "Player Haters"

It would be so much simpler to attribute this standard of "groove" to some guy who never committed himself to a loving wife and the kids they birthed together, but that's too pat an answer. Miserably I must tell you that women are as hard on themselves and each other as any man could be. Sure, the first person to suggest that mothers should look like non-mothers to be successful groovers may well have been a guy, but I maintain that it's us girls who keep that preposterous notion alive and well. Even those of us who live with men who revere and respect our mommy metamorphoses can't pass a mirror without finding a flaw, droop, or fold. If truth be told, we often appraise our entire package, from head to foot to what we wear to cover those places in between and come up tragically dissatisfied. This mommy dissatisfaction is really a composite of several little misfires that come together to create our identity bonfires.

Admit it, the standards we set for ourselves and other women are tougher than anything men could dream of. Ask a Girlfriend to describe a woman she knows but you've never met, and she'll say something like, "She's about thirty-two, a little overweight, and wears shoes with chipped heels," or "She's about my age, really thin—you'd HATE her!" I have Girlfriends who would chop their tongues off before describing a woman as white, black, or Hispanic, but who will give you five minutes of description about the poor gal's thighs, backside, or bad hair. We're positively obsessed with other women who've had kids and managed to hide all evidence of the crime by getting thin and fit again.

This kind of calculating starts very young. The other day, one of my daughters came home from dance class, full of indignation and outrage. Apparently the mother of one of the other little dancers showed up in a cropped top. "But, Mom! She's even older than you! I think she must be about sixty-five!" Clearly the light of my life, my little girl, had not been spared that cosmic orientation for all females that teaches us to size up the rest of our species and find them either lacking or threatening. I spent the next fifteen minutes imparting a message that a person's appearance was a form of self-expression, like a drawing, and that it's never fair to judge someone by their dress. And, while I truly believed every word, there was a little voice inside my head that said, "Maybe uniforms shouldn't only be for elementary school kids."

Misery Loves Company

I had a Web site for about a year. While this may seem like shameless self-promotion, I only bring it up here because of the incredible access it gave me to Girlfriends around the world thanks to its message boards and letters. After collecting a couple of thousand e-communications, it's become apparent that women who "look at the world through Mommy-colored glasses" have three major obsessions: sex, balancing the demands of motherhood, careers, and marriage, and, yes, their bodies. So you see, I'm not alone in my physical unease. (Note: Check the Table of Contents to find the other two obsessions addressed at length.)

It's kind of pitiful, don't you think, that almost none of us fret over our commitment to the depletion of the ozone layer or consider world hunger with nearly the zeal reserved for our daily bouts of critical appraisals of how our butts look in a bathing suit or self-chastisement over the six fish sticks we wolfed off of our kids' dinner plates as we cleaned up. I'm not suggesting that we lack a certain social responsibility, since I sincerely believe that mothers are the driving force for most social improvement. I'm just bringing it up because, hey, we're all so busy and frantic most of the time that we can't even complete the first section of a newspaper—why do we waste so many moments and calories determining that we've come up short in the appearance department?

A couple of years ago my husband and I attended Back to School night at our kids' elementary school. Naturally, all the other parents were there, too, and we all crowded around the bulletin boards in the hallways outside the classes to admire the third graders' essays on "Why I Love My Mom and Dad." Call me Narcissus, but I confess, I don't recall a word that our daughter wrote about my husband, her father, but I can quote verbatim from her sweet description of me. "I love my Mommy because she is so soft and cuddly, like a pillow," it began. At that point, my vision slightly blurred and I felt myself reaching spastically for my husband's arm to regain my balance. Without even turning my head, I could feel all the other mothers' eyes on my daughter's "tribute" to me and smiling like the cat that got the canary.

"SOFT"? LIKE A FREAKING "PILLOW"? What did my little girl think I was, a SOFA? Didn't she know that I'd been in "spinning" classes years back in the days before most Americans knew the term meant something other than making yarn? Hadn't she ever seen me in my kickboxing class do a flying side kick high enough to decapitate her father? And doesn't a mother get any credit whatsoever for winning the fitness certificate in twelfth grade for going farther around the track in ten minutes than any other girl in the school? Sure, I was gratified to learn how much she loved our cuddling, but didn't she feel my pecs and lats when she hugged me? I might be experiencing a momentary lapse in maintaining my fitness regimen, but underneath my temporary upholstery lay the body of a triathlete, an iron Woman. Well, maybe not yet, but that is still certainly a reasonable goal—if only I could manage to

23

clear all the boxes of Halloween costumes and Thanksgiving decorations off my treadmill in the garage. Clearly, the Vicki who lived within did not match the Vicki who was mothering my children.

"Father Time" is Such a Guy!

I have this theory: Becoming a mother is so all-consuming that most of us can only survive by retreating from all aspects of our lives that aren't absolutely essential to the survival or our family. I call us "Mommy Moles" because it's as if we go underground for several years to live our lives below the radar of the bigger world. We don't recognize it at first because our subterranean lives can include serving on the PTA, coaching softball teams, getting promotions at work, staying current with our mammograms, and even reading *In Style* from time to time, but we are still existing in a finite number of tunnels and nests safely protected from the bigger world where the bright sun can shine in.

What no one ever tells us is, by the time we're ready to come out into the sunshine and rejoin the human race, we are significantly older than we were when we started digging our holes. There are a million books and magazine articles out there brimming with advice about losing those last few pregnancy pounds or crunching our way back to our former abdominal fitness, but they all seem to assume that Father Time went into a coma while we were gestating, nursing, and "launching" our babies. I got pregnant with our first child when I was thirty-four. From that moment on, I was either pregnant, breastfeeding, or bribing the best preschools to consider admitting us until one month before my fortieth birthday, when our fourth child was born. Add another three or four more years devoted to sibling rivalry, moving toddlers from cribs to beds and potty training, and you pretty much sum up an entire decade of my life.

One Indian summer morning about a year ago, as I was driving away from dropping off my youngest at her pre-K class, it struck me: I'd done it! I'd protected all four of them from getting lost at Disneyland (at least not permanently), I'd not only gotten them all out of diapers but had hammered in the importance of hand washing after every toilet visit, I'd imparted basic etiquette (they remembered to say "please" and "thank you" about 70 percent of the time), I'd drilled into them a healthy suspicion of strangers (okay, so maybe they were a little overindoctrinated, but what permanent harm is there really when your four-year-old screams, "Don't kiss me; I don't know you!" to your mother's best friend?), and I'd trained all four of them to touch their noses with both hands whenever a car door was being closed (I'm terrified of pinched fingers). My job as a parent wasn't complete, but we were well on our way. We could buy toys with small pieces and not worry about choking, and I could let a dry cleaning bag lay on my floor for an instant while I put my husband's shirts away without the threat of toddler suffocation.

So off I drove, nearly giddy as the world of opportunity and potential compounded intoxicatingly with my caffeine high. On the way home I stopped at the gym I'd kept a membership in, even though I'd not spent enough time in it to break a sweat in several years. I picked up the aerobics and "hip hop dancercize" schedule and bought the newest fashion in workout clothes, since the leotard and bike shorts of my heyday were now passé. When I got home, I called my Girlfriend Chasen to pitch my dream for the two of us getting our grooves back together in time for Spring Break, since even in my hypermotivated condition, I couldn't face reclaiming my body without a fellow Mole standing beside me. She was right there for me, full of optimism and ready to commit to picking up where we'd left off before she'd started infertility treatments to achieve her third child, who was now four years old.

Without going into all the excruciating details, let me just tell you that there was not enough Advil on this planet to enable me to mask the agony of complete muscular failure after one intermediate yoga class. I

25

didn't just feel the burn, I was a mortifying example of spontaneous combustion. I'll never forget the day I ran to my bathroom to take a pee pee break and, after bending my knees in preparation to sit, I fell the next two feet and landed in the bowl of water (one of my sons had used the toilet before me and had neglected to put the seat back down). My thighs were so weak and traumatized that I couldn't even stand back up to dry off without grabbing hold of the nearby towel rack.

Things didn't get much better when I backed off the rigorous exercise classes and moved on to speed walking and light weight lifting. Now, when I walked fast, I felt like I might wet my pants with every energetic step, my breasts seemed so fragile that I wanted to carry them in my folded arms, and I swear I could feel my uterus rumble when I skipped up or down a curb. That doesn't even begin to include the chronic pinch in my neck I'd developed after three years of nursing, the hemorrhoids that came and went, depending on my fiber intake or the fact that my hips had never fully returned to their sockets after delivering four babies. I could go on with stories about how light-headed I became when I bent over and straightened up too quickly, how my pregnancy sciatica flared up if I lapsed into the toes-out duck walk that I'd picked up in my first maternal journey, and how none of my athletic shoes from the good ol' days seemed to fit anymore.

Why didn't anyone tell me that, while I was off mothering, I would also be aging? The prospect of getting back into pre-pregnancy shape is daunting enough on its own, but when you add the physical wallop of getting older to the equation, it's almost more than a gal like me can bear. Heck, if I'd spent the last ten years lying beside a pool or learning to play the accordion, and never missed a single birth control pill, I'd still never be able to recapture the physical self that I took for granted in my twenties! Whenever I read anything about some celebrity mom who got right back into shape as soon as her episiotomy stitches had dissolved, I had believed that she had it made for good—or at least until her first hot flash. Experience has taught me, however, that, since most of us end up with at least two kids, a momentary visit to your favorite pair of jeans from college means nothing in the big picture. We get pregnant again, we get broadsided by the reality of parenting by "zone defense" rather than the "man to man" game we played when we had only one child and we have to go back to work to keep our little teams fed and clothed. AND we get older.

It's simply too overwhelming to address the discrepancies between my ideal me and my actual me as a whole being. Perhaps we can break this discussion down into little bites, both so that we can set realistic goals for any changes we might want to make and so that we don't just toss this book into the nearest garbage can in frustration.

Let's Take It from the Top

It's always easier to enter a cold pool slowly and from the shallow end, so let's start with hair. Aside from that bothersome period shortly after birth when most of us watch huge coils of our precious mane snaking down the drain and our hairbrushes are so full of loose strands that they resemble beavers with plastic tails, the quantity and quality of a mother's hair is not really the problem.

No, it's style, color, and maintenance that often get a little neglected once we assume the mantel of motherhood. First of all, finding the time, not to mention the discretionary cash, for a real haircut can be overlooked for months on end. A good sharp pair of cuticle scissors attacking the hairs that surround our face is often the closest we get to a professional grooming. Whatever is going on in the back of our skulls is of little or no interest. As my Girlfriend Catherine, the mother of a toddler and a preschooler, recently asked me in great earnestness, "How old do the kids have to be before we have the time or interest to blow-dry the backs of our heads?" As the mother of kids between the ages of six and twelve, I confess, I still only groom the parts of my head that I can see in my car's rearview mirror.

But it's not just the cut or lack thereof, it's what we do with the hair at hand. As I sit here writing, I have blow-dried my bangs, at least until only moist, and trapped the rest of the odd hairs in the ubiquitous pinch clip. No matter how much trouble and effort I'm willing to take with styling my hair, by the end of morning I'm feeling messy and claustrophobic by all the sweaty hair on my face and neck, and I predictably pull it all up in a messy bunch and stick a clip in it. It's my personal observation that we moms function at a rate slightly above the land speed record, and perspiration and wilt are the natural result. Anyone who's cocky enough to suggest that a stray perimenopausal hot flash might be contributing to the sweat on the back of my neck that makes my hair curl had better have the nerve to say that to my face.

If I hear one more Girlfriend tell me that she was born a blond, I will throw a peroxide bottle at her. Unless you were born pregnant, I think it's safe to say that part of getting your groove back includes a realistic appraisal of your hair color. My Girlfriends and I unanimously agree that pregnancy and motherhood, not to mention the passing of time, conspire to take some of the poop out of our hair follicles. I've dyed my hair for so many years now that I don't clearly recall my natural hue, but I think it's pretty much like the dark brown found on two of my four kids. My hairdresser frequently comments that I don't have many grays, as he hurries to cover the evidence with his little squirt bottle, but I think it's safe to assume that I also don't have the coppery highlights that my little girl has when the sun glances down at her or the warm chestnut undertones that my son has both in his hair and in his eyes. Mud. That's probably the most accurate description. Mud, with some streaks of salt deposit (as in gray).

Not only has my hair dulled, but my complexion has lost some of its former oomph. I used to be pretty much the same color from my forehead to my chest, but now my freshly-washed face has all the shadings of a papier-mâché contour map of California. Some of the changes can be attributed to ordinary wear and tear, but you'll never be able to convince me that the dark circles under my eyes and the broken capillaries on my cheeks aren't part of my sacrificial gift to maternity. The lunar eclipses under my eyes are like a barometer of my sleeplessness, my premenstrualness, and my haphazardness in remembering to pick up another tube of concealer the next time I gas my car at the station next door to the beauty supply store. As for the capillaries, I can still remember feeling them explode during all those hours of pushing to get each baby out of my uterus and into my arms.

The great news about coloring is that it can restore the luster we delude ourselves into believing is our birthright, it can create a softer or more exciting frame for our drained faces and, best of all, it doesn't require any physical exertion on our part. Who cares if you were born a blond? You can damn well be one now, even if you were born with green hair. You're a woman, a MOM, and you deserve that tiny indulgence of crowning yourself with whatever color mane you ever wanted. And if you don't like it or get bored with it, you can change it as frequently as Madonna.

The bad news is that, once you lose your haircolor virginity, you'll have one more thing to squeeze into your already unmanageable schedule to keep it up because the only thing that looks worse than dull, gray hair, is lovely, shiny hair with dull, gray hair sprouting up like weeds in a rose bed. I find that my roots have to be dealt with every three or four weeks, and highlights have to be restored every four or five months, minimum. Hair color can also be an expensive endeavor, so it might be a good idea to find a Girlfriend who's willing to become your peroxide partner. The home color kits at your local Rite Aid or beauty supply are pretty manageable and not too expensive. Start out with the rinses that come out after five or six washings until you've found your best color and mastered the technique, then you can move on to the permanent colors. And speaking of permanent, do us all a favor and avoid perming your hair once you've colored it, or leave it to the professionals, because there are only so many chemicals a strand of hair can take. It's never a good idea to think of your hair as just another "crafts" project. You can always hide the decoupaged kitchen chairs, but you have to wear that frizzy orange tumbleweed cap on your head for months until it's long enough to put up in a pinch clip.

Think Like a Dancer

It turns out your mother was right about the beauty of good posture. After years of hunching over an armful of baby, especially to nurse, lots of us moms look like we're developing our dowager's humps several decades ahead of schedule. Add to that two or three hours a day behind the wheel of a car as the family chauffeur, and you have the spinal fortitude of a flexible soda straw. My Girlfriend Mindy is forever coming up behind all of our growing daughters and chirping, "Don't forget the string!" It has been her personal contribution to the girls of our tribe to teach them to imagine a string running up their spines and out the top of their head, pulling them up straight like a bunch of marionettes.

Not only are there obvious vanity reasons for stranding up straight and keeping your shoulders pulled back, but allowing your vertebrae to collapse onto themselves sets you up for everything from chronic neck-aches to tingling in your fingers. Speaking for myself, some of my biggest spinal damage is sustained while I sleep. It began when I would fall asleep with a baby at my breast. Of course, I could just as easily doze off while standing in the line at the Department of Motor Vehicles, waiting to renew my license, or during a particularly lengthy sexual encounter—but that's just between us Girlfriends.

Ever since then, I've seemed to fall asleep in the nanosecond between getting under the covers and my head actually hitting the pillow. There could be a nest of tarantulas on my pillow and I wouldn't have noticed. That means I have spent about ten years sleeping in whatever position I landed in the moment unconsciousness overcame me. Then, of course, there have been the thousands of nights when our marital bed has been invaded by the little migrants we lovingly call our children. Since most kids under the age of six sleep horizontally, I've adopted a sleeping posture that defensively avoids their feet in my face while clutching the edge of the bed with the dedication of a rock climber trying to avoid falling into the abyss below.

So now, as I realize that it's up to me to keep my backbone strong enough to not only support me, but my entire family, I've begun to pay more attention to how I prepare for sleep. I actually stretch a couple of times before I lie down, and then I try to stay awake long enough to make sure that I at least begin the night with my spine flat on the mattress and the pillow flat under my head. I may awake to find myself sharing a bunkbed with an eight-year-old, his Bugs Bunny parachute cloth pajama bag, and his collection of professional wrestling figures, but at least I would have started the night out with good intentions.

It's one big blur between adolescence and chronic lower back pain, so indulge me while I remind you to protect and strengthen your "pelvic girdle." I wish I had a buck for every Girlfriend who has had to take to the bed after trying to make the bed. It might have something to do with the strain on our lower backs that the full belly of pregnancy causes, or it might be the passing of time, or probably it's both. All I know is that if we succumb to the tendency to sway down around our tails, we are just asking for an intimate lifetime relationship with our chiropractors. Not only that, but letting everything down there hang loose makes us look even more potbellied that we absolutely need to. My Girlfriend Janet, who was a dancer and is so beautifully pregnant with her fourth child that she posed for a magazine cover, insists that the secret to her long, lean look is her habit of isometrically squeezing her abs whenever she is just standing or sitting around. I'm sure she is also sneaking a few thousand situps into her routine and not telling me, but I've tried her isometrics and they really do work. Just lengthen your torso and crunch every muscle between your pelvis and your shoulders. And while you're at it, throw in a few Kegels, too.

And speaking of Kegel exercises, the news about them is that we are wise to continue that regimen of internal fitness for the rest of our lives, or at least until we've learned to embrace Depends as part of our daily armor. According to my mother, an original Girlfriend, who is refreshingly candid about such things, the giggle-pee reflex just gets more sensitive with the passing of years. I gave my best efforts at describing Kegels in *The Girlfriends' Guide to Pregnancy*, but they're important enough to bear repeating.

You can strengthen what is known as your "pelvic floor," which gets seriously traumatized by pregnancy and vaginal delivery and, yes again, by time, by clenching and releasing the muscles you use when you stop the flow of urine midstream. To be completely graphic, you can get the full "range of motion" by trying to "hug" your sexual partner's organ while it's inside you. Ask him if he can feel you tightening around him; if he can, you're on the right track. Once you know the maneuver, you can do it anywhere, anytime. One of my favorite repetitions is to stay clenched through an entire red light when I'm stopped at a traffic light. These internal gymnastics can make sex more satisfying for both you and your partner, as well as giving you the bladder control that is so important in civilized society.

The Skin You Live In

Granted, I didn't have my first baby until I was thirty-four and my last when I was thirty-nine. Granted, I have the skin of a person who was mistakenly born in sunny Southern California when she should have lived with no more sun exposure than offered in the Arctic Circle, or at least in the constant moisture of the Emerald Isles, where my fore-bears stayed moist and rosy. But still, four babies later, this body belongs to a stranger. I first noticed it when I would dance up to a mirror, a baby's cheek against mine, only to feel the room begin to spin when I acknowledged how much environmental damage I'd sustained and how perfect he or she was. Babies look like just-washed peaches; you could take a bite right out of them. I look like I've been following Moses through the desert for the last forty years. Okay, let's call it an even thirty-nine, just among us Girlfriends. Freckles, moles, laugh lines, and broken capillaries interrupt my landscape, but only round mounds upon round mounds, punctuated by eyelashes and dimples, define a baby's face.

My Girlfriends insist that I'm holding up quite well and that I'm aging slowly, but I tell them the same thing, whether it's true or not. Besides, once you know and love someone, they remain ageless, espe-cially if you see them on a regular basis. It's only occasions like high school reunions or bumping into a childhood friend during your kids' soccer tryouts when you realize that at least THEY have put on some serious mileage. It takes a tremendous amount of wishful thinking, if not a dangerous level of delusion, to think that they didn't think the exact same thing about you, no matter how they might have protested to the contrary.

Something else seems to be happening to my skin just as I stand here perched on the cliff, ready to take a headfirst dive back into my groove pool; I'm getting pimples again! Look, I put my time in during my adolescence, picking at my zits, and napalming them with Stridex medicated pads. It was a big price to pay, but at least these little erup-tions manifested themselves on an otherwise perfect canvas. Ask me how happy I am to be getting breakouts AND wrinkles at the same time! Maybe I got the occasional breakout before I ever had kids, but I've idealized my former self so much by this point that I hazily recall a complexion as smooth as a baby's tushy. Now that I think about it, even my babies had terminal diaper rash, so I am clearly romanticizing the whole thing.

Anyway, T-zones, broken capillaries, crow's feet, and minor eruptions to the contrary, I've learned that my skin needs to be coddled to thrive. My Girlfriend Shannon has the loveliest complexion of all my mommy friends of a certain age, and what follows is her prescription for the care and feeding of that delicate tissue. The first weapon in the fight against skin imperfections is keeping it clean. Since my whole body seems to be dehydrating like a raisin in the sun, I've stopped using drying soap on my face. I love a mild cleanser you can get at the drugstore called Cetaphil, and I wash my face two complete times each evening, even if I'm so tired that I have to pull a chair up to the sink and sit down. I've also stopped using washcloths on my face, since they are abrasive and tend to make my rosy cheeks look positively pissed off. Shannon does, however, recommend using a washcloth on your lips at least twice a week to remove the chapped stuff that accumulated when you've eaten your lipstick off several days in a row.

I've also started washing in tepid water, for the same reason, since really hot water seems too harsh. Then I put on some heavy-duty moisturizer that's greasy enough to stay on my face all night, but not so greasy that my hair sticks to it like I'm covered in lip gloss. Hey, if Sophia Loren and Lena Horne swear by a lifetime of slathering their faces in Vaseline or Crisco every night, that's a good enough testimonial for me.

If I've learned one major lesson in caring for my skin as I've grabbed for my groove, it's been to treat my neck as lovingly and diligently as I treat my face. Horror of horrors, it turns out that the old French wives' tale is true, a woman's age is given away by her neck and hands. My hands, well, they're a lost cause. I try to keep them moisturized and covered in sunblock, which is somewhat easier these days now that there are SPF-fortified hand creams on the market, but motherhood and its concomitant germ phobia have turned me into an obsessive hand washer, so my paws are perpetually exposed to the elements. My neck, however, is much easier to protect. Not only can you grease it up from your collarbone to your chin without the dreaded shine that is so unattractive on your face, but you can generally depend on your neck not to betray you with pimple outbreaks.

No Surrender!

We have a choice here, Girlfriends: we can either roam the earth mildly dissatisfied with our bodies, or we can wake up and smell the gym socks with the realization that these bodies will be our personal vehicles for another half a century. Face it, we aren't trading these babies in for a newer model, so it might pay to get a new paint job and change the oil and tires for the long ride. Yes, we survived what we hope was the biggest physical ordeal of our lives, but the race is far from over. There will be other challenges along the way, I promise you, and we owe it to ourselves to get into some sort of fighting shape.

Eating to Live, Just Barely

Don't get me wrong. I honestly don't care about whether you lose or gain any weight—at least as long as you don't care. But if you do want to effect a change, you'd better start now because it just gets harder as the sands of time pour down. But I'm going to play the odds and assume that most of you, like me, secretly believe that an essential element in getting our grooves back is in getting some control over our physical appearance, even if that doesn't include ever being able to wear our wedding dresses again (and zipping them all the way up). I get more mail from women yearning to lose their "baby fat" than I do about any other single topic.

Since it goes without saying that none of us has more than an hour every day, or maybe four times a week, to devote to a fitness routine, any advice I give you now acknowledges that limitation. Remember, I'm not a doctor, a certified fitness instructor, or a nutritionist. I'm just a mom who's come clawing back after four forty-pound weight gains with four children. **Please don't take anything I say as gospel. Run any of my suggestions by your own doctor.**

There is one single exercise that all women can do, no matter how busy, to help drop a few of those resented pounds: Clenching Her Teeth. That's the bottom line here, Girlfriends; you have to cut way back on your caloric intake if you want to lose a pound. Think about it, you can walk with the treadmill at a 6 percent grade for forty-five minutes four times a week, and the total calories burned will equal about one pound. That might translate to the sensible loss of four pounds in a month except for one little catch; the more we exercise, the hungrier we become. If you, like me, dash out of the local gym and into the nearest coffee store for a grande iced latte to sustain you through afternoon school pickup and drop-off at the orthodontist, you may have improved your cardiovascular fitness, but your caloric burn is a mere fizzle.

Even those annoying women who swear to you that they eat anything they want do not eat it *anytime* they want. The first thing we do is we kill the between-meal snacks. Not such an easy thing to do, since most moms skip one or two meals a day and live only on snacks. I used to pull over to the side of the road after I'd pick my kids up from school and hysterically scream, "Turn over any leftover pudding cups or bologna sandwich crusts to Mommy RIGHT NOW!" since by that point, I was running on the fumes of that latte I just mentioned. The first step I took toward fitting into my old clothes, or new ones with a size I found acceptable, was to absolutely halt all eating that was conducted standing up or in a moving car.

I've also changed my entire philosophical commitment to protecting my home from wasted food. In other words, every time I reach for some uneaten chicken tender on my kids' plates, I imagine that they've licked it already. Hey, if I've learned one thing after years of feeding kids, it's the wisdom of giving them very small servings and offering seconds rather than heaping their plates up like it's an all-you-can-eat buffet in Atlantic City. That way, what they don't eat, or lick, can be dropped into some Tupperware and offered up again at another time. Since my husband works too late to make it home for dinner with the kids during the week, I force myself to make myself a plate and sit down to eat with them. When my plate is empty, I'm done. The end. No ice cream as a palate refresher or reward for being a member of the Clean Plate Club. Not only does eating early give me the opportunity to chat with the kids about their day, but it also ensures that I've eaten at least three or four hours before I go to sleep. Perhaps even more important, it sets an example for my kids that we eat to live, not live to eat.

The third dietary weapon in my arsenal is my protein breakfast. You and I both know there is a tremendous controversy going on pitting carbohydrates against proteins, and I haven't taken a strong stand one way or the other. I have, however, replaced the bagel or buttered toast and coffee of my former breakfasts with two scrambled eggs and a couple of pieces of turkey bacon. I still have the coffee (it's my drug of choice) and I have fresh-squeezed orange juice, but I cut the juice by a third with bottled water. If I were really disciplined, or at least paying attention to my cholesterol, I'd probably replace the eggs with egg whites, but white eggs look too much like curds and whey to me. But enough of my Little Miss Muffet syndrome; the truth about the new breakfast is that it's immediately satisfying and keeps me feeling like my engine is stoked all the way till lunchtime.

When I feel my weight creeping up, I eat for lunch and/or dinner a giant bowl of vegetable soup with some rice thrown in, AND NOTHING ELSE, except a glass of nonfat milk. On those blessed days when I'm able to sit down in my pants without the top button piercing me, I use lunch to fulfill my bread quota. I absolutely love a cheese sandwich, but I slice the wheat bread very thin and pile it high with things that crunch, like pickles, cucumbers or even sunflower seeds on a bed of lettuce and tomato and a moderate slathering of mayonnaise.

Since I don't run a short order kitchen, I eat what the kids eat for dinner, but without the buttered pasta, the Rice-a-Roni, or the dinner rolls. That may mean I'm doubling up on the meat loaf or take a leg and a breast from the chicken that has given its life for our family, and I pile up the vegetables, partly for the nutrition and partly to demonstrate to my kids that green and orange foods are not poisonous.

On those rare but glorious occasions when I dine out with my mate, I order any damn thing on the menu. After all, it's a celebration, and I never want to turn into one of those tedious women who engage sneering waiters in discussions of whether the fish can be grilled rather than broiled and the salad dressing set on the side. We both love the presentation of a great meal and we make a big deal out of tasting each other's selection. Then, once my husband has tucked into his potatoes gratinée and sautéed lamb chops, I go into slow motion. My goal is to take three bites from each food served on my plate. The rest gets packed up to be taken home. This is a technique I stole from Dolly Parton, one of life's great Girlfriends, although I've never met her. She explained her noticeable weight loss by saying that she tastes everything on her plate and finishes nothing. I'm still waiting for that method to give me a Dolly-like bustline, but in the meantime I'll settle for the waspish waist I can achieve with the help of the right undergarments.

The biggest sacrifice for me, personally, has been to learn to watch an entire movie without eating at the same time. When I see that big mountain or the revolving globe that signifies the beginning of a film, my fingers start rummaging around for things to put into my mouth in a steady, rhythmic fashion. I went through a stage of uncontrollable nailbiting, and I actually considered giving up movies altogether, but I finally discovered a way to satisfy my oral fixation during a THX moment—sunflower seeds in their shells. I learned this one from my Girlfriend Sonia, who is so addicted to this parrotlike way of eating that you can't sit down in her car without Dustbusting the seat first. You have to admit, there's a certain Calvinistic beauty to a food that makes you work that hard to get to the eating part.

Everything I'm sharing with you is my optimal program. Don't believe for a second that I live by those rules day in and day out. But it's the foundation for my acquiescence to the fact that my body needs far fewer calories to survive than I wish it did.

"Oil Can, Oil Can"

Getting some of the pounds off doesn't do a thing for giving you any more agility than the rusty Tin Woodsman, nor does it provide the weight-bearing exercises that have been proven to help ward off osteoporosis or give you enough stamina to hold your own in a three-legged race with your seven-year-old. All it does is make you slightly less self-conscious about putting on the clothes for those activities. That's where some kind of fitness program comes in. This is the fun part, or at least it should be. My Girlfriends have committed to all sorts of physical endeavors, all of which were selected for pleasure rather than for maximum caloric burn. Corki has her own horse and rides every single day. Mindy practices Tai Chi on the front deck of her country home. Shirley and my sister-in-law Janet have committed to golf with the devotion of Moonies, Lynette and Jamie are runners (who are clearly addicted to endorphins), and Lili and I have become yoginis.

This is a very important part of getting your groove back, Girlfriends: Since there are very few moments in a day carved out for pure enjoyment, we've all decided to pick an activity that tones up our bodies while we're distracted by the fun we're having. My Girlfriend Shelli, for example, loves to chat with her Girlfriends, but hasn't had time for a lunch out with them in three years. So now she hikes through her neighborhood with them. They move as fast as they can without getting so breathless that they can't gossip or compare concerns about public versus private schools for four-year-olds.

Most of us agree that we are looking for something different from our fitness than we did ten years ago. We're pretty simple in our goals; we want to be able to bend over to tie a child's shoes without making a grunting noise, we want to be able to climb a flight a stairs with a sleeping toddler in our arms without needing oxygen resuscitation at the top landing, we want to be able to wave goodbye in summer shirts without quaking an underarm pouch that looks big enough to hold our wallet and car keys, and we want to be able to get out of bed the day after exercising without rushing for the antiinflammatories. Most of all, we want relaxation and a break from the frantic pace of our days.

A Little Pampering Wouldn't Hurt, Either

I truly don't think I felt much of my body from the neck down for several years into motherhood. My body was like an army tank that barged through all terrain while I manned the controls from my small seat in the turret. Bang into a table, step on rocks, cut my fingers on the tape on FedEx boxes, I felt none of it. A major part of getting my groove back has been in reinhabiting my own body. Once I discovered my personal physical expression, which is yoga, I started to become interested in actually doing an occasional nice thing for my body. A long hot bath took on meaning far beyond personal hygiene. I started getting pedicures, not just to keep my toenails shorter than Howard Hughes's but for the massage that was thrown in for the price. I've even begun to teach my very generous daughter to do a scalp massage.

Here's the greatest payoff of all, Girlfriends: Once you regain your physical senses and the ability to take pleasure in your body, you are just a stone's throw away from wanting more sex and liking it a lot. But there's more about that in Chapter Eight.

If Your Body is a Temple, It's Time to Check the Rain Gutters

As my husband so dispassionately stated not too long ago, "Vicki, you simply cannot die on me." Well, I suppose I could if I had to, but I could see his point. I have responsibilities to people other than me that are best fulfilled if I stay walking on this earth. It's the same for you, I'm certain. That means that all the ways in which we neglect our personal health and upkeep are not private sacrifices. We may think that we're at the bottom of the needs chain as far as getting physicals or echocardiograms, but if we don't stay the strong little engines that can, all the other cars of our train will come rolling to a halt in Toyland, and that's not as good as it sounds.

How can we moms, the very same ones that keep a written diary of our children's vaccinations and growth charts, justify not getting a pap test and mammogram once a year, for heaven's sake? Yet we do it all the time. What are we thinking, that a colonoscopy is just another indulgence like a visit to a spa or joining a book club? WRONG! Are we just going to hope that our inability to turn our head all the way to the right is going to just disappear by ignoring it? I once had a period that lasted twenty-seven straight days, and I only called my gynecologist because I needed a quote for one of my columns. I guess I just thought that chronic menstruation was simply a feeble cry for attention and shouldn't be rewarded.

What would this world be like if we looked after ourselves as if we were one of our own children? The mind reels at such nosebleeding heights of self-indulgence. But think about it. Most of us are blessed with kids who are positively thriving. We, on the other hand, are falling apart and in need of regular medical intervention. Staring us in the eye is a loss of bone density, faltering hormones, suspicious breast lumps, and menopause—what woman in her right mind wants to enter that jungle without a paid professional at her side?

These Are the Bodies We Deserve, If We're Lucky

A couple of days ago, when I indulged in another one of my deluded attempts to get fit in the fastest and most frantic way possible, I joined a very "happening" yoga class. For any of you who has been in her mole hole so long that she hasn't learned the lingo of America's latest fitness craze, there is a yoga posture called Downward Facing Dog, or Down Dog, in which you form a sort of bridge by standing with your feet at the back of your mat and bent over at the waist so that your upper body is supported on your straight arms in front of you. Think of the position you'd assume if your child wanted to be the train and you were the tunnel for him to go through, and you'll get the picture.

Anyway, I was hanging out in the Down Dog position, trying to catch my breath and keep my arms from quivering under my upper body weight, when I noticed this was a good posture from which to check out the people who were standing behind me in the class. I'd already checked out the thirty or forty people who were Upward Dogging in front of me, and been mightily depressed at their agility and trim athleticism, but this was my chance to both hang out and get to know the people who couldn't see me looking at them because they were busy evaluating the row of people behind *them*.

One young woman comes to mind because she epitomized the yin and yang of the physical sacrifice of motherhood and the heroic rebuilding Girlfriends achieve through fierce determination. She was incredibly svelte and strong. Her upper arms had great definition and her thighs even had those fabulous "dents" on the sides of her upper legs and hips that genetically superior women have. She even had a perfect pedicure and manicure, not to mention a tan that didn't seem to have any strap lines. She was also a mommy, of that I was sure, because she recognized me and said something sweet about my books. Okay, so getting back to the Downward Dog, just as I was about to move on to the next specimen stretching beside this woman, I noticed that her muscle tee had bunched up on her tummy a bit, us all being upside down and all, and I could see her upper hips and sides. Gently striping her up both sides were the pale horizontal lines of stretchmarks. Not just one or two, but enough to make her look rather like a tiger.

All I can tell you is that it touched me so deeply that I welled up with tears and one drop rolled over my forehead and fell to my exercise mat. I don't know how else to describe it but to say that I was overcome with how noble and heroic she looked to me.

You'd think that I'd be smugly satisfied to find a mark of imperfection on that incredible human specimen, but I swear to you on my children that I would have willingly worn those stretchmarks across my own face if it meant I experience her beautiful body and being. Her stretchmarks were like medals of valor. They were the single indication to me that she had lived a life that served far more than just her physical perfection. She'd obviously surrendered her body to a baby or two, and she was a Girlfriend; a real life example of someone who'd lived in the mole hole and come up to reclaim part of her being for herself. At the end of class, the only thing that kept me from going over to her to tell her how amazing I thought she was was my own inability to get my legs out of the pretzel pose we'd assumed for a moment of meditation and I'd frozen into. In retrospect, I think God was working one of his small miracles in preventing me from making a fool of myself with my sentimentality. Still, if I ever meet that potential Girlfriend again someplace where wine is being served, I will thank her for showing me what a champion looks like.

What's a Mom to Wear?

*I*n the six years since I started writing books and columns about pregnancy and motherhood, I've received thousands of letters from
women. About 95 percent of them can be divided among three cate-
gories: How can I be a good enough mother; How do I lose this extra
weight; and, What's a gal like me supposed to wear? Nearly all the other
letters are plaintive questions about how to live with in-laws. We'll hit
on all these pressing issues in this book, but this chapter is devoted to
Mommy Fashion.

I've pretty much given up shopping for myself in stores and malls.
First of all, I tend to get all light-headed and sweaty when faced with the
endless opportunities of a retail experience. Second, I haven't been able to
enter a place of commerce in twelve years without being overcome by
the pressing need to get my sons new socks and pajamas or buy my
daughters sneakers that fit feet that grow like there's yeast in their shoes.
Even if the kids are all caught up in their attire and school supplies, there's
always my husband, who is facing a summer with nothing but black

sweatshirts in his closet or a winter with seven Hawaiian-print shirts, three pairs of sagging khakis, and some very scuffed white gym shoes.

Believe me when I tell you that I've actually gotten into the car and headed to the mall full of resolution that I won't buy a thing for my family until I've got my own neglected sense of style back on the path of fashion consciousness, but I invariably get waylaid in a Hallmark store. And since every mother knows you can never have enough cards for kids' birthdays or enough Halloween, Christmas, Passover, or Fourth of July decorations, I can spend a hundred dollars there without even feeling it. I'm usually so tired, distracted, and strapped for time at that point that I have to go running frantically into the parking structure to catch my breath behind the wheel of my car—the place I happen to feel most safe and secure these days.

When I'm feeling really really disciplined and focused, I will force myself to walk into one of the two gigantic department stores that bookend most American malls, filled with a feeble sense of purpose to address my own scruffy appearance. Why is it that cosmetics are always the first department you have to walk through to get into one of those emporiums? The artificial light and the crowds hurry me to the nearest sales clerk, where I buy a tube of the same lipstick I've been wearing since disco was king. I must have forty of those lipsticks by now, but it's not a complete waste since I lose several a month to the recesses of the floor of my SUV and pockets of windbreakers that I've left on the softball field. Not to mention the two or three my girls take for their stage makeup for their dance team or to spruce up their My Size Barbies. Occasionally I will make it to the lingerie, which is always adjacent to the makeup, but I never manage to buy anything. I just couldn't imagine trying on anything that was actually designed to FEATURE my abdomen, upper thighs, or freckled chest.

I just have to wonder where they're hiding the stores for women who are youthful, still interested in sex, on a budget, and dealing with breasts that will still make milk, even though they've not been in use for five years. Then there are my other critical concerns for fashion: It has to be comfortable, even during my PMS week; it has to be machine washable; it has to be free of any beads, flowers, or sharp buttons that would impale any child who needs a hug or to be carried to bed; it can't wrinkle so badly during carpool that I look like I've slept in my car; it has to be easily removed so that I can go potty several hundred times a day; it can't give me a wedgie, can't show my midriff, and it has to make me look thinner than I really am.

And those are just my personal standards. My kids, who are sophisticated enough to edit the Fashion Do's and Don'ts in a popular young women's magazine and keenly aware of a mother's potential to embarrass and humiliate them, have a whole other set of standards for my clothes. Consider this:

My Girlfriend Maggie, who is the mother of a twelve-year-old girl, is constantly trying to help her daughter find a way to master her homework by applying it to her real world. Recently, her daughter Mellie had a vocabulary test that included the word *conspicuous*. Maggie asked Mellie to put it in a sentence, and Mellie replied without taking a breath, "Mrs. So and So is *conspicuous* because she wears clothes that show her boobs."

Now, Maggie and I both know this "conspicuous" mom; in fact, we went to school with her, and we admire her tremendously (read: enviously) because she has such a gorgeous figure, even after birthing three kids. I can't speak for Maggie, but take it from me, I would dress as conspicuously as having my hair aflame if I could look that good. The problem is, as my husband so succinctly put in one day when I presented myself in tight (is there any other size?) white jeans and a muscle T-shirt, "Vicki, there comes a day when the old kit just doesn't work anymore. You have to get a new bag of tricks."

I considered striking back with a mention of the tiniest evidence of love handles embracing my darling Jimmy, since I refuse to go silently into this midlife, but I just skulked back to my closet to find a pair of roomy khakis and one of my five Banana Republic white blouses in deference to my obvious fashion crisis.

The dress code that has been set forth by my kids is something like this:

1. NO NIPPLES.
2. NOTHING THAT MAKES NOISE, LIKE BANGLE BRACELETS, NYLON PANTS, OR SHOES THAT FLAP LIKE MULES.
3. NO ATTENTION-GRABBING PATTERNS.
4. NO HATS, UNLESS THEY ARE BASEBALL CAPS WITH BENIGN LOGOS OF POLITICALLY CORRECT TEAMS ON THEM. NOTHING EMBROIDERED WITH MOTTOES LIKE "BAD HAIR DAY" OR "IF YOU ASK ME AGAIN, I'LL BITE YOU!"
5. NOTHING THAT A SIXTH-GRADE GIRL MIGHT CONSIDER WEARING. (The logic being, I suppose, that this is THEIR moment in the sun and any attempt on my part to join into the fun ruins the fad for everyone involved.)

In spite of these restrictions, I've had several moments of optimism over my years of parenting and desperately grabbed on to a Pollyanna-like attitude that fashion was still my friend and ally. That there had to be some smart retailers who recognized the value of appealing to a woman whose credit card usually got approved and was part of the fastest growing faction of the U.S. population, the baby boomer. Even with this kind of resolve, I have been insecure and confused enough to rely on the superior advice of a Girlfriend who seems to have her look mastered. In my life, that person is my Girlfriend Lili. Lili strides right into any store with such courage and focus that she makes a big game hunter look like a wuss. She has tremendous style and taste, and she also happens to have a healthy sense of entitlement to indulge herself and her needs more than twice a year. We usually select a store with a restaurant inside so that I can fight the hypoglycemia and caffeine drop that invariably hit me when searching the sales racks. If we really select our store carefully, there may even be a place to buy a stiff drink, should push come to shove.

I follow her around like a dog, holding my arms out to collect all the garments she has snatched off the rack and thrown over her shoulder at me. None of it looks like it is an obvious mix and match, and that's a huge problem in itself. Is anyone besides me old enough to remember Garanimals clothes? They were the kids' separates that were marked with different jungle animals on the tags. It was so simple: If you bought all giraffes, you could get dressed in the dark and still be assured that you wouldn't leave your house wearing purple paisley leggings, an orange T-shirt with a gorilla face on the front, and a pair of flip flops. Giraffes went with giraffes, lions with lions, and monkeys with monkeys. It was brilliant.

The closest thing I've found to dressing like Geranimals is the Gap. If you buy all your essentials during a single season (and who really has time to shop for themselves more frequently than that?), chances are pretty good that all the pieces will blend together. With the Gap, there are usually khakis, pants and skirts, and whatever color or pattern combination that their wizards have selected for us Mommy lemmings to follow them to the shore in this time of year.

But if you venture out of the Gap, you're pretty much on your own in the matching challenge. Even its sister store, Banana Republic, presumes that we know how to pull together a sarong-cut skirt, a lime-green sleeveless T, and a denim jacket to make a fabulous fashion statement. As if! I've tried a couple of scientific systems to keep me sartorially synchronized, like drawing stars with a Sharpie pen on the labels or inner seams of separates that are ludicrous alone, but stupendous when pulled together. My problem is that I can never remember how many stars connote a finished ensemble. I can find the skirt, the pashmina-like scarf, and one of the shoes with a star drawn on the insole, but I usually give up in desperation and pull on a white oxford-cloth shirt because I've forgotten about the fourth piece, an adorably funky gypsy-cut blouse that defines the whole look.

One day, in a gesture of grand generosity, Lili actually volunteered to put each complete outfit on the floor and take a Polaroid of it. She even took pictures of all acceptable variations on the theme. The problem was, I could never manage to find the photos while I was dressing in the dark to begin a day that would start with volunteering for Language Arts in my kindergartner's class and end up with me standing on a windy soccer field to watch my sixth grader defend his school's honor. I confess that I've never even aspired to wear one of those outfits fashion magazines are so crazy about, where they take off the jacket, add a string of pearls and dangly earrings, and insist that you can meet your mate for an evening affair without even stopping home to pick up one of those tried-and-true lipsticks you've got in every shoulder bag you own.

The Fundamentals

I consider myself fortunate that I have two women and three teenaged girls to pass on my ill-conceived purchases, since I make several of them. The things I buy because some nineteen-year-old salesgirl told me they make me look "hip" or much cuter than her own mom ever looks, I usually give one game try to, then I either catch a look at myself in a window reflection or feel them creeping up uncomfortably during my countless hours of driving or sitting in chairs designed for children under the age of seven. At this point I pass them to my thirteen-year-old Girlfriend-in-Waiting, Caitlin. The clothes that I buy because I'm certain they're classics, only to discover when I'm wearing them that they encourage all people under the age of thirty to call me

Mrs. Iovine, I give to Caitlin's mom, my Girlfriend Mandy, who happens to be a successful and admired attorney, to wear to court. That usually leaves me with what I had before I went shopping: a pair of Levi's 501 jeans, a pair of J. Crew khakis, and three white T-shirts, one sleeveless, one short-sleeved, and one with long sleeves.

I guess that the process of elimination indicates pretty forcefully that every mom should have two pairs of utility pants and three neutral cotton shirts in her closet. But what fun is that? Sure, you never show up looking like a sixth grader or a hooker, but you also show up looking invisible. There must be a few more things that can be relied upon to round out a sexy, intelligent, professional mother's wardrobe.

From the Inside Out

Indulge me, Girlfriends, while I point out to all those moms who've been in a coma since Stage Three Labor—you cannot wear maternity panties one instant after you've stopped bleeding after delivery, and you must give up the psychic comfort of nursing bras as soon as your child is able to drink from a cup and you are able to pop your breast above or below your own cup to feed him. I know that maternity fashions are getting pretty stylish. I have even seen some great black lace nursing bras. But if you, like me, became attached to the soft white cotton of a bra the size and weight of a bulletproof vest, you'd best be shopping for a sports bra or a supportive but sexy little number that unclasps in the middle so that you can still put breast to baby, but still be a contender for showing breast to mate.

Not too long ago I had the fun of co-hosting a network morning show, and I got to narrate a lingerie fashion show. I swear on a stack of Bibles that it had never occurred to me in a decade to buy panties and bras that matched until that national epiphany. My first thought was that pretty undies would come in handy in the Loehmann's communal dressing room or if I were in a car wreck and doctors would be judging my undergarments, but even a slow gal like me soon saw the greater benefits that sexy underwear offered. My husband recently caught a glimpse of me in silky maroon panties and a matching bra, and you'd have thought I'd marched out with a sash reading "Miss California" draped across me.

There seems to be something very arousing to men in the concept that we care enough about how we look to those few special people who are privy to our privates. Hey, what did I know? All I can say is, pretty panties and matching support garments have great erotic appeal. Once I learned that, I, too, began to feel pretty snazzy in my fancy undies. They were my constant reminder that, if I was lucky, someone other than a medical professional would see me in my skivvies and be turned on.

I've been wondering: Do you think I could get away with wearing Sheer Energy pantyhose permanently? You know, like the Laker Girls or Miss America contestants. In fact, I've been thinking of writing to the makers of L'eggs to see if I can interest them in making their pantyhose turtlenecks. I have about two yards of skin that I have no use for and I'm desperate for the elasticity that I swear I had before I grew up to be the woman I always wanted to be.

I could have sworn that pregnancy was the biggest challenge to my personal sense of style. First of all, I had cellulite creeping up the backs of my legs from ankles to waist within two weeks of a positive result on my home pregnancy test. Second, my behind matched my belly pound for pound all nine (ten) months of gestation. I'm not even going to start with my double, then triple chins, which I swear to this day were more pronounced with daughters than sons, but that's another subject. Still, experience eventually showed that far greater fashion trials lay ahead.

During gestation, my "regular" clothes were packed up and stored in boxes in the garage to make room for all the bought and borrowed clothes that were sufficiently ample to drape my belly and bottom. Unlike the pregnant gals I occasionally see in celebrity magazines, I never once considered my pregnancy as a fashion plus. But more about resurrecting those old clothes a bit later.

Getting back to the concept of body-length pantyhose: My favorite garment these days is the New Millennium's version of long-line girdles, legging-type spandex undergarments called "body slimmers." Lots of people make them, in all price ranges of course, but I've been totally satisfied with the ones that I buy from the J. C. Penney catalog. They give extra support over the tummy, boost up the booty, and often have the extra added feature of firming panels over the "saddlebag" area.

If there is one inalienable right afforded to us mothers under the Girlfriends' Guide Constitution, it's that we have earned the right not to hold in our stomachs. First of all, no one can remember to do it all the time, and all it takes is one relaxed moment to let the world know that our trim tummies were a fraud all along. I don't know about you, but no matter how many Ab Isolators and Tummy Crunchers I've bought during bouts of insomnia I was trying to cure with infomercial shopping, the effort it takes to hold my overtired abdomen up tight against my lower spine requires such serious sucking in that I swear I could break my own ribs from the inside out.

I wear these slimmers instead of panties a lot of the time, which works out pretty well since I rarely wear skirts these days, because I invariably have a Visible Panty Line that is so severe it can be detected beneath wide wale corduroy trousers, even the full-cut ones. Something frightening has happened to obliterate the geographical demarcation between my bottom cheeks and my upper thighs. My Girlfriends Jody and Shirley have been trying to sell me on the idea of wearing thong panties for about ten years, but after three massive episiotomies, I just can't stand the idea of clothing that is so blatantly intrusive. They insist that you don't feel the permanent wedgie and, as if this were a deal clincher, they point out the fact that Pamela Anderson not only wears them but endorses them. I don't even know where to begin to list the discrepancies between Pamela's anatomy and my own. . . .

Now that my bustline has finally submitted to Newton's Law of Gravity, I've become much more interested in bras and camisoles than ever before. Before I had kids, not to mention nursing them for about three years total, I loved my perky little breasts. I admit it, I loved pulling on a tee and bouncing off to face the day—all four of my eyes facing forward. Now that a couple of those eyes have a distinct downward gaze, I've had to wear bras for reasons that aren't just seductive. First of all, I look a little hunchbacked without a bra, as if the weight of my mammary glands pulls my shoulders and upper back forward toward the pavement. Second, I continue to be optimistic that I can protect against further bosom drop if I prop those suckers (no pun intended) up with the proper underpinnings. And third, now that I have kids who are old enough to find me an endless source of potential embarassment, it has become one of my most essential grooming responsibilties to avoid showing any hint of "nipple action." Yes, these very same offspring who were eager to suckle me till they left for college are now obsessed with making sure that I don't leave the house with any evidence that I am a mammal.

As lovely as I think those matching bras and panties that I recommended to you are, I still don't find them the most comfortable of garments. The Gap sells these stretchy camisoles that I'm particularly fond of wearing instead of bras. What can I tell you? I just can't face a whole day of breasts that are lifted and separated. Sometimes I'm just more comfortable pressing my boobies tightly against my chest and pretending that they're not even here. Not only is a spandex camisole sentimentally reminiscent of the little undershirts we wore as kids, but they have the added value of not emphasizing the fold of skin that gently drapes over my bra band in the back. I ask you, where the hell did THAT come from?

Bra or camisole, it's up to you and your genetic composition. Either way, I think it's safe to say that 99 percent of the mommy breasts I've seen that have not been restructured by a skillful surgeon need some kind of elastic undergarment, both for support and for modesty.

Moving from Maternity Into the Groove

An essential part of getting our groove back is forcing ourselves to recognize that we are more than life-sustaining appendages to our children. We make a statement about how we feel about ourselves by how we present ourselves, not just to the other patrons at a snazzy restaurant on a Friday night or at work, but to our mates and, most importantly, to US.

Getting back to those prepregnancy clothes that I had lovingly stored in my garage: Here's the bad news, Girlfriend—way too many of us mommies become so attached to a certain style that worked for us over a year ago that we fail to notice that the fashion train has left us standing at the station. Almost all of us, no matter how much we embrace our pregnancy voluptuousness, become almost irrationally attached to our body and style images from before we started retaining more water than the Hoover Dam. The whole world may have moved on to capri-length pants and animal prints, but if our last fashion experience from our pre-mommy era was pleated khakis and oxford cloth shirts, then that's our personal style Mecca.

Most of us are so hungry to reclaim our former sense of "normalcy" that we don't have any concept of the passage of time—all we want is to be the gal we used to be. I remember trying on my old favorite pair of jeans about thirty times after my first baby was born before I could get them buttoned, but when I did, I felt like I'd achieved my former glory. It never occurred to me that my beloved denims weren't necessarily cool anymore, nor even flattering. I just wanted the old me back so badly that I was desperate to squeeze myself into any-thing that looked and felt familiar, like a talisman from my former life.

Look, I realize that most of us don't have enough money to justify buying new wardrobes after the birth of each child. The financial bur-den of having kids is daunting enough to make us all wonder if we can ever justify buying another pair of panties, let alone anything we've seen in *Allure* or on *Ally McBeal*. Nearly as overwhelming is the challenge of finding the time to go shopping, not to mention the hideous experience of appraising ourselves in the fluorescent lighting and three-way mir-rors of most changing rooms. Still, we owe it to ourselves, not to men-tion the people who have to look at us, to stop deifying our former fashions.

The biggest excuse I hear from moms for not attending to their "looks," after the universal complaints about insufficient funds and lack of time and interest, is the fact that they are "waiting until they lose that last ten pounds." No one wants to invest a dollar or a moment in cloth-ing that they hope will be obsolete as soon as they find the time to join a gym or the discipline to stop eating all the uneaten macaroni and cheese off their kids' plates. Here's the news, Girlfriends: You're not invisible to the rest of the world just because *you've* stopped looking in the mirror. It may take hanging up your birthing saddle for good and getting your youngest child into a full-day preschool program, or win-ning the Super Ball Lottery, before you can find your way clear to make yourself your biggest remodeling project. In the meantime, if you think that it's okay to recycle old maternity tunics and leggings every day, you're selling yourself way too short.

I think it should be an obligatory part of postpartum recovery for mothers to pass on their maternity clothes to their pregnant friends and to pile up the leftover panties and leggings, douse them with gasoline, and dance around the bonfire. Yes, you're a mother, you're a hero, and you deserve to take a step back from some of the superficiality and frivolity of fashion slavery. Still, if you completely give up the ship where your appearance is concerned, you give up a part of yourself. Getting your groove back requires acknowledging that you have been forever changed by becoming a mother and that you embrace your future as this new person, not that you are pretending like none of this has happened and you are trying to move back in time. Remember, the road to maternity is a one-way street. You won't ever go back to being the gal you were before you invested your heart in a tiny new human. And anyway, why in the world would you want to?

You owe it to yourself and all of us who love you to invest in at least three or four separates that fit you right now. Twin sets and full-cut blouses will still be useful even if you lose twenty pounds, so all we're really talking about are a couple of pairs of pants and a skirt. As much as I adore the concept of passing our clothes down to our Girlfriends who are behind us on the maternity mile, I really do think you must buy these four essentials for yourself from the current fashion racks. You and I both know that Target is a haven for trendy pants with elastic or drawstring waists, most costing less than $30. All you need is a black pair (this is the only exception to my "no black clothes" rule) and another neutral, like tan. They can serve you through at least a ten-pound shift in weight while still making you look hip and like a participant of this world, here and now. I'd stay away from jackets and blazers and look for loose-fitting knit tops and sweaters since they'll look good even if they get a little big for you. If you buy a jacket that you hope will fit you in your new, svelte form, for now it will probably pull open over the bust, giving the impression that you are committed to a day of shallow breathing, and creases across your back like a Shar-pei. And if it fits now, when you lose that notorious ten pounds in a few months you'll look like Columbo.

The single greatest fashion illumination I've experienced in the last couple of years is how flattering pants and skirts can be if you wear them a size larger than you can squeeze into. In other words, just because you can zip and button a size eight or ten doesn't mean they look good on you. I know it's emotionally difficult to own up to the bigger size, but the better choice is the next size up, after you've had the dry cleaners hem them and take in the waist if necessary, because you always look thinner and sleeker if your skirt or trousers don't cling to every inch of your anatomy like a wet suit. Not only that, but if you look like your clothes are a tad loose on you, people will think you're shrinking and compliment you on your weight loss. Besides, once you own an article of clothing, it's yours to do with as you want: Just cut the size label out when you cut off the other tags, and no one needs to be the wiser.

You owe it to yourself, and those of us who look at you, to devote at least enough time to put together at least two "perfect" outfits for daytime wear. I know that the trend in workplace fashions is on the slippery slope of informality, but part of getting your groove back is acknowledging that you're not going to be admired for your cleavage and great pedicure anymore. You have earned the right to be chic and dignified, rather than cute and funky. Unfortunately, that takes a little more planning than throwing on a tube top and sandals. You'll have to spend some time coordinating all the pieces of each outfit, including shoes and jewelry, and to getting them altered if necessary. Enlist a Girlfriend or a professional shopper (always free) at your local department store for an unbiased opinion and stick with it until you've put together two looks that you can always depend on to make you look and feel great.

The Ubiquitous Little Black Dress

Everybody has one, usually for years past its life expectancy; Coco Chanel's inspiration, the Little Black Dress. I'm going out on a limb here, Girlfriends, but I'm willing to risk it—dump the dress! What's the concept behind it? Are we trying to blend into a crowd? Are we thinking that because it's black it's timeless? What kind of groove can we get back if the pinnacle of our fashion aspiration is to be invisible and perpetually out of fashion? NONE! Okay, so you can keep the dress, after all, there's always the concern that we might have to attend a funeral, but we should push it to the back of our closets and indulge ourselves in one lovely colored skirt and top or dress for New Year's Eve and the two other "fancy" nights out that we might be blessed with.

If you live in New York City, then this pill will be particularly tough to swallow, but I'm right here patting you on the back. You're a grown-up now, you know what colors bring roses to your cheeks or make your hair sparkle, so be brave and commit to color. Hey, if you can face hemorrhoids, you can certainly face pink! If you just can't overcome the feeling that anything other than the noncolor of black is like walking around with a traffic cone on, then put black on the bottom and something else on the top. Here's one place where I think you can justify spending just a little more than $20 on a top; get a crisp white, long-sleeved blouse from Banana Republic or Gap and you can wear it with everything from a full skirt to any pair of pants to over a sexy pair of panties for a little bit of foreplay.

One time, many years ago, I had the honor of being invited to a charity dinner at the Kennedy Library in Boston. I'd birthed one of my countless children about six months before, and I had exactly two outfits in my wardrobe that fit me at that moment. One was a cap-sleeved black dress with a hem that came to about two inches above my chubby knees. The other was a navy blue suit with full cut, flowing pants and a tapered jacket that, when worn without a blouse, showed off the glory of my nursing breasts and created the illusion of a waistline. I fretted for weeks that pants would be hopelessly out of place, even though I knew that the navy outfit made me look much prettier. Only because it turned out to be a chilly evening, I opted for the navy after rushing out that day to buy some silver high-heeled sandals at Nine West. Guess who was dressed almost identically to me, the walking milk machine? Jackie Kennedy, that's who! That was my epiphany: The Little Black Dress was like a little white flag; nothing more than a surrender. Girlfriends, we deserve so much more than that.

Dressing in the Dark

If you're like my Girlfriends and me, there are two standard-issue looks for a regular day. For those of us who work outside the home, there are usually two or three variations on a theme (hopefully the ones you carefully coordinated and altered) that we quickly pull on automatically in the darkness of our closets so that we can rush back to the kids' rooms to make sure they are, indeed, awake and preparing for school. The rest of us, who don't have to dress for strangers until later in the day, tend to head off to school drop-off in clothes that look appallingly like the clothes we slept in. My Girlfriend Karla used to show up with her two kids at preschool in leggings, a polar fleece jacket thrown over the nightshirt she had been wearing, a pair of sandals or a kind of after-ski boot made of sheepskin called Uggs, and a baseball cap.

Let's take a moment right now to acknowledge the value of baseball caps in the wardrobe of still-unshowered moms. There have been mornings when I wouldn't have had the nerve to leave the house, even if someone was bleeding, if it hadn't been for the cap on my head and the sunglasses on my face. If I ever misplaced those two items, I swear I would have to dig into the costume trunk in my basement and don the *Scream* mask and black hood my son wore for Halloween last year—and I'd be completely confident the getup was more attractive than my on-end hair and puffy eyes. The only drawback of leaving the house dressed like an outfielder is that bad hair becomes even worse and must be dealt with as soon as you have access to a shower nozzle and a blow-dryer.

We Don't Have to Look Like "Soccer Moms." Even If We Are

Morning school drop-off aside—since that ungodly hour is only dealt with in matching clothing and groomed hair by those moms who are dashing right off to work after—those of us who work from home, however, really ought to put a little effort into not looking like something the cat just dragged in. Once again, we moms tend to put our kids ahead of ourselves in meeting these needs, too. My Girlfriend Karen has two little girls who never leave the house without their hair perfectly braided and beribboned, bows on their dresses sculpted so deliberately that they look like giant flowers that have sprouted from her children's backs, and sneakers so scrubbed and white that they look like they've never been worn. Darling Karen, however, wears the same navy shorts and sweatshirt every day, and her hair looks like a shrub in need of a good gardener.

I feel her pain. Easter morning is my personal Armageddon; I polish all four kids, even the very modest ones, clean the insides of their noses with Q-tips, and make sure every sock is smoothly pulled into place and, in the case of the girls, folded over so that the lace ruffle lays flat. Invariably, however, I notice that we're already five minutes late for Sunday services before I've even brushed my teeth, let alone found a dress that isn't missing the hook and eye at the top.

For the last seven years, we've had an Easter morning ritual of lining the family up in front of the piano to take a photo to commemorate the one time a year that everyone is groomed at the same time—oh, yeah, and to show the passage of time. I'm always included in the picture, too, since I'm the one in charge of shepherding our flock to church. My hus-

61

band, by the way, takes the picture, since he won't go to church unless I cry, so he's dressed in his sleep attire. What's become almost as poignant to me as I look over the collected photos, almost as touching as the growth of our family is how pathetic I usually look. One year, it's obvious that I've squeezed into a dress that is such an ill fit for my nursing bazongas that they're squeezing out through the armpit holes and lifting the pearls I'm wearing around my neck. Another year the dress fit all right, but the shoes look suspiciously like a pair of terry-cloth pool mules I once bought for a trip to Hawaii.

This most recent year the dress and shoes are all right, but my hair looks like a wig. Either I had a premature hot flash after I'd done my hot roller thing or I'd worked up a furious sweat climbing under my daughter's bed to find her favorite hair scrunchie. All I can tell you is that it looked like my own "real" hair was frizzing out from beneath the "wig" of the dry hair that was doing its best to hold its smooth style. I actually considered sending the negative to one of those computer photo retouchers to correct the truth, but I thought I'd come out looking like Lady Bird Johnson, so I dropped it. The only lesson I can glean from all these years of style don'ts is to get my lazy ass up a half hour earlier and force my kids to stand at attention in the driveway for as long as it takes for me to pull myself together. Yuck!

We're all fabulous, interesting, and uniquely expressive women, so there really is no justification for anyone telling us that there is a single style that works for all of us. Okay, that political correctness duly noted, I know I would give anything for a clothing fairy to sneak into my closet some night, steal all my unattractive or ill-fitting clothes, and leave me with three or four things that all looked good on me. Honest, I sincerely wish we were issued uniforms like the crew on the Starship *Enterprise* so that I would never again have to stand before my closet, surrounded by mounds of things I've tried on and discarded, and yodel into the empty hanger space, "I haven't got annnnnnyyyythiiiiiing to wearrrrrrrr!"

Who Are Our Fashion Role Models?

You all know that Cindy Crawford, that divine human being, has started offering mommy guidance in several ways, from fashion to fitness to finding the perfect baby carrier. I love watching her and actually write down most of what she says, believing that I might achieve some of her style if I just follow the recipe. I've asked hundreds of women if they think that they can approach Cindy's greatness with her generous help and secrets. Interestingly enough, most of them say, "No," but they like to have someone like her out there raising the bar for the rest of us. I guess you could say they see Cindy as an "aspirational" model for moms. Well, I guess that makes me the "perspirational" model for moms. Yeah, we'd all like to look like her, but those of us who are grateful to learn that Gold Bond powder keeps our thighs from making farting noises when we sit on unupholstered chairs have a whole other kettle of fish to fry.

Since I work from an office in my home, I keep myself from losing my mind in the solitary pursuit of writing by keeping the television on quietly beside me. In the last year or so I've become obsessed with *The View,* that show with the five women chatting around a table and chaperoned by Barbara Walters. More specifically, I've become obsessed with their clothes. Meredith Viera is my age, and I think she looks pretty darn good, but she likes skirts more than I do and I'm a little bolder about color and design. Star Jones has the color and the variety, but she's a little too fancy for my life. In my dreams, I dress like Lisa Ling, but I'm not nearly as fond of my bare midriff or upper arms as her youth allows her to be. Still, there's something casual and funky, but still pulled together about her wardrobe. Joy Behar looks like an incredibly stylish aunt I'd like to have, but all the big blouses and capris aren't for me quite yet. And Barbara, well, Barbara looks and is the woman I want to grow up to be. I don't know if there's any hope of that happening, since I still wear pigtail braids and ponytails much more often than any woman should.

63

Oprah, too, always looks great and comfortable. I know her clothes cost more than most sports cars, but she does look comfortable and groomed all at the same time. Groovy Girlfriend Supreme that Oprah is, she occasionally devotes an entire show to telling us how to find clothes like she wears in knock-offs from Target, A.B.S., and Old Navy.

I bring up my TV fascination because daytime talk shows tend to be the only place where I regularly see fashionable women who look like they could be dropped into my life for a day and look just fine. It was television, for example, that showed me that I had to own at least one pair of strappy sandals. I have toes that look like Vienna sausages that have been painted bright pink at the ends, so I honestly prefer closed-toe shoes. Still, my gals Katie Couric and Ann Curry regularly show their tootsies to the whole nation from May till September, so who am I to argue? Between you and me, I often identify more with Al Roker at 7 o'clock in the morning, but that would be the death of my groove.

The daytime Girlfriends have also taught me a lot about accessorizing without jangling so much that you sound like a band of gypsies has entered the room or swathing yourself in a scarf so big that you look like an entry in the Iditerod. I pay close attention to their lipstick colors, too, since I embraced Russian Red by MAC when Madonna began her Material Girl Tour and never knew it was time to stop. If I were to depend on fashion magazines, they'd tell me that lips were "neutral" this season. Well let me tell you what neutral looks like on these mommy lips of a certain age: NOTHING. Time and childbirth seem to have removed all natural rosiness from my sweet little mouth and left me with lips that are indistinguishable from the skin on my chin. If you can find the time one of these days, stick around to watch the credits at the end of a show that has styles you can imagine wearing and look for the fashion sponsors' names. Even if the clothes are provided by Saks Fifth Avenue, you might have a Saks within driving distance so that you can drive by and see what the real thing looks like. Then you can head back to Target or Contempo Casuals for a knock-off.

Let Your Fingers Do the Shopping

If you hate to shop for yourself, or are completely inept at it, I'm with you. That's no longer an excuse, however, for us to show up in our pajamas (unless they're silk, of course). Ever since my last baby was born, six years ago, I have spent at least one night a week putting myself to sleep by reading catalogs. I usually have to use my Itty Bitty Book Light, since my husband is entering the Land of Nod, and I go into a sort of trance with page after page of fashion. I fold over the corner of any page that has something I can imagine leaving my house in and then throw all the magazines onto the floor before I go unconscious. The key here is to review any choices in the unforgiving light of day over my second cup of coffee. This protects me, and our family assets, from whatever delirium clouds my judgment when I'm snuggled in my bed, or from giving in to whatever my older daughter has chosen, since invariably, she's lying right beside me in bed while I do my nocturnal shopping.

Until I get used to a particular manufacturer or designer in the catalogs I like, I forge ahead and order my best guess for size and cut since I return about fifty percent of what I order. Never feel guilty about following my lead in frequent returns because insiders within the mail-order business tell me that clothing is the most returned purchase of anything available through catalogs or on the Internet.

Speaking of the Net, I'm getting much more comfortable buying clothes online now, too. The most important thing you want to know about online ordering is the return policy of the site and its reputation for fulfilling your orders in a timely fashion. You can find out about the differing sites from your net-savvy Girlfriends, in *USA Today* or *People* magazine or several other on-line sites that devote sections to e-commerce ratings for consumer satisfaction. Of course, you will only want to use an established site with the now nearly universal access block to protect your credit card information from a disgruntled and deep-in-debt order placer who would love a trip to Vegas on your MasterCard. This kind of shopping is much safer than your natural protective instincts may lead you to believe, however, so you can order from well-known and long-established shopping sites even more confidently than you can place a phone order with your favorite department store.

Top Ten Fashion Items
Mothers Don't Need

10. Different little matching bags for her outfits. We must pack to survive, as well as keep our arms free to pick up little people or to hold their hands while crossing streets.

9. Pierced belly buttons to show off under our shortie tees.

8. Shortie tees.

7. Any article of clothing that blows open in the wind or is held up with one single tie at the shoulder.

6. Any shoe that can't be worn for four hours straight without needing an Advil, unless, of course, you have a limousine and a folding chair at your disposal.

5. Blouses designed to highlight the black bra underneath.

4. Any article of clothing not made of a recognizable fabric. That means no gold mesh halter tops, no vinyl hipsters, and absolutely no feathers on anything unless they're on your hat and you're dressed as Peter Pan or Pocahontas.

3. Anything that's in style now that you wore when it came out twenty years ago. There's an unwritten rule called "No Backsies" where retro fashion is concerned.

2. Tuxedo jackets and bowties with no dress shirt underneath.

1. Anything you buy on vacation in Santa Fe, Hawaii, the Bahamas (unless it's from a European designer in a duty-free store), or from a bridal design shop.

Who's Been Sleeping in My Bed?

It's a Conspiracy of Silence

I used to think that the single biggest lie off a married person's lips was how often they still had sex after their kids were born. Now I know that that little fib is a pasty white one compared with how often they misrepresent the sleeping habits of their children. More specifically, the biggest secret in America is how many parents still have kids sharing their beds at least two times a week. I certainly haven't read any government-funded studies on this matter, but my unofficial tally leads me to believe that about 75 percent of the parents on this planet with kids not much shorter than they are regularly find themselves ascribing to the Family Bed philosophy. This is either because they have considered all the options available and chosen this one, or because they are just so darned tired that they'd rather roll over and make room for visitors than get up in the middle of the night and re-Ferberize their midnight ramblers each and every time they stop by for a nocturnal visit.

Let me break the ice for the rest of you by confessing here and now that my husband and I have spent at least half our parenting life sharing our bed or making a bed on the floor. Of course, we have four kids aged twelve and under, and there should be some sort of mathematical credit for each individual sleep faux pas—in other words, if we'd only had one child, our statistics would probably look better, but our failure has to be considered in multiples of four. Still, we have a revolving bedroom door that seems to swing endlessly during those precious hours between *Nightline* and the morning news. I'm not proud of this, but I swear, we're not alone in our nighttime lifeboat.

It didn't start this way. I read the book about the comfort and nurturing offered by the Family Bed, but my husband was in lock step with me when I announced that no child, beloved as he or she might prove to be, would ever be allowed to encroach upon the sexy sanctity of our marital bed. I nursed my babies, some more than others, but that's another book, and I recognized the convenience and reassurance of having my fragile infants near me at all times. That's what bassinets were invented for; you have the baby beside you, but you feed him, change him and put him back into his own personal real estate throughout the night.

The Ferber Dream

Then, when the babies were about five or six months old, out came the books about getting them to sleep through the night in the comfort of their own cribs. I sincerely believed (and still do, at least on a philosophical level) that children needed this kind of tender teaching, even if it occasionally felt like tough love. Learning the gift of putting oneself back to sleep and self-comforting was a blessing, no matter how you cracked it. After all, most of us devoted parents fully intended to prepare our darlings for the delights of sleepovers, of school bud bonding through overnights at Astro Camp in sixth grade, or the ability to accept those full scholarships we expected to flow from fabulous colleges more than a thousand miles away. Okay, I admit that many of us would admit under torture that there was a side to us that yearned to accompany them on each and every one of these forays, but our better selves kept us naggingly in check . . . I would have sworn it.

It may have been six years since I last pulled up a chair in the hall outside the room of a howling infant, with an egg timer in one hand and a bottle of Advil in the other, but I remember it like it was last night. It's all a marvel to me, to this day, that I kept the faith—three nights with every one of my four babies—timing my reentries into their rooms to utter words of encouragement and a pat on the back, then leaving the nursery before I succumbed to the ardent desire to crawl into the crib with the miserable little tyke to offer the comfort that both of us wanted so badly. My husband opted out of this early life lesson. In fact, he usually took to his bed with all the pillows over his head. On the few occasions when he furiously marched down the hall to see how we were doing, he limited his remarks to such comments as "Are you out of your ever-loving mind?" or something to that effect.

But it did work, even without the full support of the Daddy side of the family. Each one of my Mommy-addicted babies eventually learned the lesson I was supposed to teach and slept alone in their cribs all night, barring any unforeseen events, like a smoke detector chirping that it needed a new battery or one of those dreaded double-ear infections. I was exonerated; not only that, I was heralded among the girlfriends. I had Ferberized my babies! God forbid that I should wear this medal of valor alone, however; my pillow-headed husband started spreading the tale of how "we" had taken a firm stand with our kids and taught them to sleep through the night in their own beds. You're talking to a woman whose mate tells the world that "we" also had a C-section with our first-born. Funny, I ask him to show me his incision or to demonstrate the total failure of his abdominal muscles and he comes up short. All I can suppose is that when he uses the term "we," he must have a mouse in his pocket.

So, for heavenly month after month, each darling cherub child slept placidly in his or her own crib. It was a thing of beauty. Reclaiming the marital bed was, without a doubt, one of the first and most significant steps toward making room for some grooving to take place in it. Then one day, one by one, they each discovered that by simply swinging a pudgy leg over the crib side and hurling their entire body behind it, they could be free. Sure, it involved a short free-fall and an abrupt landing on the carpeted floor, but once the landing was achieved with no serious injury—they were free!

I used to worry that an escaping toddler would go to the uber danger zone of the kitchen, perhaps to toast a Pop-Tart or boil some water. Or perhaps they would head straight for the bathroom to turn on scalding water or dive headfirst into the toilet bowl. I spent countless hours and dollars baby-proofing those areas to try to head off those disasters. But more often than not, it wasn't the kitchen or the bathroom the little wanderers were seeking; it was US! (Usually ME!) Toddlers who found freedom had one thing on their minds: finding Mommy and Daddy. Their padded little feet allowed them to travel in silence until they were close enough to breathe into our faces.

The first few times when I awoke, because I was sharing oxygen with a milk-breathed baby, I freaked out. I thought I was suffocating in a butter churn! Not only were they full of their entitlement to suck the fresh air out of my space and make me fear that I was getting menopausal night sweats prematurely by lying their incinerator bodies on top of me, but they seemed wide awake and game for anything we had to offer. What did they expect to find, a magician performing on our bed or a Candyland game set up on the comforter?

Where was Dr. Ferber now? Was I on my own? Was I supposed to dig out the old skills of getting infants to sleep? What good would that do when I now had kids who rivaled Houdini in his escaping prowess? Give me some credit for trying. I took each toddler back to the crib, careful to keep all lights low and conversation to a minimum, dropped him back in with a blankie and a bottle of water (don't come after me on the bottle thing while I'm baring my soul about my family bed, Girlfriends!!), and walked out the door with full intentions of returning ALONE to my bed. I usually made it all the way back under my still-warm comforter and resumed my coma before my toddler finished the bottle, tossed it over the crib side like an empty beer bottle, and prepared to swing that pudgy leg over the rungs yet again.

The Mind was Willing, but the Body Failed

This is when all hell broke loose in my meticulous parenting plans. I just couldn't do it all again. My feet were too cold, my sleep too fragile, and my husband too comatose to go through the drill again and again of returning my errant child to his bed. Okay, I offer my full confession: a second visit to Mommy and Daddy in the wee hours almost always culminated in my offering the interloper a quick boost up and over me into the middle of the bed. From that hour on, we suffered pudgy little pork chop feet in our face, baby breath up our nose, and very short arms laid indiscriminately across our heads. Shall I give you the rest? Hmmmm. I don't know; will this ever be used against me? Okay, okay, I break:

I Actually Enjoyed It!

You can mock me, but I don't care. I found the smell of Dreft in the baby's jammies had a narcotic effect on my husband and me, and we slept like poked and smothered BIG babies. Sure, the hours of REM

73

sleep were curtailed, but the hours of what I call "mother hen" sleep were delicious. I was content in the knowledge that all my chicks were in one basket and we were safe . . . at least until the next chick left the hatchery.

By the time subsequent siblings started their inevitable march to our bedroom like recently hatched sea turtles struggling to the ocean, I was totally bolluxed up. It was debatable whether we had enough room to share with one wiggle worm, and pretty evident that no sleep could be had with two, or later three and four, furry little puppies squirming for territory. Clearly, new criteria had to be found, AND FAST!

But that was just the problem. You'd think that the youngest little darlin' would have the inside track, right? Not necessarily so, I'm afraid. The little ones aren't even the most comfortable to share a bed with, so they really don't have a measurable edge in the sleepy-time Olympics. For one thing, the youngest little visitors don't usually have the story-telling skills that are so persuasive to delirious parents. They might offer their best shot, "I need Mommy and Daddy 'cause it's dark," and granted, that's pretty pitiful and persuasive. But a four-year-old gener-ally enters with real or feigned terror about a dream in which "A mon-ster ate Daddy and he's just waiting until I close my eyes to come after Mommy and me!" As a parent, honestly, which child do you sacrifice at a time like that? Not only that, older kids are actually easier to share a bed with because they understand that the head goes on the pillow and the feet go down under the covers. Toddlers look at a full-size bed as a trampoline-cum-painting canvas upon which they should express them-selves from the middle out to all four corners.

Things only become more complicated from there. How in the world do you close the inn to a six-year-old who just can't possibly sleep because she's afraid of school, especially Ryan, the class bully? And what about the eleven-year-old who actually says he has "insomnia" because of the pressures of making the soccer team AND getting a good grade on the social studies final? Besides, he usually enters our bedchambers with his four-years-younger sidekick, his little brother, who has complied by having a nightmare, too.

Is a Lock on the Door All It Takes?

Keep in mind, I've been writing magazine and newspaper columns on this issue (and several others), and I've gotten more letters reminding me of the invention of the lock for bedroom doors than I care to count. Hey, I might be overtired and overmanipulated by my kids, but I'm not so far gone that I failed to notice that piece of technology. In other words, I'm not quite as dumb as I may sound. I am also not as indifferent to the value of my marital intimacy as these well-meaning writers may think. I just wish that each and every writer had been forced to divulge whether they 1) had parented a child in the last twenty years, 2) were mothers or fathers (nothing personal; I just have this nagging suspicion that men are more inclined to make blanket statements about childrearing than moms because it's us moms who have to do the enforcing and clean up more fallout than Chernobyl left the next morning), and 3) any children they did parent are willing to consent to follow-up interviews so that I can see if they are as well-adjusted as their parent suggests.

Sure, I have most modern conveniences in my house, including locks on several key doors, but the only ones I regularly use are those that lead outside the house. First of all, I have a "no locking" policy for all members of this family under driving age because I have spent far too many hours looking in my five or six junk drawers for the skeleton key to free a toddler who has locked herself in the bathroom or to barge in on my older son and his friends before they've had enough time to tie up my younger son and throw him onto the roof. One of my worst nightmares is not being able to rescue a child behind a locked door with water running in the tub or the sound of a match being scratched against a box.

According to the better parents who write to me and proclaim I'm a victim of wimp mothering, kids are smart enough and resourceful enough to recognize a locked door to Mom and Dad's room as a sign that they must turn around and handle their problem alone. Sounds good on paper, but what about the three-year-old who has just learned to awaken when the sensation to go potty presents itself, but who can't face a darkened toilet alone? Which would I rather have, a night of sleeping in the nude with my beloved or a toddler curled up outside our door with wet jammies?

And what about those monsters? Everyone knows that monsters can be outrun by a child, but that they will surely catch their prey if they are stopped outside a locked door. It doesn't take total recall to be able to conjure up our own childish visions of our parents unlocking their door in the morning to discover nothing more than a pile of tiny kid bones and a "blankie" draped alongside.

We *close* our bedroom door now that the kids are old enough to come in and find us, and we don't need to be able to hear them breathe in their own rooms, but it really means nothing. Not only that, but I still haven't thrown out my baby monitors, so I know they're coming as soon as they throw off their covers. Just like moms can tell from a baby's cry whether it's tired, hungry, or in pain, I can tell from the vibrations on the floorboards which child is running my way and how urgent the visit is going to be. What do the door-lockers suggest I do—ignore these early warning signs and go back to sleep? I'm already awake and on alert before the doorknob has been turned, so what difference does it make whether they finish the trip or not? No matter how you crack it, it's *sleepus interruptus,* so what difference does a locked door really make?

The Marital Sacrifice

I'm not oblivious to the toll this takes on my relationship with my mate. We still want sex, and we want it more than we get it. Not only that, we want intimacy, we want cuddling, and we want to pretend that we are still boyfriend and girlfriend, in spite of the four little snorers who share our home. I can't promise you that all this midnight rescuing doesn't come at a price. All I can tell you is that I've calmly explained to my own husband that I could more easily adapt to widowhood than being divorced, so if I catch him looking for some fetching little buttercup who still sleeps in the nude with her mascara on, I'll just have to kill him. A clean solution, but not the one I would choose.

I really love and like my husband, and I pray that parenting hasn't been the kiss of death for our marriage, but even with seventeen years under my belt, I can't guarantee that my way is the right way. So far, I think the biggest thing I have in my favor is the fact that my mate is as tired as I am. I know straight up that I couldn't stay awake even if Antonio Banderas delivered my milk in the morning and promised to wait in my pantry until the family went to school and work. I might go so far as to lead him upstairs to my bedroom, but I can't be certain whether his amorous advances would prove scintillating enough to get me to stop watching the second half of the *Today* show on the bedroom TV. Pitiful, I know, but I accept your pity and hope for a brighter future.

Bedtime Fashions

I have dressed for bed like a fireman on call for twelve years now. That's a big sacrifice for me, because I adore high-thread count sheets and change my bed twice a week just to feel the smooth percale against my skin. Ever since I graduated from college and communal living, I'd slept nude. It was spectacular. No nightgown creeping up to settle around my neck like a noose, plenty of fresh air for my private parts to breathe, and the self-soothing feel of rubbing my shaved legs slowly up and down between the slick sheets. Oh, yeah, and when my husband came along and started sharing my bed, he liked it, too.

Not only is there a sense of liberation to sleep in the nude, but it is a distinct call to attention for the sexually active. If you cuddle and something stirs, you know it right away; no wondering if he has a banana in his pajama bottoms or is just happy to feel you. Breasts, buttocks, and all the good things that are attached nearby are right there, available for fun and games. Even an idiot knows that climbing naked into bed with another person is an open invitation for touchy-feely.

We don't have that anymore, at least not for the time being, and I'm really sad about it. Even at his most uninhibited, by husband never slept completely nude; he has this cold feet thing that sends him to bed in big white athletic socks, but I could get him out of those babies in under ninety seconds, even with one arm tied behind my back. But now we dress for a different kind of action. I don't want to lay 100 percent of the blame on the doorstep of parenthood, since we live in temblor-prone California and have been forced out of our bed and onto the street or into the yard at least four times that I can remember. Still, it is Amahl and the Night Visitors who are more motivating than any old earthquake.

I may be a love child at heart, but I just don't have the emotional fortitude required to deal with a whimpering child when I'm naked or clad in nothing more than panties and a muscle tee. First of all, my oldest son first noticed my breasts at the age of three and unabashedly stares at them so intently that he is often unable to get the words out to describe his fear or need. If modesty weren't enough, let's not forget how *cold* one gets if she's leading her little one back to his bedroom, visiting the bathroom (since all women who've given birth must use the toilet every time she shifts in the night), and turning off a few lights during her nightly wanderings.

If you actually surrender and bring your child into your bed, it's even creepier not to have several modesty layers between you and your cuddling baby. Go ahead, you free spirits, and tell me how uptight and unnatural I am. It falls on deaf ears. Once I've stopped offering my breasts as a source of sustenance, they no longer belong to anyone but my beloved mate and me, not necessarily in that order.

Where my husband is concerned, his ubiquitous socks and a pair of boxers will usually suffice. My daughters are pretty fond of his chest hair and may put themselves back to sleep by digging their hands into it, but that falls within acceptable boundaries to us. Still, the issue of staying warm, whether it's his turn to get up and kill the monsters living in the tub or when the monkey in the middle of the bed has pulled all the covers off us and cocooned himself in them, has to be considered.

Lovers and Other Strangers

As kids grow up and become more social, they have this inexplicable need to bond with their friends by spending their sleeping hours together. That means, on any given weekend in the Iovine household, there can be up to four or five small, unrelated people sleeping under our roof. If you haven't experienced sleepovers yet, let me be the first to lay down some surprising ground rules. Even if you and your mate have established a relaxed bedtime dress code for your own family, everything must be seriously reevaluated by the time someone else's child comes over for the night.

Think about it. Do you honestly relish the thought of a five-year-old going home and asking her parents why little Jessica's mom "wears the kind of panties where they look normal in the front but are just a string in the back"? Or would you really like the entire first-grade class to learn that you sleep in an ugly T-shirt that "shows your whole bottom"? If you think that your miniature visitors won't give a fashion report to his or her parents within ten minutes of pickup the next morning, you're living in a fool's paradise. I've had parents call me the next day to ask if it was true that I had fifteen pairs of never-worn high heels in my closet, that our dogs are allowed to eat off our dinner plates, and that we drink wine, not just during dinner but after.

Now that we're all so conscious, too, about sexual improprieties where kids are concerned, one of the biggest parenting nightmares you can head off with this warning is to have a little girl go home to tell her big, burly dad that when she and her tiny hostess couldn't sleep because the mean daddy in the *Sound of Music* video scared them, they rushed into the hostess's parent's bedroom and climbed into a bed with a daddy who was "practically naked." My conscientious mate wears sweatpants, a T-shirt and, of course, the socks, to bed whenever a sleepover is in the making. Can you blame him?

That's a big consideration when we become parents: Our kids bring strangers into the family bed. Just as it takes a village to raise a child, it takes two modestly dressed parents to supervise and soothe the little people who show up on our doorsteps with a sleeping bag and a duffel in hand. Not only do we owe it to the little guests to make them feel safe, or later, to let them know that all their movements are being surveilled, we owe it to ourselves to protect our reputations from any revelations that are sure to be shared by these little town criers.

The bottom line is this: Getting our groove back requires dressing for the part, day and night. For as long as we must occasionally dress like camp counselors, we still live with the mind-set that some of our nights are to be spent like Welcome Wagon hostesses, not like lovers. Thank God for the other nights.

Where's Mr. Blackwell When You Need Him?

You know me and my perpetual search for comfort in all aspects of my life, so you know I'm not going to get up on my soapbox and order you all into your nearest Victoria's Secret. In fact, my young and very sexy unmarried-but-living-with-a-hunky-actor Girlfriend, Michelle, tells me that see-through nighties and garter belts and the like are only supposed to be worn *before* bed; after the fun and games, lots of child-free women across this country slip back into drawstring pants and a cotton camisole. Turns out, wearing plaid flannel pants and a hoodie is not only acceptable fashion noir, but it's actually hip.

The point here is to capitulate onto the need for more coverage, but not to throw out all fashion and grooming with the baby's bathwater. Remember, baggy flannels can be dropped with the simple release of a drawstring and a little sleep tee can be short and loose enough to allow inquiring hands to reach up and under it at will. My best advice, if it's a welcome wagon night, is to pretend like you're preparing for a night of romance, even if you're still dressing like a surf bum. Take a bath and rub on lots of yummy-smelling body lotion. Wash your hair and leave it loose. Forget the moisturizing gloves and the Breathe Right strips unless your sleep partner is out of town. Think of it like high school; you might look presentable enough for that cute guy in algebra, but your clothing should never be so restrictive that you can't concentrate on the Pythagorean theorem.

Why Is the Bed So Significant?

In the beginning, sleeping in a bed that allowed visitors was more a decision of convenience than anything else (well, that baby smell *was* pretty intoxicating!). When I was nursing my babies, occasionally I fed them in my bed and fell asleep before I could think to get up and put them back in their own beds after the Fabulous Ferber years, and during the toddler years, I often just caved by their third visit to Mommy and Daddy's bed and would have let them hang from the ceiling lamp if they'd just be safe and quiet.

But there was something even more powerful about lying in the dark with all my chicks in one basket. It felt so *safe* and so *precious* to have these times that I knew wouldn't last forever. My husband hums the theme song from *The Love Boat* whenever he comes into the bedroom and discovers all four kids and me under the covers, sharing popcorn, and watching a video of *James and the Giant Peach*. To me, it's not so much the *Love Boat*, as my own personal life raft. All my heart is contained in one flotation device, bobbing on the seas of change and growth.

As the kids have become more independent, going off to spend a weekend with family friends who live at the beach, attending middle-school retreats, and staying out later for bar mitzvahs and thirteenth birthdays, I feel so torn. On one hand, I want to celebrate their confidence and adventurous spirits and to do some celebrating alone with my husband. On the other hand, I am beginning to see how this movie will play itself out; they'll go away more and more, finally never to come back to my bed again. With that in mind, I'm pitifully grateful when my oldest son deigns to lie down on the bed after coming home from a party to tell his dad and me about who he danced with and if anyone suggested playing Truth or Dare. And I love giving my baby girl, my six-year-old, a warm bath, dusting her with powder, blow-drying her hair, and wrapping her up in my down comforter until she falls asleep in our bed. Then we move her back to her own bed before we grown-ups reclaim our adult retreat.

It's less and less common for my kids to need the safety and cuddles our bed provides. You'd think I'd get down on my knees and thank Mr. Sandman for giving me my rest back, but I haven't yet. I'll tell you who *has* been getting his sleeping groove back, and that's my husband. As much as he has loved being able to fall asleep against the velvet upper arms of our children who still have the scent of shampoo in their hair, he's loving reclaiming his turf. I'm sure he wishes I was as resolved about it as he is.

Okay, so I'm not there yet. I *am* taking my own baby steps toward letting them be independent and letting my mate get a little more dependent than he's been allowed to be in thirteen years. Right now, I'd say I've progressed to a point where I can put all the kids to bed and expect them to stay there, but it takes me about an hour each night to complete my tucking-in ritual. The girls share one room and the boys another, so after I've made my first round to put bottles of water beside each bed, fluff up the pillows, and tuck each big baby in, administer nose spray to my two allergic offspring, rub cream onto chapped lips, and inspect everyone's fingernails, I spend about twenty minutes in the girls' room reading *Anne of Green Gables* to them and the next twenty minutes reading *Harry Potter* to the boys. I then change into my own sleep attire, brush my teeth and deal with my complexion, and then I go back into each room to make sure everyone is really sleeping, that our second son (the one with adenoids the size of tennis balls) isn't mouth breathing, and that the youngest is still facing up toward her pillows rather than sleeping upside down or on the floor. Then I'm ready to meet my life partner for a little "tucking in" of our own.

I figure that at this rate, I may someday be able to deposit each of these little angels off at college without needing to check myself into the nearest mental institution. My endlessly tolerant and loving husband trusts me that by that time I will be ready to be his girlfriend again. Sounds good to me, too.

The Mothers' 24/7 Workday

*F*or those of you particularly pressed for time, let me cut to the core of this chapter. I'll give it to you now in one sentence, and then you can come back for the details some sleepless night or during several episodes of bathroom reading. Here it is: **You CAN have it all, just not all at the same time and depending on what your personal definition of "all" is.**

Please, feel free to prove me wrong by your own example if you want, but the Girlfriends and I are here to tell you that we've been performing this juggling act for several years now, and there are dropped balls all over the place. In the early days of television there was *The Ed Sullivan Show,* a variety lineup consisting of everything from the Beatles to a mouse puppet with an Italian accent who always wanted Ed to kiss him, but my favorite regular was this overcaffeinated guy who would spin plates on sticks that were planted in a line on the floor. While they were spinning, they would stay in the air like flying saucers, but his job was to run up and down the line, shaking each stick just enough to keep the plates from succumbing to gravity and shattering on the floor. I feel like that guy must have felt my pain. My husband phrased it more sweetly recently when he told me that I was the family hummingbird: I was never seen perched calmly on a branch, chirping a lovely melody, but rather moved from the "flowers" of each of my kids, him, my work, and the business of running our home, emitting a frantic little buzzing noise. Either analogy gives you the general sense of the frenzy that is my Girlfriends' and my life.

In theory, I love having a career. In fact, I love it nearly as much as having children. Okay, just between you and me, there are times when I like it more; unlike parenting, jobs can be left at the end of the day, jobs let you know annually whether you're performing well, and jobs force you to at least consider putting on pantyhose and adult clothing. In the big picture, however, I love my children more passionately and essentially than I love my job, and that's a new little wrinkle wrought by motherhood and its changing priorities. Until I actually became a mother, I never understood how perpetually torn and distracted I would be—when I'm home, I worry about work, and when I'm at work, I worry about what's going on at home. I never seem to be fully present wherever I am.

Like many of you, I worked for several years before I had kids and I intend to continue working long after they've gone off to some dot com college or joined the World Wrestling Federation. As an adult, I defined myself by the work I did, and I just assumed that becoming a mom would be the second part of my hyphenate: Writer-Mother or Attorney-Mother or Community Activist-Mother, or whatever. I could and would have the best of both worlds—after all, that's what I'd been promised since I first read *Ms.* magazine.

Don't get me wrong, I'm not Pollyanna sitting here at this keyboard. I know from experience that all jobs are not equal and their significance in the family coffers varies from family to family. Granted, I like writing books more than I liked a previous job as a corporate attorney, and the attorney job was a big step up from the job before it, when I wore a wench's costume that displayed my meager cleavage and maximum booty while I served cocktails I'd never even heard of. Then again, being a wench was a big step up from my job as part of a cleaning and refurbishing crew of college housing. To this day, I still don't know how college kids can make so many holes in the ceiling without a rifle, but I don't want to pollute my brain thinking about it too much.

Once I found a career that I thought I could devote a significant portion of my future to, I wasn't completely clueless about the sea change that motherhood would bring into my life. I knew that I'd probably need the six weeks maternity leave that my employment package guaranteed me (if not to recover from my effortless delivery and mastery of nursing, then to write all my thank-yous for baby gifts and concentrate on losing the last of my pregnancy poundage before slipping into my nonmaternity work clothes), and I planned to be stricter with myself about quitting work at the end of the day to get home for some quality family time in the evenings. Aside from that, and the undeniable need to find some good child care to bridge the gap, I felt completely up to squeezing and stretching my time and attention to embrace a job and a baby or two (or four).

Living up to Expectations

The next time a woman tells you that, with a little time management, lots of self-discipline, and regular ingestion of Ginkgo Biloba and Metamucil, you can run a Fortune 500 company while raising polite, well-adjusted little achievers in a clean home with fresh laundry and a couple of balanced meals a day and maintain a marriage brimming with newfound romance and passion, do me a favor and give her a good whack upside the head. If I thought I was the only one letting her plates crash every single day, I wouldn't even admit it to you, let alone write a chapter about it, but I've made it my life's work to interview every single working mother I've ever met to see if any of them are shard-free, and I've come up empty-handed.

The single most appalling thing that happened to my work ethic and dedication was the birth of my first child. I'd thought I was prepared, but I never expected a tiny little preverbal critter to make most of my other interests in life seem, at least in the beginning, colorless and insignificant. I was personally attending to the perpetuation of the species, and there wasn't a personal injury suit alive that seemed as urgent. Even my Girlfriend Emily, a plastic surgeon, often finds herself torn between wanting to devote an afternoon to finding just the right decorated birthday invitations to match her three-year-old daughter's dancing fairy princess party motif and performing yet another mini-lift on someone who is distinctly NOT a dancing fairy princess.

Still, Emily, like I, has enjoyed the stimulation, professional respect, and satisfaction of a job well done, and, of course, the money the pursuit brought her long before she'd discovered the joy of theme birthday parties. I suppose there are some of us who are in the blessed situation of being able to reconsider our commitment to our careers once motherhood came along, but how were we supposed to do that? Did we just up and quit, with never a look back? Did we try to backpedal a bit and cut down to part-time or job-sharing? Were we delusional to think that the world would wait for us to kick-start our kids and then return to our former jobs? The employment pool is crawling with other people who are falling all over themselves to fill the vacuum we would leave, and you can bet they don't plan to step aside once we've had our fill of being the Brownie troop leader for a year.

Exactly When is it That We Can Have it All?

Just like my Girlfriend Nikki says that there are certain windows of opportunities for forging deep friendships, there are also traditional windows for merging motherhood with work outside the home. According to the statistics (please don't ask me *which* statistics, since I can't remember where I read them right now), over half of the women who have babies return to their jobs as soon as their negotiated maternity leave ends. The anecdotal truth, as least among the Girlfriends I've talked to, is that they often resume their jobs outside the home much sooner by being connected through phones, faxes, and the Internet. All I can say is, it's a good thing most hospitals prohibit the use of cell phones for fear of their interfering with pacemakers and other high-tech equipment, or there would be a lot of laboring women handling crises at their offices in between their panting and hee hee breathing.

If you want to get the lowdown on returning to work right after having a baby, please consult *The Girlfriends' Guide to Surviving the First Year of Motherhood*, in which I give a very colorful, and apparently still traumatized, account of experiencing postpartum depression on the job, having your nursing breasts stage a mutiny and let down during a sales presentation, and managing to keep a swing shift when you haven't been to sleep because of a colicky baby.

Then there is another category of mothers who don't necessarily need or want to return to work after a six-week leave to pay the rent and keep food on the table or to keep their companies from going into the toilet in their absence. This is the vast gray area in which choosing to return to work is a complicated formula consisting of personal fulfillment and commitment to the job, multiplied by the hope of eventually owning a home, having at least one vacation a year and putting a little something away for the newborn's eventual matriculation to college, and subtracting from the sum the total cost of hiring support people to stand in for you as childcare and household maintenance providers.

So many different factors determine when and if a woman will return to the workforce. For some, going back to work seems natural after they've finished breastfeeding and their children can walk and talk. For others, an unexpected divorce or change in their partner's financial status will rush matters along. Then, getting the kids into school for a major part of the day signals a good time to ease back into work. And still others find themselves registering with an employment agency when their teenagers don't want to talk to them or be seen being dropped off by them at school. The last group of women entering the workforce are those who've successfully pushed their little fledglings out of the nest and discovered they have a lot of wisdom and energy to put somewhere outside the home.

Then again, there is always the very real possibility that even your best laid plans will be broadsided by another pregnancy. For as long as you're still ovulating and copulating, you have to allow for your house of cards to collapse and accept the new hand that heaven deals you. Like Sally said, the nature of motherhood is that getting your groove back may have several false starts. For the sake of *Getting Your Groove Back*, let's arbitrarily assume that those of us who didn't return to work outside the home within the first year or two have either slipped back into the workforce or are considering it now that all our kids have been successfully established in preschool or kindergarten.

I once answered a letter in my *Los Angeles Times* column in which the mother felt that the world had conspiratorially agreed that even the most devoted and fulfilled stay-at-home moms only had a "divine doctor's note" to be excused from working for money until their kids started school. Then, evidently, her "free ride" was over and the kid became custody of the public school system and whatever after-school activities her community had to offer. I told the writer that I hadn't noticed my own parenting responsibilities diminishing just because my kids were old enough to know better than to put a fork in the toaster or the dog in the microwave. On the contrary, my Girlfriend Shirley's mantra, "The bigger the kids, the bigger the problems" was proving even more accurate a prediction than "Red sky at night, sailor's delight."

This letter really struck a nerve; in fact the only two issues that inspired as much reader mail were whether kids under the age of seven should be allowed in restaurants that don't give out crayons with the menu and whether a woman should tell her Girlfriend if she thinks the Girlfriend's mate is having an affair. It was obvious that many stay-at-home moms felt that society believed that devoting oneself to full-time mothering was a free ride that they were only entitled to for about five years. If a woman had been trained as a doctor, a lawyer or day trading chief, then deciding to "give it all up" and parent full time was like welching on a deal. Sure, civilization would accept, even encourage, mothers to devote their big brains and valuable career experience to the lesser demands of raising their offspring, but once the kiddies were out of the house in the hands of professional teachers for six or seven hours a day, it was time for Mom to put the bonbons back in the freezer and get a real job again.

We're Our Own Harshest Critics

Even if society wasn't yammering at them to start punching the clock again, "Girlfriends with choices" (meaning anyone who'd grown up watching *Family Ties*, in which Elise Keaton was always available to share heart-to-hearts with her four kids over a glass of orange juice and work as an architect) have historically beaten themselves up for even considering letting their bar memberships lapse, their union status move into "inactive," or their employment contracts expire. Look, I realize that for many of us, there is no choice about working for money or not; if we don't, the kids don't get designer sneakers, all the utility bills come in pink envelopes, and we don't qualify for a Costco or Sam's Club membership card.

The world is usually incredibly enthusiastic about this group of mothers having jobs—heaven forbid they should need federal or state assistance. But for the group of women who *could* stay home with the kids, assuming they can get a third mortgage on the house, forego all vacations till the year 2050, and color their hair at home, the decision is murkier. And for women who yearn to work simply because they want independence, fulfillment, and the satisfaction of knowing that they've made an impact beyond their own carpool, well, the world is torn between those people who view them as self-sacrificing and those who view them as selfish.

As long as the rest of us aren't asked to pick up their kids from Indian Guides meetings or assume their hours as hot-lunch volunteers, we don't care what career decisions they make. The minute we feel imposed upon to pick up their slack, even those of us with "Sisterhood Forever" tattoos on our ankles, however, start making snarky remarks about certain people with certain misplaced values.

Take it in Baby Steps

With nearly thirteen years of experience in the motherhood fox-holes, I've found that one or two truths have become obvious to me. One of them is this: It's always wiser to plan your parenting in bite-sized chunks rather than for the full eighteen-year sentence. Since raising children is life's biggest ad lib, you owe it to yourself to expect to learn on the job and change course accordingly. For example, even if you began promising yourself from the time you started baby-sitting that you'd never "plug up" your own baby with a pacifier, you should feel completely entitled to reconsider just as soon as you've given birth to your second child and your first has become obsessed with taking up nursing again, at twenty-two months of age. Or, if you criticized your own beloved sister for allowing her toddler daughter to sleep in Mommy and Daddy's bed and then awoke one day to discover that you'd been sleeping on the floor beside your own baby son's crib for three straight months, you should know that you're allowed to rethink your position.

The same is true with work outside the home. I'm going to say it again, at the risk of you throwing this book into the trash compactor: Motherhood is a marathon, not a sprint. You may end up with several starts and stops in your professional résumé before your kids are old enough to pick out their own clothes, and that's completely fine. One of the best insights into getting your groove back is realizing that how you get through your day today is not a life sentence. You get to reinvent yourself and your life right up to the time you consider the hosts on QVC your best friends and care whether Regis Philbin has stayed true to Joy. Judging by my own Girlfriends and me, there are several times when career and family collide ferociously enough to make you combust spontaneously. Just stop, drop, and roll, then get up and try again when you're ready.

A Good Scout is Always Prepared

I've already mentioned that old Yiddish expression that translates into something like "If you want to make God laugh, tell Him your plans." Well, the older I get, the more I wish I spoke Yiddish. Like nearly every woman I've ever met who faced impending motherhood, I spent about thirty-two of my forty gestational weeks making plans, particularly about how to smoothly integrate a brand-new human being into my already filled-to-the-brim life.

First, my husband and I'd evaluate the individual chores that composed the running of our tight ship and reassign them so that I had more free time to devote to the baby. Second, I'd ask my mother-in-law to come out as soon as I felt my first contraction. Third, I'd work as close as possible to my due date to have more time for postpartum recuperation. Fourth, I'd start freezing casseroles in my fifth month so that I'd have enough enchiladas and turkey-noodle concoctions to last till Armageddon. Fifth, I'd stay in touch with the world at large by asking my office to copy me on all faxes and give me phone messages at the end of every day (this was a couple of years before e-mail).

Then, at about twenty-five weeks into my first pregnancy, I was told by the ultrasound technician that I had a condition called placenta previa. From that moment on, I was put on strict bed rest, only getting up to use the bathroom or to go back for another sonogram. What?! Were they kidding?! I hadn't even begun shopping for the nursery furniture, let alone freezing any casseroles. In case I didn't get it, the doctor drew me a picture—I get up and run around like I'd planned and I could hemorrhage and lose the baby, and maybe even my uterus. So, in bed I stayed until the final doctor's visit, when they performed an amnio and determined that the baby's lungs were developed enough to breathe here on earth and my C-section was scheduled for dawn the next morning.

If I'd listened, I'm sure I would have heard God chuckling quietly in the atmosphere. Bed rest, C-section, premature baby, colic, and a good bout of mastitis should have been sufficient to clue me in on the precariousness of my motherhood/career plans. With all this evidence, however, I still persevered in my devotion to slipping this uncooperative little baby boy into my wild and wonderful working life. Sure, there might be a few hiccups in the beginning, but everything would lead to smooth sailing by the time I went back to work four weeks after having my tummy turned inside out and stapled back together . . .

Okay, so four weeks weren't enough, but it wasn't for lack of enthusiasm. I still believed that it was my job to ease my baby into my universe and it was his job to be a good sport and play along. After about three months postpartum, when I entered the neighborhood grocery store with my baby cozily sleeping against my chest in a front pack and started weeping because I couldn't remember what I was supposed to buy in such an emporium, I started understanding that this baby was not only NOT fitting into my universe, but he had created his own and was daring me to come on in.

Renegotiating the Marital Contract

In a conjoined, but not fully integrated, universe lives my husband. I don't want to spend too much time in this book talking about Daddy's adjustment to sharing his sunshine with a new little baby or two because I've hammered that nail to death in previous books. Even though, after nearly seventeen years of marriage and thirteen years of motherhood, I still haven't managed to integrate any of the romance tools into my life that all the experts suggest, such as making "dates" with my husband and scheduling child-free vacations, I do at least know what I'm supposed to do to keep the marriage torch lit, and I thought we were doing pretty well.

Then last year I took on a new business. In addition to my work as a writer, I decided to branch out into the dot com world. After all, my youngest was in kindergarten all day, and it seemed like the time was ripe to redirect some of my energies. I took an office away from home and hired employees. I left home after the kids went to school and worked till dinnertime. Then, after dinner and homework with them, I'd do my family chores and return phone calls and send e-mail. No big deal for a woman who just three years earlier had finally thrown away the baby potty and the leftover Pull-Ups, right?

How could I have been expected to know that my husband had been counting the days till the last kid was successfully launched into academia so that I could return to the "good ol' days" when I could not only think about what to feed my husband for dinner, but actually go out, pick a chicken, and lovingly pluck it for his delight? I was absolutely stunned to learn that my mate had considered the previous ten years as a temporary distraction *from him*? Call me oblivious, but it never occurred to me that my husband might be quietly yearning for the return of the girl he married, just like a scene from *Lassie Come Home*.

As any of you with a business of your own knows, shit happens! I had a handle on my days some of the time, but other times my assistant called in sick, my computers all crashed, and I now had to find time for meetings with bankers, human resource experts, and potential clients. Without going into all the hairy details, suffice it to say that I was even more busy than I'd been when I had an infant and several toddlers underfoot, and to say that my husband took it on the chin is like calling labor "like bad menstrual cramps."

"You are violating our marriage contract," my mate explained to me one night, his body emitting desperation through its pores.

"What are you talking about?" I screeched back at him—a little too defensive, perhaps, but with twenty years of women's liberation standing behind me. "Are you saying that it's okay for YOU to pursue your dreams and test your mettle outside of this house, but not for ME?"

"No, I'm just saying that when we decided to have kids, you didn't have this other career. If I'd known then that you planned to be Martha Stewart in ten years, I would have been a little more careful about the condoms! You can't just birth all these kids and then leave the house and expect them to raise themselves!"

"Well, what about you chipping in a little bit more? Why do YOU get to come home at night and read all the mail and take a shower before even asking if the kids have homework? Why can't you pick up the slack for me?" I courageously continued.

"Because I was the hunter-gatherer then and I'm the hunter-gatherer now. If you expected to become a hunter-gatherer, you should have given me some warning!"

I've relived this moment a thousand times since it happened, and I've got to concede, he has a point. Not that I'm saying his point necessarily applies to anyone outside my house, but I had changed the rules with very little warning. As I've consulted my Girlfriends, I've learned that almost ANY abrupt changes in domestic responsibilities are dangerous. The first time I informed my darling co-parent that I was too busy to attend the meeting for all parents of kids on my son's sports team and that he'd have to go instead, you'd have thought I'd suggested he quit his job and burn the house down. As far as he was concerned, since I was the one who opened the mail from school and put the significant dates on the calendar, the monkey was on my back. After all, I had the whole semester to get the rhythm of extracurricular activities, and he couldn't even remember the names of all four of the kids' teachers.

I'm not sharing the inner workings of my marriage with you to condemn him or convince you of my righteousness; I'm mentioning it so that you can be better prepared than I was when it happens to you. I knew my mate very well before I married him and had still four more years to have him etched into my brain before the babies starting tumbling out of the sky. He hasn't changed a whit, except to become more loving and generous through becoming a father, and it was sheer folly to think he'd suddenly become interested in the school hot lunch program and Grandparents' Day celebrations.

This renegotiation of the marital contract works both ways. I've been in elevators, conferences, and dinner parties with men who are just as appalled by their wive's reneging on their promise to return to work after their six-week postpartum checkup. "We had it all worked out," they indignantly maintain. "She knows we can't get by on just my salary, and now she's acting like I'm an ogre for suggesting that she 'abandon' our baby and go back to work. If I'd known she was going to put all the financial pressure on me, I would have insisted we wait to have kids."

You can't really blame these guys, either. Look, *we moms* had no way of predicting the overwhelming addiction we'd feel about our babies once we met them face to face; how could they have a clue? As much as they love their kids, many otherwise wonderful fathers find this maternal devotion a little unsettling, if not downright irrational. They can't be expected to know our cosmic connection with our offspring, to feel our ache when we haven't held them in three hours or know our secret belief that no one on the planet can possibly care for our babies with the love and intuition that we provide.

Robbing Peter to Pay Paul

In my own defense, I truly didn't know how incredibly hard my new job would be; it knocked me to the mats within two months, but I didn't know how to control the monster. I still don't. The only advice I have for you, whether you are facing a mandatory return to work right after giving birth or choosing to rejoin a world in which people speak in whole sentences and don't eat with their hands: **Try to bite off a much smaller piece than you feel ready to eat.** Careers are a lot like kids; they're much more work than you ever think they'll be.

Something's got to give, and if it can't be your job, then it's going to have to be your home, your social life, your marriage, or your expectations. Your marriage is the last thing to be thrown out with the bathwater, so you'd better get strong about bowing out of several of your other life busy-ness. As I've said before, no fairy godmother is going to come in and miraculously relieve you of dirty dishes, unopened mail, and overtime hours, so it's up to you to set the limits.

Your first course of action is to make a realistic appraisal of what you absolutely must do to to stay physically and mentally healthy. As the locomotive pulling the family train, you have to stoke your own fires. **The first priority is setting realistic goals for getting enough rest.**

You can tell me from now till the cows come home that you can exist on six hours of sleep a night, and I'm going to tell you that you're a delusional martyr. (Hey, if I can't give it to you right between the eyes, who can?) That means you're going to have to employ tough love to get your kids to sleep by 9:00 and yourself in bed by 11:00.

My Girlfriend Donna, who has been married for about twenty-five years and has a daughter who is a sophomore in college, emphatically believes that **one of the keys to a successful marriage is going to bed at the same time as your mate as often as possible.** When she first shared that with me, I panicked, thinking it meant that an enduring marriage required sex every single night. When I shared my anxiety with her, however, she reassured me that sex was just one of many options. What's important, she maintains, is getting into a rhythm with your lover that allows a few minutes of intimacy before you collapse into your nightly coma. That can mean a little chat, a little of Leno's monologue, or, yes, a little hanky-panky.

You'll find it a lot easier to keep to your evening routine if you **set up barriers against the outside world after six** P.M. My Girlfriend Marty has a firm rule about not taking phone calls once the dinner preparations have begun. She just turns on her answering machine and ignores everyone from long-distance carrier salespeople to her Girlfriends to her kids' friends until she gets the kids off to school the next morning. I'm so impressed with her self-discipline, but it's a possible dream for all of us. Think about it; once you have "all your chicks in one basket," meaning at home with you, what could anyone have to tell you that can't wait till morning? Everything else is just a distraction.

If exercise is essential to your well-being (as I wish it were for me), you're going to have to steal that time from something else, like your lunch hour or an extra hour of sleep in the morning. Knowing mothers as I do, I'm going to bet that you haven't actually sat down to an hour-long meal at noon for years, but you're going to have to find another time to do your banking, pick up the dry cleaning, or attend your Jenny Craig weigh-in. This will work most of the time if you compromise by devoting no more than three days a week to fitness (take the stairs at work and play tag with the kids after school if you have energy to burn on your off days). Remember, we're not talking about the rest of your life, Girlfriend; we're just getting you through this mommy adolescence.

Surrender half of each weekend day to family business. Saturdays are notoriously frenetic with sports, shopping for shoes (which must be done almost every three months), sleepover pickups, and finishing up any leftover homework. Try to schedule one personal maintenance chore for each Saturday afternoon, like getting a trim and root touch-up or putting your summer clothes in boxes to make room for your winter wardrobe. Saturday afternoons are great times for Dads to take the kids to get the car washed or visit Home Depot and maybe a drive-through lunch at McDonald's.

Weekend afternoons, especially if you're lucky enough to find an hour when all the kids are at sports practice, birthday parties, or in the care of some other mother, are also a long-standing tradition for my husband and me to excuse ourselves for a "nap." While I completely subscribe to Donna's wisdom about going to bed each night with my husband, we see a lot more action during "afternoon delight" than after dinner, after homework, after baths during the week.

Here's an odd one for you: **resist the temptation to sleep late on Sundays.** Sleep experts all agree that going to bed and getting up at the same time seven days a week is more restful in the long run than trying to catch up with all unfinished work on weekend nights and sleeping till ten in the morning. If *Saturday Night Live* is the highlight of your weekend, then videotape it. I'm sorry, but you've got more important demands to meet the following day.

I used to be pretty hit-and-miss about taking my kids to religious services, but my middle son and daughter told me recently that they liked being in church "because it's where they feel safest in the world." Believe you me, we now get there three weeks out of four, and it turns out that I feel safe and sound there, too. This is one of those commitments that I thought I made for the sake of my children, but that turned out to be just as nurturing to me. Now we try to devote Sunday mornings to prayers and rituals, then breakfast. The rest of the day is informed by that. My "holiness" tends to wear off by lunchtime, but with that kind of kickstart, I don't feel quite so guilty about retreating to my desk in the afternoon to get ready for the week ahead . . . or sneaking off for some of that afternoon delight.

Easing Back Into Work, Big Toe First

If you've postponed returning to work outside the home until now, here's my best advice: **try part-time first**. This will be hard because as soon as you get your sea legs, you'll probably want to take on more responsibility, but promise me you'll wait until the next time you and the kids all get the flu and the septic tank overflows in one week before you take another bite. (Sorry about the eating and toilet analogies in the same sentence.)

When I suggest that you consider part-time work, I also mean you should try to **create a buffer between you and the total functioning of your department or business.** The word here is: Collaborate. A partner, a job-sharer, or a superior who can cover you when you get the call from school that your kid's pearly permanent tooth is in a glass of milk and on the way to the hospital, along with the kid, is a tremendous insurance policy. I don't know about your work, but even if I were a fireman, I'd drop the hose and go running to the tooth, and it would be nice to know that someone else can keep the water flowing without me.

A couple little things happened out there in the job market while I was spoon-feeding strained vegetables to my kids, like the Internet, e-mail, and video conferencing. I knew about computers, which may not seem like much to you, but I have several Girlfriends who still don't know what AOL stands for. Since I'm handing out free advice here, let me mention that **the transition back into the workforce might have gone a tad more smoothly for me if I'd taken the time to learn the technology first.** This doesn't have to be that difficult. You can offer to volunteer in your kids' school office to pick up the knack for caller-conferencing, cutting and pasting on computer, and keeping a virtual filing system. Or call your local community college for their night course list—it's just teeming with classes in everything from desktop publishing to the fundamentals of sales and customer relations.

Even those of you who returned to work right after your kids' birth might be inclined to check out the nearly-free classes of a community college, YMCA, or church/synagogue. Think about it, you're approaching the next stage of your life, and maybe getting your groove back includes finally getting a job that you really like. Besides, getting away from the house one or two nights a week can be more invigorating and inspiring than four cups of coffee and an *Oprah* episode. I promise you, it will blow your mind to meet all those new people with dreams and aspirations besides getting a good night's sleep.

One last thing I'd recommend: **Find yourself a mentor.** Ideally, you'll cultivate a relationship with a woman with children who is navigating the seas of motherhood, marriage, and career. She doesn't have to have it down pat; she just has to be smart, generous with her wisdom, and more experienced than you. I have a Girlfriend who has been a network news reporter for nearly twenty years, and she recently told me that the most amazing thing had happened: All the young women who worked with her now spent more time asking her how she dealt with baby-sitters, mommy guilt over missed recitals, and sticking to a fitness regimen than they did asking how to phrase a killer question for an interview or where to set the cameras to capture all the shots. She said she felt like the Mother Goose of the news business. Great Girlfriend that she is, she shares everything she knows, but she's a little surprised that other working moms still don't have this balancing act figured out. I guess we were all sort of hoping that our daughters would never have to evaluate "quality time" versus "quantity time." The good news here is that you're no more behind the learning curve than any of the rest of us, Girlfriend.

Down in the Coal Mines

After all the years I'd spent trying to get pregnant, you'd think that my colleagues and superiors at work would dance around a tribal fire upon learning that I was finally "with child." Well, they did, for one night, but after that, it was stiff upper lip the rest of the way. Unless you happen to have a job where spontaneous vomiting, unpredictable crying jags, and chronic pantyhose itch are considered "value added," you may find your place of employment a little less hospitable than you'd hoped.

First of all, I never recommend that a Girlfriend take her home pregnancy stick to work the day after it gets its stripe. As joyous as the news truly is, there are several other considerations, such as whether you've negotiated a maternity-leave-with-full-pay-and-the-option-to-extend-at-no-pay-but-with-the-right-to-resume-work-without-losing-seniority-priviliges-or-your-benefits-package. Second of all, I find that most bosses, whether male or Girlfriend, can't help but wonder how your growing distraction will affect them. It's amazing how quickly men who can't even count the months between now and Christmas are able to calculate your gestation in a nanosecond and realize that you should be in your transition phase of labor right about the time of the company audit. Hey, lots of these coworkers are parents, too, and rejoice with you that Mother Nature has smiled on you; they're just a little worried that the Great Goddess has completely kicked their fourth quarter in the ass. It's no reflection on them, just their inability to understand any upset that does not involve their own child.

The other bit of nefarious advice I give my closest Girlfriends is to tell your co-workers and supervisors that you definitely intend to resume your career with even more energy and devotion after your baby is born. For all I know, you might even have believed it when you said it, but now, as we reevaluate our lives to get our grooves back, I'm pretty confident that you've realized how insincere you really were. If you returned to your for-pay job shortly after your baby was born, you are already keenly aware of the compromises and professional gymnastics being a working mother requires. If returning to your career after four or five years of concentrated mothering is part of getting your groove back, then you're still an innocent to the ways of the "little white lies" and "working from home" exercises in optimism. Let's bring you up to speed on those mommy concepts right now.

What They Don't Know Won't Hurt Them

I'm telling you that you can work for a children's developmental toy corporation and have a mommy/Girlfriend for a supervisor, and you will still occasionally find yourself wondering how to get out of an afternoon staff meeting in time to be with your little girl when she "flies up" from Bluebirds to Campfire Girls. As supportive as your work environment might be, there comes a time when a working mother has to choose whether it's wiser to explain that she has to take half a day off work to find out why her child has refused to take his morning dose of Ritalin or to just give a little white lie about a root canal or a repeat pap test that she needs to take. If you decide to share the bit about the reluctance to take prescribed medication, you're already revealing a lot more about your family life than you might have ever hoped to. And if you have to mention that you've chosen Ritalin as a coping mechanism for your child, then you open yourself up to a bigger debate than whether you should excuse yourself from half a day of work; you must be prepared to defend your and your husband's decision to medicate your child with a controversial drug and probably get into a discussion about whether attention deficit disorder and hyperactivity are overdiagnosed in this performance-driven era.

Gosh, it gives me a migraine just thinking of the land mines a well-meaning mom might trigger. It makes it a lot easier to see why the best explanation for missing an afternoon at work is your fictitious need for a biopsy. No one, especially a man, will press for more details about a medical procedure that involves needles, scraping of cavity walls, or slicing. I don't know about you, but my Girlfriends and I would much rather talk about our own real or imagined medical conditions than about those of our children. We'd rather state flat out that we have a breast lump than to whisper our fear that one of our kids has asthma, even if only because, superstitiously, we don't want to attract the evil eye to our kids. My Sicilian in-laws and husband have taught me over the years that it's acceptable to the gods to fib endlessly about your own physical condition, but when it comes to the babies we must repeat "He's just wonderful, Gobblessem." That keeps the bad spirits from taking any notice of the amazing blessing that is your child. I'm pretty comfortable with it, myself, these thirteen years since being admitted into the Mama Mafia, but I'd never want to suggest you behave in any way foreign to your own beliefs.

What a Girl Wants, What a Kid Needs

Here's how we moms see it: Our kids would prefer it if we didn't work and yearned only to devote our lives to shadowing them in their own exciting endeavors; to applaud when appropriate and to nurse boo boos when necessary. They may be mildly interested in certain aspects of our work, like the fact that we have access to a color copier or can spiral-bind their homework on the office machine, but they are only perfunctorily interested in whether our work fulfills us or makes us happy.

If we could be happy spending the entire first semester *on campus* building and painting the sets for the Spring Sing, they'd be even more joyful.

There's nothing wrong or spoiled about kids who expect their parents to be happy with the same things that make them happy. Life will barge in soon enough to let them know that they're not the Sun Kings and the rest of the world their adoring planets, so I see no reason to make it my job to teach too much humility at this point. Compassion, sure, but humility is a little premature for those of us trying to get our grooves back after we've introduced our babies into the bigger world.

I bring up the "work from home Friday," really, to show how unaware most workplaces still are about the vast responsibilities working mothers have shouldered. Yeah, your best copy writer may be spending a couple of valuable hours of her working Friday standing in line at the Department of Motor Vehicles, but that's because those are the only hours that make sense. Saturdays are too crowded and take twice as long, plus most soccer and Little League games are scheduled on weekends. Any woman with half a brain realizes that getting her driver's license renewed on Friday morning frees her up for much more concentrated work on Saturday, when her mate or a fellow sports mom, can take her budding Mia Hamm to the game and she can sit quietly at her computer.

She Needs a Plan

Our days take more planning than the invasion at Normandy, but two things will get us through most days: a thick skin and a schedule. Beginning with the thick skin, you'll spare yourself several months, if not years, of agony, if you just take the Girlfriends' word for it that your kids won't think you're giving them enough time and attention until they're about thirteen years old, and wishing you'd vaporize for about four years and leave your credit card and a full refrigerator behind.

106

Never begin a conversation with a question like, "Did you miss Mommy this afternoon when I missed your practice?" or "Did any *other* mother miss the spelling bee?" I promise, you'll be devastated by the answer. Even if the darling child never even noticed your absence, he or she will muster up some tearful answer just to play you like violin.

An incredible book was published in 1999 in which the author asked kids all the questions we working mothers have wanted to ask, but were too afraid of the answers. It's called *Ask the Children*, by Ellen Galinsky. This woman spent five years surveying kids and parents (but we already know what *they* guiltily said) about their attitudes toward the parents' work and how it affects family life. Surprise, surprise, surprise, as Gomer Pyle would say, kids are pretty fine about Daddy *and* Mommy working outside the home as long as the parents aren't overly conflicted about it. Turns out, kids may manipulate us a bit, but they actually take their cues from us about our work.

The most important lesson I learned from this book is to always characterize my work positively in front of my kids. In other words, instead of saying, "Did you miss Mommy at practice today?" I'm almost always certain to get a better response if I say something like, "Gosh, I feel so great about the meeting I had today while you were at practice. How was your day?" Banished forever from my parental vocabulary is the phrase, "I would have . . . but I *had* to work." I don't want my kids growing up to think that work is like a prison sentence, nor is it an overwhelming, unseen force that stands between them and my complete devotion to them.

As for the schedule: If you can establish some sort of routine for every day, not only will your kids relax into the predictability, but you will, too. It's one thing, for example, to have your child standing in the carpool line expecting a big reunion with Mommy and quite another for her to discover that the sitter is sitting behind the wheel. Plus, if you'd planned to be there and got caught at work at the last minute, I bet good money that you had to do a lot of scrambling to dig up that sitter without notice. Don't you think all three of you would be significantly more relaxed if you'd planned this in advance? No one expects us moms to be clairvoyant and the unexpected will happen with expected regularity, but a general pattern of Mom being available on Wednesday afternoons, Monday and Thursday mornings, and all weekend might be something you can strive for.

She Needs Another Plan, Too

Kids are ferociously smart and adaptable. They also understand the art of negotiation from a very young age. If you have a Plan A, go ahead and tell them what Plan B will be, in case Plan A crumbles into little pieces. Even a three-year-old will catch your drift when you say, "I will try to finish my errands in time to help Ms. Singer and the class with the macaroni art project, but if I don't finish in time, we will read *The Stinky Cheese Man* together before dinner." The most essential part of this promise, particularly for very young kids, is to be pretty sure you *can* fulfill Plan B. Do your best to avoid being vague about the day's plan or acting as though you have no control over where you'll be or when you'll be there. Kids can deal with a lot, but they really need to feel like you have at least half a clue about what the universe will be throwing at them. Remember, you're Mommy the Monster Killer.

Making Peace with the Twenty-four-Hour Day

Long as a standard mothering/working day may occasionally seem, it still is punctuated by your family's needs, your required presence on the job, and the coma that you fall into sometime between getting the kids to bed and answering your office e-mail at home. Go ahead and knock yourself out trying to find extra hours in each day, we've all done it. Tell yourself that even Winston Churchill lived on four hours of sleep a night, and *he* was in charge of restoring peace to Western Europe. Or, if Winnie is too distant a memory, feel free to buy the myth promulgated in your preschool group that you're surrounded by mommies who sleep six hours a night, get up at five A.M. to get their fitness training in and pack organic lunches for the kids, drive carpool, and head straight to the office. If you aren't ready to take the Girlfriends' word for it that they're either suffering from sleep deprivation–induced flights of omnipotence, then be our guest to try emulating that lifestyle. Sooner or later you'll have to at least consider that you've been sold a bill of goods. I sincerely believe that any human who does not spend at least seven hours a night in Lullaby Land is a potential serial killer, but hey, that's just me and my lazy crowd.

You will probably start your combined life of mothering and working outside the home with a schedule that would make General Patton (okay, enough of the World War II examples) get all warm and tingly inside. Those early-morning hours are particularly alluring; the kids and husband are still sleeping, the phones aren't ringing, and even the lighting is flattering as it comes in all rosy through the windows. What better time than this to read company memos, fill out student health questionnaires, and catch half an hour on the treadmill? So whose fault is it, Girlfriend, when you show up for work at nine and are certain that if you don't get your hands on a *grande latte* in thirty seconds you'll have to hide in the backseat of your car and catch a nap until lunch? The fact that you've gotten two loads of laundry done and entered the names of everyone in your first grader's class on your computer contact list is thrilling enough to get you through the pupil handoff and onto the freeway, but it isn't nearly a good enough buzz to keep you going till lunch.

I have a hundred Girlfriends who still ascribe to living a full and productive day before the crows have cockadoodledooed, put in another productive day on the payroll of their jobs, and then face those hours between six P.M. and bedtime as yet another day. Well, speaking only for myself, Girlfriends, I'm over it. I've learned over the years that there is not a single person on this earth (aside from my Girlfriends, who have absolutely no influence over my career and who rarely turn to me for mothering) who will take me by the hand from time to time to tell me that I'm doing a fabulous job at work and at home and should find some quiet time for myself.

Say "No" First, Ask Questions Later

I have a secret to share with you: It's always best to answer "No!" to any question posed to you, then take your time to reconsider. As a mother, you may already partly understand this wisdom. If you're anything like me, you can answer fourteen or fifteen questions from kids during one quick car ride to the orthodontist. Thirteen out of fourteen times you'll nod and make some sort of "uh-hummm" noise, but your Mommy Radar will shake you out of your stupor when you detect that a significant question has been zipped in your direction like "Can I have cereal for dinner tonight and eat it in my room?" or "Am I allowed to hit Jordan in the arm if he touches my stuff?"

"No!" you instinctively respond. What harm can that answer ever wreak? There's not a kid on the planet who won't ask you again in about thirty or forty seconds, giving you plenty of time to reconsider. Well, take that innate wisdom and apply it to all the other forces in your life asking your for time, money, or talent. I guarantee, they'll all give you the chance to change your mind, should you be so inclined. Start with paper responses; it's easier to build up your "no" muscles if you don't have to see the other person's face. The next time your child comes home with a backpack full of volunteering opportunities, either throw them away or write "No, thank you" in the response box. Then when you get the follow-up call from the teacher or room parent, be firm. Try saying something like "I've really enjoyed all the time I've spent in the kindergarten supply room, organizing all the tempera paints and cleaning the brushes, but I have already committed my personal time for the next semester."

If you're anything like me and my Girlfriends, you won't leave well enough alone. You'll feel a deep compulsion to divulge your hourly plans for the next twenty weeks like a patient talking to her therapist. Saying "no" is like lying—the shorter the explanation, the better. Trust me, it gets easier with practice; as my Girlfriend Chris's church pastor told her, " 'No' is a complete sentence." Even if you see the wisdom of that statement now, it's a long guilty journey to live by it. Keep in mind that you aren't shirking any responsibilities or obligations. An essential part of getting your groove back is recognizing that you are not the heart that beats to keep the school functioning, Parents' Association meetings well attended, and the space labs in orbit.

After you've rehearsed for a few weeks or months with all written requests for your time, take a deep breath and move on to your Girlfriends. This sounds sacrilegious, I know, but think about it—how many times a day do your precious Girlfriends ask you to pick up their kids, meet them at a boutique to approve their purchases, or join in those hateful chain letters? No, no, and NO! Your friends may be shocked and dismayed at first, but, trust me, if they're paying attention, they may learn a valuable life lesson here. Hey, you just might help them find their own groove! No need to be harsh, but you must actually utter the "n" word several times in the conversation. Otherwise, they'll think you're waffling and can be coaxed out of defining your own life. Silly girls.

Okay, now it's time to try out the art of declining at work. This requires a certain amount of suss, since we all know that the workplace is generally inhospitable to hearing that you aren't willing to donate a lung for the cause if necessary. The key to successfully saying "no" at work is to make sure that you are not shirking any part of your mutually-agreed upon job. If, say, you take a job that requires you work one Saturday a month, saying "no" to that Saturday just because your in-laws are arriving and need to be picked up at the airport just won't fly—pun intended.

In your next staff meeting when your superiors are asking who is willing to write the office newsletter or organize the company picnic, sit on your hand—break your own arm if necessary, but don't go waving your hand in the sky like a giant flycatcher. Either someone else will rise to the occasion, or, Lord have mercy on us, the company picnic may have to take a bye. Really, is eating funky food in a mosquito-ridden park more important than spending time with a wonderful book or visiting your own precious grandmother in the nursing home? Come to think of it, is that crummy picnic worth staying up all night stuffing deviled eggs when you could have sex and go to bed before Leno? In the big picture, Girlfriend, I promise you will miss the sex and sleep far more than the eggs.

If you have the chops to say no to your church, your school, your homeowners' association, and your colleagues, you're officially ready to close in on the loves of your life—your family and yourself. Let's say you have followed the volumes of suggestions for a happy marriage and made a date with your mate. Let's say, too, that your twelve-year-old son and his four friends lost their ride to the Chili Cook-Off Carnival. Pragmatism should reign. If the Chili Cook-Off lasts for more than one evening, you are well within your rights to decline the lovely chauffeuring invitation and offer to pick up the slack the next day. But let's be real here; if this is the only night for the undisputed cultural event of the year, you might just have to move your date over a night and go to the carnival. Stay in practice, however, and say "no" first, then let them beg you or bargain a little bit for the privilege.

After you've peeled away all the layers of obligations, duties, favors, and commitments to the rest of the world, you are left with the hardest person of all to say "no" to—YOU. "I know I have a temperature of 102 and green stuff coming out of my sinuses, but I have to get up out of this bed and get to my spinning class!" Or "I'd give anything to drive down to the beach and walk along the sand, but that would be such a big waste of time, what with all the photographs still in baggies in my drawer, waiting to be placed and captioned in albums." My husband says that most mothers are like sharks; they drown if the don't keep moving forward. It's as if we're running in so many directions that we're terrified of sitting down and staring at the clouds for a moment. I don't know about you, but I secretly fear I'll never be able to get up again.

Once a month, each Girlfriend should have a No Day, in which she does nothing but what she enjoys. This is harder than it sounds; I, for one, can't even remember what I used to do for fun. But I've recently started digging around in my rose garden and I found my old needlepoint stuff and I'm slowly getting the hang of just grooving. Walking, too, is a great No Day activity because it fools your guilt into thinking your accomplishing something, when really you're just taking your imagination out for a spin. If a whole day is impossible to come by, claim at least two hours a week for escaping into a book or taking a nap or singing along to Broadway show tunes. Whatever you do, don't answer the phone—it's sure to be someone calling to ask you to do something. Or if you must answer, Just Say No!

Neither Here nor There

The single most striking difference between fathers who work outside the home and mothers who work outside the home is that fathers seem to take off their parenting cloak and hang it on the hook in the backseat of the car for the day, only to put it back on when they pull into the driveway at home that night. Working moms, however, wear that heavy old cloak around day and night; they shower in it, they sleep in it, and they sweat in it no matter how air-conditioned the workplace may be. I don't want to make too broad a generalization, but I don't think my husband or the husbands of my Girlfriends simultaneously perform surgery and wonder whether their four-year-old daughter is getting along with the preschool bully. I don't notice my husband calling the school nurse from *his* office to see if our son has remembered his inhaler or if our daughter has been drinking enough water during a heat wave.

My Girlfriend Barbara, is a well-respected cardiologist. Do you know what that means for her? It means she has held more hearts in her hands that just about anyone I know. While she actually has someone's life in her hands, she is as focused as a laser, but when she's sitting late in her office doing paperwork, she's wondering if her two little kids are eating their dinner. She lives within walking distance of the hospital, so she occasionally pops home to get some cuddling and maybe give the kids their bath, but even when she's up to her elbows in bathwater, she is thinking about that unfinished angiogram report on her desk. It's that shark thing again: Her mind can't stop moving from the tasks she's doing to the tasks that need doing.

This curse of never really being in the moment does have its benefits. A woman's ability to wrap a birthday gift, talk on the phone, and defrost a ham is legendary. We all know the genetic brilliance that makes women capable of multitasking when most men have trouble putting on their shoes and watching the morning news at the same time, but it also makes it very difficult to follow the Zen wisdom of "Be Here Now." I feel more like a hyperactive border collie chasing down all the sheep in my life than like a graceful flower, accepting both the rain and the sun on my face. If I feel rain, I must dash upstairs to my kids' closets to see if their slickers still fit, run out to the garage to see if I ever remembered to get my windshield wipers fixed, and sprint around to the backyard to bring in the mattress pads I'd stripped off the bed to air out over the hedges.

So far, I've not discovered that glorious Girlfriend who has mastered the ability to find peace and satisfaction in doing the one thing she is doing at that time. I'm going to take that as a sign from above that it isn't gonna happen for me either, at least not in this season of my life. But, that's the pearl of wisdom about "having it all," Girlfriend; you can have it all, but all in its own sweet time.

What-SAHM-atta You?
or
The Stay-at-Home
Mother

About a year ago, Girlfriend readers of my magazine and newspaper columns started identifying themselves with the Internet-efficient acronym "sahm." In my mind, it's only been a year or two since people were giving themselves clever names for their c.b. radio use, so I figured a sahm was some cute little nomenclature for Web users. After it had shown up about a hundred times, however, I wrote back to one of the writers and asked what sahm was and to make sure it wasn't some sly sexual term or veiled insult, like your column is "stupid and makes me heave."

Stay At Home Mom is what it means, the writer graciously informed me. Pretty clever, huh? I immediately pulled up my old e-mails and reread them, putting this acronym in context. What struck me was how significant this description seemed to each writer who used it. Sometimes it seemed sort of boastful, as if showing that the writer was particularly committed to her role as mother and wife (usually in that order), and sometimes it was used almost apologetically, as if to suggest that she might be out of touch with the world outside her domestic realm or not quite fulfilling her potential as a descendant of the feminist movement.

Girlfriends who had jobs outside the home often devoted a sentence or two to describing their work, their duties, and how many people reported to them, or how significant their income was to providing for the family. Interesting, isn't it, that the women who worked in the home didn't even waste any unnecessary words naming their occupations, but had shortened them to the barest initials. No mention of hours spent commuting with kiddies, preparing an endless stream of meals that were punctuated only by the loading and unloading of the dishwasher and another trip to the grocery store, no estimations of how much money was not being spent hiring outside help (which, in my crude accounting, still counts as an asset against the family's wealth) and no mention of the time spent ministering to other members of their extended families—the people who would preface every little request with "Since you don't have to be at work, maybe you can do me a little favor. . . ." I guess it's just a given among moms what the drill is, and no one really feels the need to get too specific about the same ol' same ol'.

Call me delusional, but I sort of thought that a surefire indication of women's liberation would have been the abolishment of any distinction between women who worked outside of the home for money and women who did not. To tell you the truth, I would have thought by now we'd all be prima ballerinas or astronauts, grow our own vegetables, stop shaving our underarms and bikini areas, and have as many kids as our co-parents were willing to share fifty percent of the responsibility for (or none) and that we'd have a woman president by now, but, hey, I went to Berkeley when it still offered Women's Studies as a major. Okay, okay, you can stop laughing now! I began to smell the coffee about fifteen years ago, and I still keep going back for refills.

Still, no matter what the universe was telling us to the contrary, I assumed for quite a long time after marriage and motherhood that, among us Girlfriends there existed a sorority and support system for all

our choices—as long as they didn't include poaching off another Girlfriend's marriage, beating our kids, or being racist. My first few years of
motherhood were spent cocooned with my inner core of new-Mommy
Girlfriends who shared my distraction over such dilemmas as fruits versus cereal for an infant's first food, nationwide recalls of certain car seats,
and how to fill out an application for preschool that showed a three-year-
old to be college prep material. We'd all had jobs before we'd acquired
husbands and babies, and I guess I just assumed that most of us would
eventually go back to them once we got our children off the launching
pad. I really couldn't see much past my baby's next inoculation, let alone
predict what we'd all do once we'd gotten our grooves back.

What difference could it possibly make? We moms were joined spiritually and deeply dependent on each other emotionally. Nothing as
meaningless as whether my Girlfriend Marla would be going back to
lawyering after her maternity leave or whether my Girlfriend Margaret
was eager to get back to her life as a magazine editor could come
between us. Every one of us had gone through the mommy metamorphosis and emerged forever enslaved to our offspring. The rest of how
we played out our lives was just a sort of color commentary to fill in the
blanks between broken arms and bottle mouth. Every shared playdate,
every weight-busting hike, every check-in phone call started out with
news flashes about the kids. Then, if there was time, we'd discuss other
people's kids, then our husbands, then our jobs. In the automatic triage
of motherhood, careers only figured in those early shared meditations
when the two Girlfriends who were sharing worked together or one of
them had a day care crisis.

Dissension in the Ranks

I will never forget the moment that I stood in the parking lot of the
preschool that had so chritably accepted our family. It was one of those

get-to-know-you receptions that preschools are so fond of throwing. You know the type: held between five and seven P.M. so that they can get away without serving you dinner or cocktails (and in my case, early enough to have me pacing back and forth in growing rage as the minutes tick past and my husband still hasn't shown up, since his workday rarely ends before seven), populated with scores of other couples who are smiling and talking effortlessly with the school director about such things as "creative play" and "undirected education" (all consisting of women with big eager smiles and men who are clearly more commited to fatherhood than my own truant husband), and who all seem to know each other and have already scheduled a semester's worth of playdates for their little darlings. God, I get edgy just recalling them.

I tread back on those squirmy memories (and recollections of the fights my husband and I used to have the whole drive home afterward) only to bring up this one observation; the larger group would always eventually divide like some giant amoeba into two vague, but still obviously separate groups—those with mothers who worked outside the home and the sahms.

As a writer who works from home, I was uniquely able to move pretty seamlessly between the groups. To the working moms, I was one of them; concerned with carpools, extended day care, and worried about how many days I could carve out of my work schedule to volunteer in the classroom. To the sahms, I could blend in like a chameleon and volunteer to have the end-of-year party some afternoon in June at my house, give my name to be part of the emergency phone tree, and offer to help distribute school sweatshirts for the annual fundraiser.

Sensing that my cover as a double agent would be blown by looking too stay-at-home, with a pair of jeans and a shirt topped with a theme-decorated sweater vest, or too woth (Work Outside the Home) in a gray suit with pearl necklace and matching earrings, I always tried to split the fashion difference right down the middle. I'd wear my jeans, or some other pair of casual pants, but I'd wear a jacket and be fully accessorized for these meet and greets. Neither fish nor fowl, I'd move with equal awkwardness between the splitting molecules of motherhood and eavesdrop and nod as conversationally cued, ever tongue-tied and yearning for a nice glass of cabernet.

School Just Widens the Gap

Armistice between the woths and the sahms has still not been fully achieved, at least not in my years of mothering. It turns out that there's a nasty little civil war brewing between the sahms and the woths, and the early school years just deepen the rift. Every fall I come home from school orientation with my arms full of supplemental reading, permission forms, and volunteer packets for the ensuing year. Whatever happened to the days of my own youth when sending your child off to school meant you didn't have to hear from them again till summer? I can literally count on one hand the number of times my own parents showed up on campus when I was a kid. Back-to-School Night and dislocated collarbones are the two major events that come to mind.

My kids, however, have about thirty days each of such voluntary servitude. We begin the school year with our Separation Exercise, when parents move from sitting in tiny chairs inside the classroom, watching the kindergartners do their morning routines of naming the date and describing the weather, gradually moving outside into the hallway and then out to the parking lot, where we have the distractions of our car phones to help keep us occupied until eleven A.M., when the teachers decide we aren't essential to their survival anymore.

Mothers who have offices, check-out counters, or scheduled lunar landings to get to either suffer the shame of showing up late and leaving early or strong-arm their mates into filling in on this watch. No matter how much we all try to "be here now," the atmosphere quickly moves from unified misery to our working and nonworking confederations as soon as one mom's cell phone rings and she excuses herself with tremendous embarrassment and exposure to some corner or the little girls' room to reschedule a patient's open-heart surgery or explain to her boss that she's "just finishing up with my biopsy and should be back at work by lunch."

Things don't get much better as the year progresses. No classroom nowadays seems to be able to function without one or two parents chipping in. Let me take this moment to grab every state and federal legislator by the neck and personally throttle anyone who has even considered reducing the funds directed toward our kids' education. I could go on for an entire chapter about our failure as a nation to support the people who teach our kids, but that would distract me from the matter at hand—our survival as the Federated Sorority of Mothers. Not only are we "invited" to help in language arts and community service, there are more field trips scheduled for our tots than your average travel agent sees in a year; all of which seem to need parental supervision. Add to that the predictable "Moms and Muffins," "Holiday Latke and Gingerbread House Party," "Mother's Day Slide Show," "Spring Sing," "Take Your Daughter to Work Day" and "Family Tree Oral History Presentation," and any Girlfriend's Filofax is full.

It will quickly become obvious to you, the teachers, the principal, the other parents, and all the kids in the class which moms are devoted to the old Alma Mater and which are selfishly hoarding their time for other pursuits, be they punching the clock at their jobs, committing to regaining a certain level of fitness, trying to wean a younger child, or caring for an ailing grandparent. Between you and me, the teachers and principal are usually pretty understanding and respectful of parents with demanding lives, and even the kids are incredibly resilient and nonjudgmental—it's often the other moms who are the harshest critics. "Oh, how are you, Vicki? We haven't seen you around here in so long!" one may mention when you show up at school for the fourth time of the year, and it's only October. Or "Who's going to take Rebecka home after Fiesta Friday, since we all know her mother works and won't be able to come before carpool?"

I can't tell you how many nights I've levitated to the ceiling from a sound sleep, panicking from a nightmare in which I've left one of my children standing beside the school in the carpool line as the moon rises and all other signs of life have disappeared. That would be bad enough, dealing with my poor child's feelings of fear and abandonment, but in MY dreams, there's always a teacher or administrator standing there beside him, with a protective arm over his shoulders and an accusing look on her face. What unspeakable thing does this say about my mothering that I'm convinced my nightmare would be less upsetting if my child were standing there alone? With my own little orphan, at least I might have a chance of salvaging the situation with the promise of a visit to Disney World or dinner at Pizza Hut for a whole week, but what could I ever do to make things straight with the adult who saw through me, who knew the true maternal failure that I was? The only nightmare that would be worse for me would be Adrienne Johnson, room mother to all sixteen of her kids and weaver of all her own fabrics for her family's clothes, standing with her protective arm around my child. If that ever happened, I'd never go to sleep again.

If You Don't Believe Me, Watch Television!

Statistics vary, according to whatever point they're intended to prove, but even the most conservative indicate that at least two-thirds of all mothers eventually work outside the home. You'd never know that from watching T.V., the source of all my popular culture information. On my favorite shows, *Malcolm In the Middle*, *The Sopranos*, and *Everybody Loves Raymond*, the moms are all so overwhelmed keeping their kids from killing their baby brother, finding out what dad really does for a living, dealing with a meddling mother-in-law, or, well, killing the baby brother that they must do their flossing and tweezing during commercials (like I do) since they don't have much time left for themselves during any given episode. Now that I think about it, I never realized until just now how common fratricide is in television programing, but I digress again. . . .

It's not much better for my kids, who live on Nickelodeon. There's Lucy, Carol Brady, Marge Simpson (or is she on Fox?), and Mrs. Cunningham. If pressed, I think I can come up with at least one episode each in which those moms have appeared in an apron. I think the Rugrat Angelica has a working mother, but she seems to have had her cell phone surgically attached to the side of her head, and she's more caffeinated than a Starbuck's management trainee. Besides, Angelica is a conniving brat—clearly a reflection on her mother's distracted parenting performance.

Look, I grew up in the sixties and early seventies when television still clung to the notion that dads stayed with moms, dads had one career with job security (until the episode when Bud lost the gold watch presented to Dad at retirement), moms kept their floors clean and their hair wet-set and back-combed, and still always had time to listen to their kids' problems after school. We had a few years of reprieve when Elise Keaton went back to work as an architect (but, with someone like Alex P. Keaton around, who wouldn't feel like there were already too many responsible adults on the homefront?) and Roseanne opened a diner to supplement her mate's unpredictable construction income.

But I distinctly feel we're coming full circle. It's as if all my little playmates from the sandbox are suddenly *running* the networks and perpetuating their extended fantasies about moving in with the Bradys or the Cleavers. This observation would be just another "so what?" bitch if it weren't for the fact that several of those sandbox buddies are Girlfriends. What is it that we don't want to admit? Why haven't we kicked this mythology in the backside?

To Work or Not to Work, That Is the Question

Let's get one thing straight: All mothers outside of Buckingham Palace work harder than Sisyphus, whether they get a paycheck and a 401K or not. For this little chat among us Girlfriends, however, I will refer to "work" as what we do outside the home for money or karma or whatever other remuneration you can think of. What's critical is that you have a set of clear-cut responsibilities besides your domestic ones. Some of us have the "luxury" of choice, whatever that means. I guess it suggests that we only go back to work if the family will be on welfare without our income or that none of us will ever see a vacation or hope to pay a semester of college without our income. Giving your full attention to your home and family is a marvelous thing, at least in measured doses. And fulfilling your professional dreams, even if they are no more lofty than being able to supplement your monthly spousal and child support payments, is empowering and wonderful, too, especially if you know you can quit if you want to. You know it and I know it: Both of these pears have their prickles.

Right now, as I've settled into writing this chapter and noticed that Jay Leno is already on, I confess that I'd love to shrug off all my professional responsibilities and "simplify" my life by devoting myself to wifing and mothering. Come to think of it, I'd love to shrug off the need to rise before noon, to fold fitted sheets, and to remain true to the high-protein/low carbohydrate diet I've dedicated myself to in hopes of dropping those last ten pregnancy pounds, my last pregnancy having occurred six years ago. Of course, I'm about a year into this project and too tired to quantify this effort compared to those months that are of "homework."

Let me add that when I don't have a book deadline, I am equally overwhelmed with the concerns of my family, my friends, and my community. It's as though I'm a vacuum just waiting to be filled by someone's needs greater than my own. I have worked for my family and for my career, and I promise you, I've never had a moment's peace in either endeavor. A genetic mutation occurred during my first pregnancy that threw my throttle into fourth gear, with no speeds between it and idle.

It's a Girl Thing

When did this crisis barge into my life? I fully recall going to high school and college, sitting cheek by jowl beside all sorts of boys who took the same classes and got the same education. Nobody told us the curriculum was different for us girls. We prepared for and fully expected the same lives and opportunities as the guys. Not one single teacher took me aside to say anything like "You know, all this will come to a screeching halt once your milk comes in!" or "Make sure you really memorize this stuff because you may not have time to finish your degree until your youngest child is in college, too." Heaven forbid that one of the lectures would be devoted to preparing the boys and girls for the cumulative effect of ninety consecutive sleepless nights with a colicky baby or the mutual blame game that occurs when your darling preteen has been to a party that included marijuana. I just went along, from high school to college to law school thinking I was exactly like the guys in my class, only a little prettier. Was I ever set up for a fall!

Some gals take to motherhood like a duck to water. I did not. Don't get me wrong; I loved my baby, and after three years of infertility, I considered his arrival as magical as the Virgin Birth except with the fun of sex thrown in. I was a lawyer by training, but I had already cut back on my professional obligations during my infertility treatments, so I could have gone on for a year or two without worrying about getting back into the work mode. My Girlfriend Jennifer, however, another attorney, had gotten pregnant the moment she and her husband even considered parenthood and she hadn't orchestrated any such "golden parachute." Too bad. Nearly thirteen years later Jen is still pursuing her career as a preeminent litigator and daydreaming about expanding her herb garden and photographing the native birds in her canyon, while I am unable take the time to even taste an herb, let alone grow one, and I've never really noticed that there was more than one type of bird in my neighborhood—they all look small and brown to me.

Since the day I threw Jennifer's baby shower and officially cut back on my own work (remember, we're talking outside the home here), she and I have both insisted that we were getting ready to do what we "really wanted to do." Her nirvana has consistently lay in quitting her job and settling into the rhythms of her home. Mine has been to get my kids adequately prepared so that I can jump headfirst into more books, more columns, more television appearances, and more, well, MORE. Here's the news about Jennifer and me: We are both still doing what we were doing thirteen years ago, just with the added confusion and prestige that comes with years of experience. If you ask me, it's not because either of us is lazy or fearful of change; it's just that we're both happy with, not to mention accustomed to, our lives, as imperfect as they may seem. I think we both know that the essence of our lives, at least for now, is to know that we can have it all, just not all at the same time.

I have other Girlfriends, like Michelle and Theresa, who work outside the home because they are the ones who win the bread. Michelle is a single mom and Theresa is the mother of two who has decided with her husband to put the family energy behind her career while he takes the Mister Mom job. Unlike Jennifer and me, Theresa and Michelle got over their conflict of "Who should I be when I grow up?" years ago. I also have Girlfriends, like Miranda and Carla, who considered work a suitable pastime until kids came along, but upon conception, never looked back. Our mommying lives are still playing themselves out, but it's clear to me that not one of us is confident that we've made the right choice. The universe has this funny tendency to throw unexpected things our way—divorce, our mates' business setbacks, our own eagerness to escape the occasional tedium of motherhood, or opportunities that seem too good to refuse, all conspire to leave us constantly renegotiating our parenting contracts.

I recently received a letter from a reader of my newspaper column asking whether it was her "obligation" to get a job once her kids were all in school and she could carve some time out of her mommying schedule. Since she seemed to be happy making her family her career, I didn't see any reason for her to believe that her youngest child's enrollment in full-day preschool meant that she needed to enlist with an employment agency. This letter was particularly poignant to me, since my youngest had just started kindergarten, and instead of feeling the liberation I'd expected, I'd kissed her goodbye and dropped her off at school, and then taken to my bed until I picked her up with her brothers and sister . . . not just that day, but for nearly a month.

So, when I gave the reader my wholehearted endorsement to redefine her home life to, say, include some activities that made her happy— what the hell? Why shouldn't she take a needlepoint class or create her own homepage?—it seemed like harmless advice to me. Besides, I yearned to know that such a smooth transition to "mature" motherhood was possible for her, if not for me. Little did I know that there are about six million other mothers out there who were as conflicted as the writer and I about justifying their career choices by the baby-sitting needs of their kids. Judging from the volumes of mail I got, even Girlfriends who love their lives as sahms feel that their decision to stay home is only legitimized by the public's interest in their keeping their toddlers out of traffic.

One Step Forward, Two Steps Back

As best as I can tell, a lot of the controversy about choosing to stay at home full time was precipitated by two critical events. One was the study spread throughout the media that maintained that babies have their highest learning curve between birth and three years of age and the other was the tragic lawsuit between the two doctor parents and their young nanny who cared for a baby who died suspiciously. All of a sudden, it was universally declared that no woman should leave her child for a moment until he was ready to get his draft card or her first prescription for birth control pills. Unless, of course, the mother was the only thing standing between her family and federal aid to dependent families, in which case she could work 24/7 and get total societal endorsement.

Maybe it's because sahms are in the minority, and all minorities feel unsupported and picked on. A sahm Girlfriend only has to attend a cocktail party, be asked by a total stranger, "What do you do?" and watch his eyes go as unfocused as an optometrist's patient after his pupils have been dilated to know that her life's work is as interesting as low tide to most people. There have been countless parties when I've responded that I pose for Web pornography or am researching a book on rediscovering the G-spot just to provoke some interest. Next to teachers and nurses, full-time mothers seem to be the most underrated group on the planet; you can't live without them, but you don't want to hear the details. The only job that gets less respect is being your husband's mother.

The most common complaint I hear from Stay at Home Girlfriends is that their working Girlfriends take advantage of them by asking them to baby-sit their kids, pick them up from school when they're running late, and assume that they know whether the science teacher really is as mean as her kids say she is. They're right, really. No working mother can seriously believe that she will consistently be able to meet the demands of her kids' school, dance, and karate routines. If every mother who was honest enough to confess that she might miss one carpool obligation or would never be available to do extra photocopying for the teacher that was stipulated in parent orientation stood up and walked out of the room, the competition for preschool and voucher-popular public schools would be decimated.

Having been on both sides, I honestly think that sahms would leap into the fray for their working Girlfriends over and over again if they felt that they got slightly more respect than Rodney Dangerfield. Rather than get flowers and thank-you notes and endless gratitude from the working moms who quickly grow dependent on the sahms' reliability, those Girlfriends who stay at home and make good on Hillary Clinton's philosophy that it takes a village to raise a child often find their deeds swept into the corner along with the rest of the woths' regrets. I hate to say this, Girlfriends, but at the end of the day, woths often end up treating their sister sahms like husbands unthinkingly treat wives. Can this be true?

Speaking of husbands, there's something else I noticed when my life was more devoted to my family than to my career, and to my own beloved mate, my co-parent, my life's companion; at the end of the day, when we get together over dinner or the smooth sheets of our bed, if he asks me about my day and I start in with a journalist's recounting of who touched whom last, whose best friend isn't her best friend today, or whose teacher complained that he was asking to be excused to use the bathroom more than ten times a day, he drifts off, even if his eyes are still open and he's winning the Fastest Finger round of *Who Wants to Be a Millionaire?*

Husbands, at least in my limited experience, are incredibly gossip hungry and equally uninterested in minor family crises or reportage. I'm far more likely to get my mate's attention with rumor that my boss is having an affair with both of his receptionists than with the report that my daughter's head circumference is in the 65th percentile for kids her age. In fact, I regularly give my reader-Girlfriends the advice to greet their mates at the end of the work day without any souvenirs of their mothering endeavors. Politically incorrect as it may be, since the days are over of meeting your mate at the front door with a martini in one hand and his slippers in the other, I have discovered over time that the very last words a mom should use to inspire some meaningful conversation with her co-parent before dinner are "You won't believe what your children did today. . . ."

Not that things have been much different when I've had a job outside the home. A few weeks ago, during a very vulnerable and sharing moment between my husband and me, he confessed that he would really appreciate it if when he shares his day with me, I could refrain from "trumping" his professional frets and worries with frets and worries from my own job. In other words, even if I've fractured both my hands and can't write a word and have been sued for sexual harassment for telling a male employee that he has been acting premenstrual, my guy would be sincerely grateful if I could set aside at least forty minutes a day, between his pulling into the driveway and falling asleep on the couch, to act sincerely interested in his life. But enough about husbands for now, let's get back to the Girlfriends.

United We Groove, Divided We Lose All Our Rhythm

This is it, Girlfriends, the big banana for all of us who have looked up out of our mommy holes for the first time in a couple (or in my case, THIRTEEN) years and wondered if we ever became the women we always hoped we'd grow up to be. You may be shaking your head and saying to yourself, "She's crazy. All I want to read is the chapter about sex!" But I promise you, if we don't handle this ambivalence and guilt about our choices for our identities, the sex part suffers, too. If we aren't satisfied with who we are and how we fulfill all our responsibilities and expectations, we are no more arousing and provocative than a mindless little girl, barely old enough to vote, whose concerns run the gamut from tube tops to Top 40 music . . . Wait a minute, bad example. What I'm trying to say is that if we don't turn ourselves on, we have no reason to expect anyone else to be able to do it for us.

131

Becoming a mother is the most transcendent and extraordinary experience I will ever know, but between you and me, I'd like to try out a couple other challenges before I've sustained total short-term memory loss and stopped noticing if I've driven the last five miles with my turn signal blinking. Remember, if we do this mothering job correctly, the kids are supposed to grow up and leave us for good. That may not seem like much of a payoff now, but hey, that's why golf and Florida were invented. We owe it to ourselves, our mates, and our kids to carve out a life of our own. I know firsthand that the "carving" occasionally hurts, like all major surgery, but that's no reason to chicken out.

Each of us will find her own way. Some of us will pursue our definition of self through careers, others through public service, and still others through a lifetime devoted to looking young and fit, no matter how many personal trainers and mini lifts that involves. If we're lucky, we may get to try many or all of these paths at least once. I've come to realize that it's nearly impossible for any of us to strike the balance between Motherhood on one side and Everything Else on the other, at least not without lots of lost sleep and soul searching.

What should be unacceptable, however, is taking out our ambivalence and chronic guilt on each other. Think of all us moms who are between the ages of needing babyproofing locks on their toilets and kitchen cabinets and menopause as "adolescents." Not a single one of us has the right to make fun of another mommy adolescent's zits or harmonica-like voice when we should be paying attention to the fact that only one of our own breasts has started developing and the other is still flat. Each of our houses is not only glass, it's as fragile as a Christmas ornament, and throwing bricks, pebbles, or even blowing a strong puff of wind at each other is against the Girlfriends' Rules of Conduct.

We're all just making up our lives as we go along. Especially now, as the first generation (and a half) of women grew up thinking that we could have it all and discovering we may not have the energy or the hours in a day to have even most of it, we should encourage our Girlfriends to keep trying to fly, and keep catching each other when we come crashing back to earth. What we learn will be our gift to our own daughters, so let's not let them think the only lesson is that they will be judged by their sisters, their Girlfriends.

Top Ten List to Rekindling the Fire

10. **Go to bed before you're tired.** Remember how in the old days you used to stay awake long enough to notice if the sheets felt like they needed changing, if not to devote another half hour or forty-five minutes to playing the Hokey Pokey? Parents with kids living in their home stay in the laundry room or on the computer until they are seeing double. Then they tumble into bed wearing whatever they put on to cook dinner. This is a romantic "don't."

9. **Go to bed naked, then put on your T-shirt and leggings around midnight** (for those mini midnight ramblers). After sleeping together for nearly twenty years, my darling husband and I have gotten a little lazy about the art of flirting, but there's no avoiding the invitation that a smooth nude body brushing against another to get the sparks to fly.

8. **Don't rule out sex over dinner.** In fact, don't discuss intimacy of any sort during the hellish hours between dinner, the kids' baths, and bed. It always sounds like a bad idea when you're looking at a sink full of dirty dishes. Reconsider at least thirty minutes after the last child has retired and you've downed half a glass of nice wine. I promise, it will sound a lot more appealing then.

7. **Smell good.** Not like detergent, not like the kids, and not like his mother. I don't know about your beloved, but mine loves the way I smell, especially if it's not like the lasagna

we just ate. If you can squeeze in a quick shower and a spritz of cologne, better still. Remember sex is for animals, and we animals lead with our noses.

6. **Shave or wax away unnecessary body hair.** Many years ago, my Girlfriend Sondra shared with me the secret that men take hairless legs and armpits to be a personal invitation for fun. According to her, this is so universally understood that saying, "I shaved my legs last night" is the same thing as saying, "I had sex last night."

5. **Spend a few minutes giggling together.** I don't know about you, but humor, even more than lust, is the tie that binds my marriage. Sharing a laugh together in bed is worth ten minutes of foreplay. Well, ten minutes of light foreplay.

4. **Don't use your period as an excuse to bow out from sex.** This isn't P.E. now, Girlfriends. We're not talking about whether you may have to get your hair wet in the school pool before lunch. Without going into too much detail, let me remind you about the many uses of bath towels followed by soaking them in a basin with Spray 'n Wash. Or, if intercourse is just too much, be creative and come up with something else (pun intended).

3. **Start the seduction at the front door.** Yeah, I know your sleeves are wet up to the elbows from baby bathwater and you hair looks like Marge Simpson's, but pausing for a real sweet kiss for that evening reunion pays dividends later in the evening.

2. **Make the first move.** Men quickly learn that there are several other people and concerns that can take precedence

over their needs. After a while, they stop bothering to make overtures, since they know that a toddler with a fever or a little daughter not getting invited to a class birthday party trumps them every time. It's our job as mother-of-all, babe of one, to reassure our beloved that we are interested and free of distraction.

1. **Remember that sex keeps you young and beautiful.** If I told you I had a face cream that could do the same thing, you'd spend at least fifteen minutes rubbing it into every pore of your body, no matter how tired or fretful you were. Sex does all that, plus it's fun, it's soulful, and it's contagious; your mate will look younger and more beautiful, too.

The "S" Word,
or
My Baby Loves
the Hanky-Panky

*S*ince I started writing this book, every single time my husband mentioned to his pals and colleagues that I was devoting myself to Girlfriends getting their groove back, they've reacted with naughty grins and
smirks. It was obvious early on that EVERYONE'S definition of *groove* is
"sex." People just assumed, and seemed delighted by, the prospect of
me, or anyone for that matter, writing an entire book about the secrets
every mother needs to know to recapture her inner sex kitten.

Even people who appeared, at least from my nosy observations, to
enjoy passionate and really "zippy" sex lives were shockingly obsessed
with finding out whether I'd discovered an extra G-spot or had invented
a magic potion to turn fatigue and chronic confusion into an aphrodisiac. It was as if everyone who heard about my private little explo-
ration hoped that I was documenting the literary version of perpetual
Viagra. They begged me to share my interview notes, they were willing
to pay for an early look at the galleys, and the particularly busy fellows
offered free concert tickets or to do my taxes for me if I'd give them a

verbal, abridged, recounting of the Seven Principles of Highly Grooving Mothers.

Why Is Sex Still a Problem after All These Years?

What's that about? Does it mean that the universal experience of motherhood, even from the father's point of view, is that the birth of kids is the death of our "zip"? Even people with only a keen view of the obvious know that pregnancy and early motherhood strike such a fatal blow to the nookie, so it's kind of boring and redundant to talk about it again now.

No, what's more compelling is the fact that the people who are reading this book at the appropriate chronological time, meaning the mothers and fathers of children who may not believe in Santa anymore, who have lost several teeth and pretended to believe in the Tooth Fairy, and who know how to eat with utensils *still* feel out of kilter where their sex lives are concerned. They're supposed to be fully recovered from the one-two punch of instant adulthood and chronic fatigue, right?

A simple and logical explanation might be that couples who have endured long enough to launch a kid or two into elementary education are simply experiencing a completely predictable cooling off of their sexual afterburners. I'm not telling you anything you don't already know when I say that eight or ten years of sex with the same person does tend to get a little, how do you say, "familiar." Nonetheless, one would hope that this should be the time in our lives when we rediscover our sexuality. We're still young enough to physically meet the challenge. Entire nights go by in which only the two of you are in your marital bed. Kids who get thirsty in the night are completely capable of getting up and filling their own glass. We have gained a real, albeit fragile, faith in our abilities as parents; no longer worrying that failure to properly wash an umbilical cord stump will lead to a raging systemic infection or that diaper rash could scar for life; and are at peace with the shift in our priorities. SO WHAT'S THE PROBLEM?

I confess right now, even after a year (okay, twelve years) of meditating on the issue of restoring one's "babeness" after becoming the mother of several babes, I've only been able to come up with two pages of reliable and reasonable suggestions for improving our Wild Thang skills, both of which are included herein. But if you've laid down good hard cash expecting to buy a book that shares enough secrets, revelations, and insights to keep the covers from flapping against each other, you might have the wrong author Girlfriend. In fact, if you find any such missive, anywhere, I'd like to be the first in line to buy a copy or twenty. I may have a pretty keen grasp of what the question here is, but I'll be damned if I hold the magic passion key in my pocket.

Speaking in my own defense, years into this mothering business, I've learned something important: Our grooves, including our sexual grooves, but not limited to them, are like different floors in a high-rise building. Each floor looks like a stand-alone department. For example, one floor can be about restoring our bodies to something resembling their former glory, another about successfully juggling childrearing and a job outside the home, and still another floor can be furnished with all the tools a couple needs to keep their marriage intact, but if any of those floors is not up to the current Metaphysical Marriage Seismic Code, good sex just collapses with the rest of the rubble if the foundation shakes because the daycare floor has started crumbling. Getting our grooves back, as I see it, is more about our ability to sustain and understand the forest; rather than take it tree by tree.

That said, let's dig in to this chapter on Sex and hope that the other chapters will cooperate by offering our family forest the sturdy foundations we will need to withstand several tremors along the way, as well as the big old 9.0 shaker that a good night of headbanging sends through the fault lines, if we're lucky.

The Blind Leading the Blind

About a year ago my Girlfriend Amelia called me in an agitated state, asking me to meet her for an emotional rescue luncheon. She wanted to talk about salvaging her sex life, now that she was the mother of three kids, the youngest being two years old, and she wanted to talk about it *now*. Never one to refuse a Girlfriend in need (kind of makes you think of Florence Nightingale, doesn't it?), I cleared my calendar and even went so far as to shower and hot roll my hair to meet her in the fancy restaurant that she chose in hopes of raising her spirits. All this in the middle of the day, no less.

I don't think Amelia would mind if I mentioned that both she and her handsome husband have always had a pretty spicy sex life. Anyway, according to my poor distraught Girlfriend, the picante was gone from her marriage now that she had beautiful and adored babies, and she was both sad and feeling slightly ripped off. After all, she and her husband had been enjoying a very sexy relationship for nearly ten years before the doldrums set in. Clearly, familiarity wasn't the cause of their lack of enthusiasm—it was all about the arrival of the kids.

Before she sent the SOS message to me, Amelia had tried all sorts of self-help measures. She and her mate had endured two marriage counselors, she'd bought a whole new wardrobe of lingerie (large enough not only to accommodate but feature her still-nursing behemoth breasts), she'd even asked her obstetrician to intervene. Finally, she came to me, the old veteran, for advice. She spoke without taking a breath or even sipping her glass of wine for a full thirty minutes before she gave me an opening to respond. But all I had to offer was this rusty nugget: "Sex is like smiling. You may start out faking it, but if you give it your best shot, a good smile will actually make you believe you're happy; likewise, a good performance of enjoying sex almost always gives way to genuine arousal."

I do want to assure you that I still ascribe to that philosophy for pre-groove women who are stuck in the morass of mommy fatigue, flabbiness, and infant paranoia. My experience in those cases has, indeed, taught me that, for many of us new moms, sexuality starts in the brain and has to work its way down to the really sweet spots. In other words, even if your don't feel particularly like choreographing a sexual encounter, the Girlfriends and I believe that you should realize on some intellectual level that sex is a good thing for a lasting relationship and you should take whatever steps are necessary to, well, get it on. I have a Girlfriend who is a member of Alcoholics Anonymous, and she told me that one of the fundamental bylaws is, "Suit up and show up," and that the rest will follow. I think the advice applies to mothers in search of their sexuality.

Anyway, Amelia shared this story about one of her more desperate measures to get the pizzazz back in her relationship; she had attended a sex techniques seminar. (No, I'd never heard of it before, either.) Actually, it sounded more like an X-rated Tupperware or Discovery Toys party—you know, where there are good things to buy after the presentation—than a seminar. Yes, you're getting my drift; a woman was demonstrating and selling marital tools that go bump in the night. I may live in Los Angeles, the frontier of far-fetched and downright funky fads, but I've since learned that these kinds of parties are popping up all across the country.

Picture this: A group of ten or fifteen women go to a party at a Girlfriend's house and are hosted by a woman who not only sells vibrators, dildoes (is there any other word for those things), and condoms, as well as sexy apparel, but actually demonstrates how to use each product to its best advantage! Wait, before you throw this book down in disbelief, let me tell you that since Amelia first told me about this kind of "entertainment," I've heard about this kind of thing from all sorts of otherwise-*appropriate* people. Everyone from other mothers gathering around the coffee urn at a PTA meeting to professional party planners have told me that sex-aid parties are the most "happening" thing for bridal and baby showers. Evidently, the woman who started this craze is not a tutor for geishas, but rather the rescue remedy of choice for so many mommy/Girlfriends eager to salvage their sexuality that she's been written up in several of the kinds of magazines that are sold right there in the checkout line of your neighborhood grocery store.

Take a deep breath, Girlfriend, because the story gets better: The chief guru of these kinds of parties specializes in demonstrating how to give gold medal oral sex to one's beloved. Maybe you're way ahead of me on this learning curve, but apparently there are several techniques for a woman to use to get her partner to see heaven. (And all along, I thought that just being a "good sport" was about as exotic as it got!) Never had I imagined that some ways were better than others. Okay, now that I've got your attention here, let me go on with my story about lunch with Amelia.

Her tale of becoming a sexual Jedi was titillating and hysterical, but once our lunch had been eaten and the check paid, I never really thought about it again. How pathetic is that? I hopped right into my valet-parked SUV and drove to take up my position in the carpool lane and never again wondered whether there existed, somewhere out there in the universe, a handbook of techniques that were practically guaranteed to make me the Mistress of the Master Bedroom. What was up with me? Did I think that my sex life didn't deserve at least as much attention as I had given to memorizing those books, *What Your 1st (2nd, 3rd) Grader Needs to Know*? Was I deluding myself by thinking my hus-

band had forgotten the special little tricks of any of his previous partners and defined his sexual appetites only by what I offered on my
menu? Did I think that, after nearly twenty years together, we could
expect momentum to keep us physically intimate? Was I certifiably
brain dead?

Who knows what was going on in my brain? Maybe I was afraid of
discovering that there might be something missing from my perfect
marriage. I certainly wasn't thick-headed enough *not* to recognize the
importance and value of making sure that my mate and I had a relationship beyond co-parenting. I truly believe what I've been telling *you*
for the last six years: It's critical to a marriage to ensure that there is
something intimate and inspiring (besides childrearing) keeping you
together; otherwise every parent of a child with a driver's license would
be single again.

You may remember my Girlfriend, from *The Girlfriends' Guide to
Pregnancy*, who performed oral sex on her beloved the night after her C-
section. At the time, I just attributed her interest in going to such
extremes to please her husband to the morphine drip she received after
the baby's umbilical chord was clamped. I never imagined that I'd have to
make any special efforts to keep the fires burning. I guess I just assumed
that the same chemistry that brought us together originally would keep
us together forever, or at least as long as all the working parts still
worked.

You know and I know that this discussion isn't really about oral sex.
It's about the bigger issue of nurturing physical connectedness between
life partners who have sustained the slings and arrows of sleep deprivation, distraction, and a little bit of laziness. I'm just using this sex party
thing to get us into the macro issue of post-parenthood sexuality. Blow
job, shlow job, it's all just a metaphor for the stuff that really matters:
growing sexually within your marriage and in spite of your kids so that
you and your mate don't spend those golden years *only* rocking on the

front porch. This isn't something that's going to just take care of itself, and it's my job to remind you, Girlfriend.

When Did All the Ardor Cool?

We've spent one or two books talking about the different sexual responses Girlfriends have to being pregnant. Some of us close up shop as soon as our biological imperative has been fulfilled. My otherwise irresistible Girlfriend, Sonia, for example, had little or no interest in repeating the reproductive act once it had already been, well, *productive*. There's a bit of irony to this because her mate found her even more attractive when she was pregnant than when she wasn't. This was the guy, after all, who'd introduced the Girlfriends' community to the phrase "arrival of the Titty Fairy" to describe the metamorphosis of a pregnant woman's breasts.

Sonia also made special efforts to slip out of her tent-like maternity frocks before her husband got home from work each evening and slip (okay, *squeeze*) into short skirts, push up bras and high heeled shoes. Not only did she change her costume, but she religiously shaved her legs, no matter how gymnastic the feat became over the months, every after-noon, just in case there was the chance of some sex that night. That's a pretty generous attitude, don't you think, considering how indifferent Sonia was feeling about the whole business?

I, on the other hand, looked upholstered from cheeks to ankles by the time my pregnancy tests came up positive. I lived in black stretch legging and tent-like shirts for about thirty weeks out of every gesta-tional period. Even if it had been as stylish then as it is now for moms-to-be to wear clothes that cling and show off their bellies, I would still have dressed for full camouflage to hide the fact that my backside was quickly outgrowing my front. I may not have looked dressed for it, but I wanted sex all the time. I'm not kidding. Once the first few weeks of morning sickness had gotten out of my libido's way, I was in a constant state of arousal.

I will be the first to admit that my interest in sex was anything but altruistic. My husband was very *respectful* of my gestational state and seemed willing to cut back on the bedroom fun and games as I grew. Just in case you don't get the picture, I outweighed my mate by my second trimester. Cellulite was usually my first indication of pregnancy. And, like most good men of Latin blood, he proudly worried that intercourse might be like a battering ram against our precious fetus. None of that cooled my ardor, however. I waited by the door for him to come home each evening. I shopped for lingerie that wouldn't make me look like a dancing hippo from *Fantasia*. I was even willing to cook dinner from time to time.

He was a real champ, my guy. He gave as good as he got, even if he was motivated more by mercy than passion, but, in hindsight, I realize that I was often asking for more than any regular guy could deliver. I'm sure it didn't make matters any less pressured, either, when I occasionally boasted while we were brushing over the bathroom sink that I'd had such vivid dreams that I dreamed I climaxed all by myself. If I were him, I would have congratulated me on my self-sufficiency and spit into the sink. Gosh, I have such fond memories of my own satisfaction during my four pregnancies that I rarely paused to wonder if it was "good for him," too.

Then came the babies, and off went all my Earth mother sensuality. In the first few weeks it was easy to dismiss my asexuality by pointing to (well, at least figuratively) my episiotomy stitches, my hemorrhoids, my raw nipples, and my chronic exhaustion. Even a male obstetrician doesn't give a woman the thumbs-up to have intercourse again for at least six weeks! But six weeks after birthing a baby, I was as uninterested in resuming our sex life as I'd been the moment they inserted my epidural. I actually cried and swore my doctor to secrecy, invoking patient-doctor privilege, when he told me that I was healing well and was ready to resume marital fun and games. What was he thinking? My nipples were still chapped, my "privates" still scared me so much that I could only approach them in the shower with a thick washcloth and my mind was totally preoccupied with whether our little darlings would keep breathing, even when I wasn't watching them.

Postpartum Repression

Even though my body felt as though I wouldn't recover even if I had six months at some phenomenal spa ahead of me, it was my mind that was my biggest sexual bogeyman. No matter what any so-called "expert" says, I still maintain, nearly thirteen years after the birth of my first baby, that Mother Nature never intended new mothers to do anything that might possibly lead to another pregnancy before she'd gotten the first one out of the nest. Yes, I'm completely aware of the fact that many women do, indeed, get pregnant again as soon as two months after the birth of a baby—my own beloved Grandma Gladys did that very thing—but I've always dismissed that incident as her succumbing to her "wifely duties," not to her irresistible sexual appetite. I still maintain, if men were sexually indifferent in this matter, no subsequent pregnancies would occur for at least twelve to sixteen months.

It's not just us Girlfriends who take a kidney (or slightly lower) punch to the libido with the birth of babies. A great number of the men I've talked to confess that they had about as much interest in sex as they had in doing early tax returns. Sleep is an obvious problem, but there's so much more to consider. First, many guys don't want to begin the sexual dance when it's pretty clear their partner doesn't even hear the music. Really, how many times can a fellow make overtures and be received by someone who responds by passing him a child with a stuffy nose?

Other guys suffer from what Freud used to call the Madonna Complex. As moved and enamored as a man might be by the heroics of his beloved wife giving birth to their child, he might be troubled by an inability to see his former sex kitten as anyone other than somebody's mommy. Remember, in *The Girlfriends' Guide to Pregnancy*, when I told you about my Girlfriend who only overcame this emotional typecasting by dressing like a hootchie to seduce her mate? Then again, there are guys who are only more turned on by having a madonna and a seductress all rolled into one package. The most romantic love letters that Ronald Reagan wrote to Nancy address her as "Mommy"—whatever rocks your boat, I guess.

Here's how it worked in my house: My mind and my body were devoted to our babies from the moment they were born. I didn't have time to return phone calls, I didn't have the presence of mind to make an appointment to get my roots done, the grocery store confused me, and I only wanted to be with my baby or other people who also had babies. Imagine what a conscientious person I was at work! Just between us gals, I often only barely knew I was even there. I was so indifferent to current affairs that I'd only read the paper to scan the headlines; if children were mentioned, I'd devour the article, otherwise I'd keep skimming. I felt like I'd seen God or something; becoming a mother had been a religious experience and I was on a mission to testify about its glories.

I was also a victim of motherhood. I spent about twenty hours a day nursing or pumping for a baby, changing a baby, soothing a baby, or counting the minutes till I could get back to my baby. If my husband thought he was going to tug on my tired body after all that, he was sorely mistaken. Wow, just writing that makes me want to get up and kiss him all over for putting up with me. As devoted as I was, I sometimes yearned to escape from everybody who wanted something from me. My fantasy was to run to my car and climb in, lock all the doors, and drive off with Bruce Springsteen's "Born to Run" blaring out of my crackling speakers until I ran out of gas. Marie Osmond, I know your pain.

If We're Lucky

I've been in love with my husband for about twenty years and married to him for seventeen. Between you and me, when I took my marriage vows, I never really understood that, if I was really, really lucky, I would never again experience the titillation of falling in lust, of a crazy makeout session on the couch, or endless hours on the phone with my Girlfriends giving the delicious postgame wrapup. Even if a more experienced Girlfriend (or my mother) had tried to spell this out for me, I wouldn't have heard a word she'd said. And you know what? I think everyone deserves to believe that romance always prevails . . . until it doesn't. Those of you who know the challenges of sustaining a love affair over a lifetime and have seen the fragility of marriage will get my drift. The rest of you will learn it in your own time.

On my first day of law school the dean gave us a chipper speech that, I guess, was intended to prepare us for the challenges ahead. "Look at the person on your left and look at the person on your right. By next year one of the three of you will not be here." I nearly vomited at his prediction, but it turns out that the odds of staying in a marriage are even slimmer. In fact, as I write this book, about half of my original Girlfriends have gotten divorced. We just never knew that moving on to this part of our lives, the part when our kids sleep in big peoples' beds and we've come up out of our Mommy mole holes to reenter the real world, would bring the daunting challenge of defining ourselves and figuring out how to sustain a marriage that is usually about five to ten years old. Trust me, keeping my marriage vital and strong is much harder than memorizing the Penal Code or understanding the Hearsay Rule of evidence ever was.

I'm devoting a chapter of this book to sex, not just because sex is always fun to talk about, or even because it's so hard to come by, but because it turns out that staying sexually active and interested is essential to keeping your marriage alive. And because it's often the second thing in our mothering lives that we neglect—the first being fitness, but we've already touched on that. Of course, if you're a single mom, there's a whole other chapter I could write about your sex life, but I'm saving that for another book.

For the purposes of Getting Your Groove Back, we have to talk about sex because, well, as they say, "use it or lose it." I suppose you could say that one's life doesn't end if she doesn't have sex, but that's not the point. Getting your groove back is about rediscovering and reclaiming all the life experiences that make you feel vital and like an active participant. Being a working mother and wife, not to mention a supporter of public television and a trick-or-treater for the United Way, often seems possible only if we cut back on all our "elective courses." Since the only part of our lives that seem fully within our control are the things we do to make ourselves feel good, they are often the first to be cut. Now is the time for us to be bolder and braver about making the selfish choices. We have to realize that we can't wait one more minute before we claim the life we always wanted because no chapter of motherhood ends before the next chapter begins.

So, with the philosophical stuff out of the way, let's get back to the lurid details.

Result-Oriented Sex vs. Recreational Sex

Unlike those of you who married because you were already in the family way or who had more to show for your honeymoon than just a photo album, a stolen hotel ashtray, and matching robes, as in an embryo, my husband I and couldn't get pregnant for over three years after we married. Since we'd been living together for a couple of years already, like many couples of our generation, we'd really only gotten married in the first place because we were ready for a family, and our infertility was tremendously upsetting. That led to an eon of nightly sexual encounters that were being undermined on two fronts. First, there was just the subtle erosion of mad passion that happens when you've memorized each other's foreplay gambits, know who prefers to be on top, and who can be counted on to get up after for a bottle of water and a towel. And second, we experienced the more direct assault of my growing fears that what we were doing wasn't working. I don't mean to suggest that I was panicking, but by the end of our first year of wedded bliss, we had undergone a series of tests to evaluate the quality of my eggs, the swimming skills of his sperm, and my body's ability to make a cozy home for both of them. Still, we didn't get pregnant.

Let me spare you the details of our three years as the Infertile Myrtles and save them for yet another book, but you can take it from me: By the time a husband and wife have been sucked into the fertility machine, sex as they knew it is a thing of the past. I bring this up now because the transformation of our sex from fun to function is so easy to put a pin in our marriage map. For those of you who get pregnant simply by sharing a water glass with a gestating mother, the change in your sex life is usually more gradual and unnoticeable. Still, if it's not infertility that creates the speed bump in your sex life, it might be a sick child an ailing parent or several unpaid mortgage payments. Anyone who is looking for her groove already knows that there are plenty of things that conspire to take the ardor out of a relationship.

If you don't think that the strains of being the bologna in your family's sandwich will affect your sex life, you're concentrating too much on the mayonnaise. As they grow, your children will come up with all sorts of crazy things to distract you from the sex goddess within. Asthma, night terrors, bed wetting, and being picked last in gym are all child-size crises that can push a parent's intimacy way past the back burner and let it fall somewhere down the wall behind the stove. As admirable as your joint commitment to your kids can be, that commitment just doesn't cut the mustard when you're in bed and feeling those stirrings.

The bottom line to my story about our three years of taking my temperature every morning and charting it, throwing out all my husbands jockey shorts, and avoiding Jacuzzis and hot tubs is that our first child was conceived in the doctor's office. Nurse Judy was the one responsible for depositing the little sperms in the direction of my naive and faintly bored egg. I recall that when I drove home from the appointment, I was so distracted that I failed to slow down for some pigeons that were in the road picking at a Snickers bar wrapper. I hit and killed one. It hurts me to this day to share this. Believing in a higher power, I knew immediately that no one who murders one of God's creatures would ever be considered worthy enough to raise one of her own, and I immediately resigned myself to accepting that this insemination, like the ten before it, would yield nothing more than menstrual cramps and a migraine in the next fourteen days. It's still a miracle to me that ten months later, we ended up with our blessed little boy.

Needless to say, our sex life had taken it on the chin far before the pregnancy even occurred. For the preceding three years, a hot night of passion usually consisted of my mate arriving at the point of payoff and me leaping out of bed to get the specimen cup and a Sharpie with which to mark the date, time, and contributor's name. After we finally conceived, we were so frightened of doing anything to loosen our baby's fragile grip within me, and so relieved not to have so much pressure to perform, that the first few months of my pregnancy were kind of a sex holiday. We'd fulfilled our destiny and we were entitled to go to bed each night with no bigger agenda than to argue over Leno versus Letterman.

In It for the Long Run

I was too distracted to realize it then, but what I've since learned was this: regardless of whether a couple's intimacy is made unimportant because of a crisis like a lack of babies or the crisis of too many babies, the commitment to stay monogamous and committed to a relationship that is deeper than being roommates is a real mixed bag, especially where sex is concerned. Everyone who's been with their mate for more than even six months already suspects this might be true. And those of us who mark the passages of our adult lives by the presidential inaugurations and the last full lunar eclipse are even more certain.

There's no doubt in my mind that marrying my husband was the most miraculous, lucky, and smart event in my life. I have loved him more with every year (and occasionally less for a week here and there), and I cherish our time together. That said, as your Girlfriend, I have to bring up the fact that there are lots of potholes in the road to marriage and maternity. In order to sustain the physical zing, you're going to have to find turn-ons that aren't based on any of the attractions mentioned in *The Rules*.

First of all, cancel the mystery. Any man who has been in the same room as you when you got an episiotomy, watched you cry so hard that your whole face puffed up and got chapped around the nose, and heard the details of your yeast infection is probably pretty familiar with you and your wiles. And on the flip side, if you've seen him through a couple of bouts of food poisoning and a head cold, chances are you know whether you married Batman or Bruce Wayne. Sure, you can dress up or play games with each other, like my Girlfriend Chasen does with her mate for some pretend mystery. Chasen has been known to put on a wig and borrow her sister's clothes and sit in a fancy hotel bar, waiting to seduce her husband of twenty-five years. Ultimately, however, they both know who's hiding under the platinum hair and that they'd both drop every pretense of seduction if their cell phone rang with a lonely child on the other end.

Second of all, you'll have to concede that you're not going anywhere. Unlike those thrilling dating years, you can't pick up and leave because something about him just pisses you off. I suppose you can consider moving onto the couch or, more frequently for moms, into the kids' room, but a good marriage with children relies on both parents agreeing not to walk out, even for a day. It would be ridiculous to think this means that you can't give him the silent routine for a day or two, or that you can't withhold sexual favors, but that's rather silly when you both know that you'll be back, talking and loving within forty-eight hours.

Third, you'll have to develop a kind of amnesia. If you don't care whether you ever see a person again, it doesn't really matter if you remind him of the time he confessed he cheated on his SATs, or the time he was rude to your old college roommate, or that you had to pick out your engagement ring without him. But if you want to spend the rest of your life with someone who doesn't duck whenever you enter a room, the ability to forgive and forget is essential.

The fourth little trick you'll have to take out of your bag of turn-ons is the fantasy that the man you're sleeping with will someday be replaced by a new, improved version. Feel free to carry on with your George Clooney reveries in the privacy of your own mind, but trust the Girlfriends and me when we tell you that people don't change, no matter how much we nag them to. I may sound like your mother talking, but I'm a lot more self-serving than I appear. If you let your mate know you think he's great just as he is, he will feel great, and anyone who feels great about themselves is much more fun to have sex with than someone who suspects he's being measured and coming up short. The reverse is true, too, of course. With that in mind, I suggest you leave this book open to this page and put it on his pillow so that he can read this message:

Any man who makes his partner feel young, pretty, and thin is halfway home to getting his deepest needs met.

This list of sacrifices you'll have to make on the altar of your marital sex life is certainly not complete, but it's a good start. Remember, part of getting your groove back is giving yourself realistic goals, and no one needs more than four things to try to master.

The Blessings of "Experienced" Love

This title sounds like a movie in which Gerard Depardieu seduces Catherine Deneuve and they make passionate, if not a tad flabby, love—oblivious to the years that have passed since their last embrace. Get that image right out of your mind! I'm talking about US, still young and vibrant people who can put one finger on their G-spot and the other on our nose without falling into a heap on the floor. There's no room for *Love Among the Ruins* here, Girlfriend. We are the women who are still considering whether to have one more baby, and have not yet moved into the spectator seats. Count your blessings and stop your pity party if you're now feeling like the advice so far has left you with a sexual future that you can predict right down to who'll go to sleep first and which side he'll roll over onto. Boy, oh, boy, are you playing the victim if you think the next forty years will play themselves out as a constantly-replaying video loop of tonight's bedtime experience. I am here to be the carrier of good tidings: No matter what the imagined setbacks there are to intimacy, it's within your power to turn it around to give yourself a magic opportunity to transcend ordinary life and jumpstart a lifelong romance that you not only deserve, but that will be the sticky stuff that holds your marriage together. The most important first step is to bow down at the matrimonial altar and thank the heavens above that you and the father of your children share the ultimate aphrodisiac—the willingness to stay together to make a loving home for your children. Just take a look around at your Girlfriends and realize how many of them have divorced in the past few years.

And you Girlfriends who have made the courageous decision to get out of a partnership with an untrue, unkind, or ungenerous man, apply what comes next to your future life partner. Yeah, unlike the other half of us, you still have all those fun games the rest of us must give up, not to mention the fun of such scandals as making out in a parked car in front of your house and steaming it up so thoroughly that you can't see when your next-door neighbor comes up to tap on the window to see if you're trying to commit suicide with carbon monoxide, and you just pray that she can't see that your unhooked bra is hanging loose around your neck.

Getting back to those married women in search of their grooves: Who can overlook a man who, after a hellish week at work, rises early, washes the tiny two-wheeler bike, oils the chain, and adjusts the little rider's helmet straps so that it fits perfectly on the son or daughter who longs to cruise without training wheels? I can't speak for everyone (though God knows, I try), but my Girlfriends and I agree that this is a sublime kind of sexual foreplay to mentally photograph and save till bedtime. Really, is there anything more sexy than a man who devotes himself to the protection, adoration, and sense of confidence to the child of your womb? If my husband truly understood the aphrodisiac effect his sweet parenting of our little ones has on me, he'd probably quit his day job to become a kindergarten teacher and moonlight as a Little Tykes Toys Assembly Man.

My Girlfriend Donna maintains that the key to keeping the home fires burning is going to bed together at the same time. My Girlfriend Chasen adds her own little twist to that wisdom. Chasen says that couples should go to bed *naked* together at the same time. Of course, during our last major earthquake in Los Angeles, she ended up on the beach outside her home, stark naked and surrounded by her neighbors and their children. Still, it's a small price to pay for all those nights of feeling each other's body hairs tickle your skin, don't you agree?

Speaking of going to bed nude reminds me of the utter bliss I find in the smoothest, cleanest white sheets I can afford. The way I see it, sex starts way before the kissing and hugging part. I like a bed that is so sensuous that I feel like I'm having sex with *it* even before my husband climbs in. Now that you know who you're sharing the linen expenses with, and who might occasionally help you launder them, you owe it to your sexy marriage to get the highest thread count you can afford, the most down pillows that you can sleep on without being overcome by hay fever, and a comforter that is warm enough to make pajamas and socks unnecessary, even in January. And make it smell good, too, even if you can't possibly launder the sheets every other day. I've found all kinds of delicious-smelling talcs that are intended to be sprinkled on the sheets.

Laughter is the greatest aphrodisiac, second only to two apple martinis, and who really needs the hangover? Don't tell my husband that I've said this, but I'm pretty sure the days are over when I would expect him to be so aroused by me that he'd scoop me up and carry me into our sweet-smelling bed. There *have* been a couple of nights over the years when I jumped on his back and he carried me piggyback, but the less said about those times, the better for my children's legacy. They're already going to know too much about their parent's lives than they ever wanted to, I'm sure.

Anyway, after one of those infamous and undignified piggyback rides, we usually both tumbled onto the bed and dissolved in giggles before considering our other options. That leads me to my second sexual recommendation: Delight in being able to laugh and giggle with your beloved because it can lead to such fun and uninhibited sex. Even the most mysterious, generous, and creative lover will probably have popped all his corks by this time in your relationship. Sex will be with the man behind the curtain, NOT "The Great and All-Knowing Wizard of Oz." If the man behind the curtain isn't funny or playful or inspired, you're left with a guy with a huge green scary face asking you to collect witches' brooms before he gives you what you want.

Same goes for you, Girlfriend. Think about it: If sexuality can only be maintained when you're at the top of your game, legs waxed, cellulite banished, wearing your "thin jeans," and having a very good hair day, we're all doomed as a gender. Trust me, there is a place in sexual heaven for us happy earth moms who don't have our party faces on but still have BIG smiles on our faces. If that's not a vote in favor of long-run sex, I don't know what is.

Dress for Success

Your mother's chidings to change your underwear every day, in case you get hit by a truck, may sound prosaic with the passing of time, or you may have given up underwear entirely, like Meredith Viera. We deal with your clothes more specifically in the chapter called "What's a Mother to Wear?" but for right now I just want to remind you that there is someone besides your privacy-gene-deficient kids who sees you in various states of polished dress. Remember him, the guy who used to beg you to wear thong panties, even though you whined that they gave you indelible wedgies? Men are simple beings with simple needs—at least where simple sex is concerned. My scientific research indicates that any man over the age of fourteen likes to think that all attractive women (except their mothers) are dressed in provocative push-up bras and matching butt floss underneath their professional exteriors.

As universal as this desire and secret fantasy is, very few married men truly believe it's something that they can look forward to in their lifetimes. Think about it, Girlfriends, you have a perfect setup to play against his lowered expectations and blow his mind with a little number from the Victoria's Secret catalog. Throw in a pair of stockings and a garter belt, and you have a sex slave for the next few days. While you're out there in bad taste land, go for it and order a pair of fishnets, too. For reasons unbeknownst to me, tarty fishnet stockings are to men like a box of Snausages are to a dog.

Reach Out and Touch, Somebody's Body . . . La La La La, De Dah Dah Dum

Way too many Girlfriends tell me that they don't feel sexy because they're too fat, flabby, or too "loosey goosey," if you catch my drift. Here's the news flash on that one, my dears: Most men like sex with any woman who wants to have sex with them. Yup, that's pretty much it in a nutshell. If you are sweet-smelling and attractively dressed . . . *oh, for heaven's sake!* You can be lying there with a Lanz nightie down to your ankles and moisturizing gloves on your hands; if you are in the mood, chances are he is, too. As my Girlfriend Lori's son told me with his college sophomore clarity, "Guys are always ready to 'hook up,' as long as the chick isn't skanky." So, assuming we're several levels above skanky, we're there for the picking.

Unless you regularly light your bedroom brilliantly enough to perform LASIK surgery, there's no need to feel apologetic about stretch-marks that seem to be a line-for-line topography of the Grand Canyon. If you and your partner enjoy the party favors offered by a great set of knockers, like my Girlfriend Ann's (one of the only pair of certifiably natural breasts of a bountiful size in all of the Greater Los Angeles area), Ann assures me that no man complains if they don't stand upright at attention, either. In fact, they like boobies that curl up somewhere near the armpit like stray puppies looking for their moms because they love to rescue them. No one even has to see your backside, unless of course, you have a mirror on your ceiling over your bed. But hey, with the proper lighting, even that angle could be rather fetching. The point here is that you must remember that your men generally love your looks a thousand times more than you love them. Here's my suggestion—ignore your own nagging little mind and listen reverentially to your guy. You'll both feel happier for it.

If you feel that you just can't get past your own inhibitions about the tolls and gravitational pulls motherhood and time have taken on your poor little body, ignore everything I've said so far and dress as though there is only one person on this planet worth pleasing: YOU. After all, if you're turned on by you, or at the very least, not turned off, chances are he'll pick up on your comfort and ease and get right into the spirit. Why not try wearing a sheer short nightie over sexy undies to achieve the same effect of a filtered lens on a star of the silver screen? You can get the same feeling if he wears glasses and you conveniently hide them before going to bed. The goal here is if you're willing to have sex with yourself, you'll find someone in your bedroom (after you've cleared out all the stray kids) who shares your opinion.

One last thing to keep in mind here, Girlfriends, though you should be willing to bite off your own tongue before saying it out loud. You aren't the only one that the last ten years or so has left a little thicker around the middle and a little thinner at the top. You still want him and find him sexy, right? Well then, cut yourself at least that much slack.

No One's Keeping Score

The last thing you want to do in a relationship intended to last a lifetime is to keep a weekly or monthly scorecard. It's like I tell my kids when one of them whines about some perceived slight, that fairness cannot be measured except on an annual basis. From day to day, there will be tallies that come up short in one fairness category or another, but they should even out over the course of a year. Same thing with sex. If you feel unloved and unloving because you and your mate have gone a whole week, if not a whole month, without good hot, monkey sex, you must fight the temptation to condemn the entire time-space continuum. Not only that, but you'll put the same voodoo hex on your lovemaking that a homerun hitter puts on himself when he thinks he's in a slump.

Sex is not a performance to be measured against a national norm. First of all, the nation's normal people are probably fibbing about the frequency of their intimacies. Second of all, in this long-distance race called marriage and motherhood, there will be so very many things to throw off your average. I'm confident that, if you stay in the saddle and keep your chin up, you can more than make up for any lost points in your RBIs with a weekend away and a bottle of wine, OR a weekend at home with the movie *9½ Weeks* and a bottle of baby oil, but hey, who's keeping score in this game of life?

The important thing to keep in mind is that your sex life is a reflection of your passion and ease. It's not a measurement of your love and commitment to your relationship. I'm letting us all off the hook here, in a way, since I've been married long enough to know that sexually clicking is as seasonal as leaves changing and the days getting shorter. While I think that everyone is entitled to find their sexual harmony without my intervention or the unrealistic standards of *Cosmopolitan*, I really, really, do think that indifference about sex is like cutting your favorite seafood dish out of your life's menu just because it needs to be boned or cracked with pliers and picked out with your fingers. It may sound like a lot of trouble before you begin, but it's so delicious that halfway through, you'll wish you ate nothing else.

Till Death Do Us Part?

"Only five more sleeps!" as my son used to say when counting down the days until his birthday or Christmas or a visit to Disneyland—and now it's only five more sleeps until my Girlfriend Sonia gets married, for the second time. If you've been paying attention to the sagas of my Girlfriends, you will recall that Sonia has been one of my closest chums for about twenty years, but we really kicked into hyper-bonding mode after she and I married the future fathers of our children within two months of each other and coincidentally became neighbors. We lived within walking distance of each other, which is kind of unique here in Southern California, in sweet little cottages near the beach, and I will never forget the day that I found out I was pregnant with my first son and burst out my front door to fast-walk to Sonia's to share the news. I could have called, and perhaps I did, I don't recall, but I was a basket of boastful tidings and I needed to share this face-to-face with a mommy Girlfriend.

Thirteen years later I still remember standing on Sonia's front porch and knocking on the door. She flung it open, hugged me, then sprinted back across her living room to capture her toddler son, who was sticking the *TV Guide* between the wires of her lovebirds' cage, making the fowl fly so frantically that their birdseed was showering all of us. You'd think that such a frenzy would have given me a moment of pause about this pregnancy, but what was remarkable was the smell of her famous enchiladas baking, the sound of her wind chimes on her patio, her utter beauty and obvious joy in her life. If I could capture that moment in a bottle and sell it over the Internet, St. John's Wort would be no more remarkable than a plantar's wart. But higher powers than ours determined that this, too, would pass. A few years later Sonia was divorced.

When I wrote my first book, *The Girlfriends' Guide to Pregnancy,* all the Girlfriends were "happily married" and blissfully assuming we'd all stay that way till death did us part. National statistics being what they are, I realized that about half of all marriages in this country end in divorce. Like other grim facts of life, I knew, intellectually, that it could happen, but I assumed it would never happen in my little world. Like seeking like, I'd gravitated toward friendships with women whose lives looked like mine; we'd all married the fathers of our kids before the babies were born (or very soon thereafter), we all had mortgage payments, we all complained about our mates' failure to embrace family trips to the Oceanography Institute or the Museum of Natural History on a Saturday morning with our own nurturing enthusiasm (they always seemed to need a nap on weekends), we all fretted about our relationships with our in-laws, and we all knew that we'd spend our golden years parking our Winnebagos in our grown children's driveways for weeks on end.

I have been blessed with a core group of Girlfriends for about twelve years. Most of them were friends of mine through my first and second pregnancies, but I've collected a few more brilliant specimens along the maternal way, usually dragged along by my kids who struck up friendships with their children and taught me to broaden my Girlfriend horizons. In the earlier years, when I was pregnant or mothering infants, I tended to seek out Girlfriends among acquaintances who were also pregnant or new-mothering. Once the "shock" of maternity wore off a bit, however, I became less particular and found it easy to bond with any woman who had surrendered her heart to a little dependent, no matter what the age. In those intervening years I've picked up a few more Girlfriends from work or in the neighborhood.

Still, when I sit here now thinking about what made me such a fanatic about the value of Girlfriends in my life, I keep coming up with images of the women who got me through my first and second pregnancies. Whenever I think of that time in my life, my joy, my uncertainty, my obsession with doing everything right, my fear that I couldn't do any of it, I am more and more convinced that the only thing that stood between me and my husband's sanity was the coven of mommies who kept loving me and listening to me, long after I had annoyed them into stupors. It was a time when all our dreams were coming true. None of us had really been at this wifing/mothering/careering job for all that long, and didn't yet know that it would be so hard that labor and delivery would seem like a tooth cleaning.

Something about new motherhood seems so everlasting when you're living it. I never imagined the days when my kids would come home with school pictures in which they had six to eight baby teeth missing. I guess I always pictured them staying totally toothless forever. Our marriages, at least in my little group, were like the flannel backing upon which we told the stories of our lives with little felt characters; they were the given, the canvas on which our new lives as mothers would be painted. If truth be told, I think we were all, husbands and wives, so consumed with the babies, and integrating them into our previous lives, that we didn't have much pep left when it came to romantic issues.

My growing family's life was so inextricably linked with Sonia's, Erica's, Frannie's, Chasen's, Lindsey's and Ann's families that we didn't even need to make plans to get together. It was just assumed that at least one day a weekend would be spent as a group, the only decision being whose house we'd gather in or whether any of the kids had an infectious disease that might put a crimp in our gatherings.

Our time together was spent so unexceptionally that we Girlfriends used to chide each other about how boring we'd become since our kids were born. It's funny, when I think back on it. We pretended a sort of cynicism about the hours spent trying to get the kids to eat something from the potluck buffet, our glasses of wine lined up on the fireplace mantel so that the kids wouldn't knock them over. Our husbands would watch some sporting event or talk about the sporting event they'd all seen earlier that day, while we Girlfriends would wrangle the children, teach them not to hit each other, insist that they learn to share, all while pulling a meal together.

We'd eat like all young parents do, with the mothers jumping up every two minutes to catch a kid's spilled cup of milk or waltzing a small child on her hip while trying to get a few bites of Chinese chicken salad with her other hand, the fathers finally putting their plates aside after fifty or sixty snide looks from their wives. By about eight-thirty or nine P.M., we'd finally get most of the kids settled down on couches or in baby seats; then us "old married folk" would play Trivial Pursuit or, even more often, charades. By then, the communal glass of wine that we moms had been sharing would have worked its spell, and we would laugh so hard over charades that we'd wet ourselves, which was not such a big deal after so recently birthing those babies. Our laughter never seemed to wake up the kids, and now I realize that there is nothing more comforting to fall asleep to than the sound of your mommy and daddy being nearby and enjoying the company of people you consider close as kin.

Up until we moved to Los Angeles a year ago, I had on my refrigerator door a Polaroid of all us Girlfriends, slightly tipsy from that out-of-toddlers'-reach wine in my kitchen, each of us waving a cooking utensil. I captioned it "The Joy of Cooking." For the four years that it hung there from a magnet in the shape of a Chinese take-out box, that photo made me chuckle. Now I know what charmed me about it—it was the last memento I had of those glory days of believing that we were friends forever, that our families were immune to disaster, and that the love that sustained us all then was so durable that time would never change it. Within the next five years half of our extended family would be divorced.

Is Divorce Contagious?

I never realized how powerful a divorce's quake would be on the Richter scale of the Girlfriends' lives. What stands out now in my memory is the feeling of vulnerability among those of us who were still married. If our dearest friends were throwing in the towel, how could the rest of us ever again believe that our own marriages would defy statistics and hold together? Even those of us whose own parents were divorced cherished the notion that "till death do us part" really was binding, particularly after we threw a baby or two into the mix.

I never would have admitted it at the time, but I think those of us who were still holding on to our marital bliss worried that there was such a thing as Divorce Cooties.

Between you and me, I was usually reluctant to tell my husband about any threats of divorce, for fear it would remind him of an option he'd long forgotten. One of my worst fears was of looking like a self-deluded character straight out of a Woody Allen movie—painting her toenails in bed with a moisturizing mask on her face and nasally complaining about another man's infidelity while her husband stands in the bathroom, cutting his nose hairs, and fantasizing about sex with the kids' math tutor.

A lot of my bonding time with the core Girlfriends was spent hiking in the foothills near our homes. There was always someone in our group who had some baby fat to drop, even if her last baby had been born more than three years ago. We never talked much on the uphill journey, our breath being too precious to waste with conversation, but the entire descent was always spent trying to discover the differences between the failing marriages and our own. It's as if we were desperate to name the reasons why our dearest friends couldn't face a future together so that we could avoid them in our own fragile little lives:

"Maybe he just couldn't take her last round of postpartum depression, especially when she wore the same overalls for five straight months."

"Well, you know, *he* always thought she'd go back to work after the baby was born, and she doesn't want to now, so maybe there's too much financial pressure."

"Not enough sex, that's what it's always about!"

"He just didn't want to grow up; you know, the Peter Pan Complex."

If we could identify the germ, we hoped would could vaccinate our own marriages against infection. The scary part was that we sometimes worried that our divorcing friends were "carriers" and we were often torn between offering love and support to cherished Girlfriends and spending extra phone time with the still-married Girlfriends to remind each other of our immunity to the divorce bug. Invariably, the Girlfriend going through the divorce was missing from our hiking group, either avoiding us in humiliation, tending to traumatized kids, or taking to her bed while her parents cared for her kids, so we could talk openly about the breakup. The rest of us were like a coven of hikers who huddled together to get a handle on the reasons for the rift and cast a spell on it so that it wouldn't threaten our own little families.

The Other Woman

Ninety percent of the time, at least by my own rough estimation, one of the divorcing spouses was "outed" as having an affair. I don't want to speculate about the inner workings of other people's marriages but boy, oh, boy, did we Girlfriends ever bite into that bone and chew. Five times out six the wayward party was the husband, and we became positively phobic about the threat of "The Other Woman." I wish I could tell you that the new girlfriends (notice that I use the lower case G for this classification) were at least as old as we wives were and burdened with at least one child, but . . . NOT! They were invariably younger, thinner, perkier, and sexier (at least to the casual observer) than we were. Suddenly we all began reevaluating our husbands' colleagues at work, analyzing their credit card bills, and resenting any woman our husband described as "lots of fun" (which means she will photocopy her bare butt during the office Christmas party) or "a great conversationalist" (which means she fakes interest in every single thing *our* man has to say).

With a little more experience under my belt, I've come to the realization that extramarital affairs are not so much the cause of divorce but the undeniable symptom of a rift. They're the Krispy Kremes, not the obesity. That's not necessarily good news. In the first wave of divorce to hit my peers, there was a kind of perverse satisfaction and simplicity in labeling the floozies as forces of nature that were no more preventable than earthquakes or hurricanes. They were like the flu; they could have been avoided if the guys had remembered to wash their hands after contact, but once lodged in their systems, they could persist for a whole winter and leave the weakened fellows coughing through spring. An otherwise healthy marriage could succumb—it was just the luck of the draw.

We Girlfriends (with a capital G) used to *hate* the girlfriends! In our battened-down little minds, all marriages would survive long enough to be mentioned by Willard Scott if only there were no tempting little cuties singing their sirens' song to our otherwise tone-deaf husbands. But our anger was only surpassed by our moral indignation. What kind of woman could have an affair with a *father!*? No woman worth her

167

estrogen would even consider contributing to the breakup of a family! Those *fathers* didn't receive nearly as much of our wrath. I don't know if it's because we didn't think they were capable of more ethical behavior or if we were avoiding damning them too much, just in case the marriage survived and we'd all end up together again, playing Scrabble and sharing a glass of wine.

Picking up the Pieces

I'll tell you one thing for sure, watching your friend go through a divorce makes you a lot more tolerant of and grateful for your own marriage. Most of the time, we Girlfriends got "custody" of the divorcing mom and her kids. The only exception to that rule was when financial or sentimental considerations prevailed, such as when the guy was our husband's business partner or had been his college roommate. But, Girlfriends being Girlfriends, we circle our wagons around the mommy and kids. Most of our husbands just tried to stay out of the crossfire, but we Girlfriends took it personally.

This responsibility to our divorcing Girlfriend always turned out to be a much bigger job than I'd ever imagined. From what I've witnessed, divorce—when there are kids and cars and houses to divvy up, not to mention attempts at reconciliation and, occasionally, retaliation—takes at least two years, sometimes four or five. I'm not talking about the time between filing and getting a decree, I'm talking about the pace set by such feelings as guilt, betrayal, humiliation, fear, disappointment, and rage. Since murder is usually not an option, the divorcing spouses usually end up wielding kids and money as their most potent weapons. Don't ever let anyone tell you that isn't horrifying.

And throughout that time the divorcing Girlfriend is working through her grief with her other friends. I don't want to sound like I'm complaining, and I'd certainly volunteer to be there all over again for any one of my precious Girlfriends, but there *did* come a time when I thought that I'd scream if I heard my Girlfriend Jody rant about how Arnie still drove a two-seater car, with no room for a carseat, even though he had custody of their two little girls two and a half days a week. Look, I already hated the guy. What more did she want from me, to walk up and slap him the next time I saw him?

It was also our moral responsibility to give the hairy eyeball to the divorcing dad, the traitor, whenever we ran into him at school plays or when it was his day to pick the kids up from school. But beyond that, our responsibilities as friends-of-the-wife got a little murky. For example, what was I supposed to do when I ran into a Girlfriend's husband in Las Vegas with a cute little blonde or when we heard that another's ex, who was supposed to be "spending some time alone to reevaluate the marriage" was really living with his girlfriend and partying every night? Was this information either pal needed for her court case, or was it a further form of torture?

Who Gets Custody of Me?

Nowadays, with living together being tolerated by most churches, and even by parents, two people choosing to get married generally comes along with a coupon for at least one free baby. Sure, it also justifies the flagrant spending of money on a well-turned out celebration and honeymoon, as well as silverware that matches, a microwave, and an espresso machine. I've yet to meet a woman who didn't firmly believe that the change in status from girlfriend to wife is as significant as when the holder of a Screen Extras Guild card finally satisfies the requirements to earn a card from the Screen Actors Guild. Sure, the quality of the work might not change noticeably, but the upgrade erased that faint "L for Loser" off one's forehead. An actor is a singular featured attraction, even if she has just one line; an extra is in the movie, all right, but she's almost impossible to distinguish from the rest of the madding crowd.

When you're a girlfriend, people may like you immensely, prefer you to any girlfriends who preceded (or even succeeded you for a few insane weeks or months), and your relationship can be intoxicatingly full of tightrope walking, mixed messages, and unspoken dreams. You and his family can adore each other, or at least generally convince your-selves of your mutual affection, but you know deep down inside that your mate's intoxication with you is most critical.

It's Like *Survivor,* Only Longer

When my Girlfriend Ann married her beau, he told her in no uncer-tain terms, "Marriage is like the Mafia—the only way you can get out is to die." Seventeen years into my own nuptial bliss, it's often occurred to me that staying married is sometimes more a function of fundamental philosophy than of the degree of passion. Anyone who tells you that her marriage has been a steady crescendo of devotion and bliss from the honeymoon through housebreaking two dogs and a couple of kids is either fibbing or having an affair. Look, it's hard enough to choose a winter coat that you won't be sick of within three months; finding a life mate with whom you can willingly share a bed and breakfast through ten Presidential inaugurations is staggeringly difficult. At least with a coat you can change the buttons or take up the hem, not to mention putting it in mothballs for half a year.

Human nature being what it is, most of us find ourselves parenting children who can dress themselves and spout radio rap lyrics right about the time that we realize we're still sleeping with that guy who showed up about ten years ago and never left—or, heaven forbid, who moved into his own apartment with little or no warning. Being new parents is like being part of a MASH unit; you're so preoccupied with patching up the big wounds that simple concussions and contusions can be overlooked for a few years. Perhaps I'm being overly dramatic to make my point, as my husband says I always am, but you know me well enough by now to know that I see most clearly in black and white. If your own life got right back on track once you passed your maternity clothes on to your sister-in-law, then count your lucky stars. The rest of you: Stick with me for a few pages.

Babies: The Marital Knot, or Not

Based on personal experience, I gotta tell you, no matter how much love there is in a relationship, there are days when it takes every sinew of self-control not to change the locks and throw all his things out the window. I'm not saying husbands are more annoying or frustrating than wives, but simply that every relationship that is not conducted primarily by e-mail seems to have seasons of discontent. No matter how seriously we all took our marriage vows, I promise you, there will be "deal breakers" several times along the matrimonial path.

Ironically, one of the biggest challenges to marriage is the fruit of that love fest, *children*. Mother Nature is so darned conniving, confusing us with a smokescreen of passion and Hallmark poetry, to make us believe that having children with our beloved is the ultimate expression of our lifelong commitment. Until that first little cherub comes into your life, you forge ahead with your reproductivity like a divine bulldozer, certain that fulfilling your biological imperative can only enhance your romance.

Okay, so we accepted the chaos of early parenthood. Tall tales about mothers who nursed for six straight years and still maintained their space eligibility with NASA or who stayed awake every night for four years with three consecutive colicky kids were shared with us during our pregnancies like the postpartum equivalents of Paul Bunyan and

Johnny Appleseed. But once we moved on to the stage when the family could fly a kite together or share Harry Potter books or enjoy our offspring's talent for team sports, the fun was sure to begin. Then we'd get our groove back, right?

Them's Fightin' Words

I have watched enough afternoon television to know that statistics say money is the most fertile ground for fights between husbands and wives. While my mate and I have had more than our share of fights about how we spend (meaning that I do it and he doesn't), I can't recall any arguments that were more hysterical and painful than those about our kids and how to raise them. Nothing is more personal than how we feel about our kids and nearly any discussion about how we deal with them, and nearly any disagreement about parenting can lead to blows.

Labor and delivery should have been some indication. When the doctor performed an exam and announced that I was completely dilated and effaced and then informed me that my husband was downstairs in the nurses' kitchen buying delicacies from a Filipino nurse to keep his own blood sugar up (even though I'd subsisted on ice chips and an I.V. cocktail of pitocin and saltwater for the last fifteen hours), I was so ticked off that I had to be restrained from rolling off the bed and waddling down to grab him by the throat, pushing be damned.

Since that night we've fought about the time I used profanity in front of our kids, the fact that my husband doesn't fake an interest in church to set a good example for our children, the time I sneaked a cigarette in my office and our daughter caught me, the time my husband advised our son to "beat the crap" out of the class bully, and when I took the two oldest kids on an overnight camping trip and our son wandered off and had to be rescued by the National Forest Service.

As the children have grown up, they've begun to offer living examples of the old truism, "the apple never falls far from the tree," and that's only served to add the "picante" to our spicy parenting encounters. It's uncanny, really, the way my husband and two of my kids hum when they're nervous, leave their shoes untied all day, and cringe when they have their fingernails cut (even though my husband inflicts the "creepy sensation" on himself). If you want to know true marital discord, try sitting down at the dinner table with the Iovines when I've served three different courses on one plate and the meat is "touching" the creamed corn; my husband and at least one of his offspring will stare at the plate in abject revulsion while the other three of us tuck in without a concern for what we're eating, let alone if it's touching something else.

The feeling is mutual, I'm sure. I've sat in the Little League bleachers and watched one of my kids get tagged out at first base while feeling my husband's accusing glare burning into the side of my skull, telepathically communicating, *"You've* always run like you have cement shoes and you've passed it on to him!" And just the other morning, my beloved co-parent informed me that he'd had the worst night's sleep of his life because our daughter had sneaked into our bed and pummeled him for six straight hours. "She's just like you!" he lamented. "The sweetest, kindest, most compassionate selfish *person* I've ever met!" The only remark I've ever heard that can trump that final dismissal "She's just like you!" is "She's just like your *mother*!"

You may recall how my husband responded to the news that we were pregnant with our fourth child in six years. Completely oblivious to the romantic surrounding of the Italian restaurant I'd chosen to make my sentimental announcement and spluttering into the red candle wrapped in plastic fishnet that separated us, he gave me his now infamous appraisal of our condition, "Vicki," he said, "you are like a pie. Every time you have another baby, you make sure that the other kids' slices stay untouched and my piece gets chopped to bits."

And that doesn't even begin to factor in the conflicts inspired by two adults trying to raise children AND meet the countless other obligations and tasks that overinflate a day. Here's a good sparring scenario for you: You and your husband wake up to the alarm, about two hours earlier than your body would like, one of you dashing to the coffeemaker to grab two cups and the other taking first dibs on the shower. Just as you're standing in front of the mirror in pantyhose and a bra and your husband is lingering for an extra ten minutes under the hot water, one of the kids walks into your bathroom; his eyes are swollen and his cheeks are bright red with fever. You know it as surely as you know you are his mother that this little one is sick and not going *anywhere* except back to bed.

Round One: The argument about whether Mom's or Dad's diagnosis is more accurate. Round Two: Some rope-a-doping about whether you can sneak the little sick one into daycare or school for at least half a day without being reported to Child Welfare Services. Round Three: A rapid exchange of kidney punches about who's inability to stay home and take care of the child is more irrefutable. Cut to Round Ten: Either it's a draw, because a grandma or for-money sitter has been rounded up by eight A.M., or it's a knockout and one of you dashes off to work, late, worried about the baby, and ticked off that their parenting commitment has been called into question while the other yanks off the pantyhose and puts her sweats on before she hoarsely calls into work to say she's got the flu.

Title Bouts Waged with the Kids Ringside

That little scenario I just illustrated had to have taken place, at least partially, in the presence of the little sick one whose fever and swollen eyes started the bout in the first place. I have no doubt that you've read as many books and articles as I have that tell us parents that arguing should be done in private, particularly when it's heated and about something more personal than whether the Lakers can beat the Knicks. Okay, I see the point; what child wants to think that he's done something, no matter how innocently, that makes Mommy and Daddy get so involved in their agitated debate that his runny nose goes completely unnoticed? I guess this is as good a time as any to point out the difference in parenting when the child at the center is either unable to understand the native language and now; when he's not only fully fluent, but old enough to take sides.

No matter whether you live in Buckingham Palace or a studio apartment, as the kids get older and smarter, it becomes nearly impossible for a couple to "discuss" anything without the walls having ears. This is a good point to remember, because, while they may understand the words being said, they most likely will not understand the context in which they're said. Part of moving into this new stage of marriage and parenthood is understanding that all differences of opinion that take place outside of a locked car must be conducted with the assumption that there's an audience sitting ringside.

First thing to remember is to clean up all the language, or else I guarantee you'll hear some very choice words pop out of the mouth of your babe. Second, you must both take pains to avoid fighting in a way that looks like it can only end with one of you walking out the door and never coming back. Even if your family hasn't experienced the tragedy of divorce firsthand, your child will have several friends who *have* experienced it and shared it with the whole class. I still recall hearing my parents argue in the "privacy" of their own room, and I'd get so frightened that my world was coming to an end that I'd crawl into bed with my baby brother and wake him up so I could tell him a story to distract myself. I must have suspected our family unit was on thin ice, because, sure enough, they separated by the time I was nine and divorced within the year. My husband, on the other hand, heard his parents argue all the time, but never even paid attention, he was so confident that no one was ever going to leave. His child's intuition was right, and his parents stayed married until his father passed away. I suspect it's all in the fighting.

There are lots of books out there telling us how to fight fairly, and I think they can be very useful, if you're inclined to want to pick one up from your local bookstore. Let me give you the *Reader's Digest* condensed version, at least as I see it, to hold you over till you get a moment to log on to Amazon.com: Keep the fights to the issue at hand. In the example given above about who's going to stay home with the sick child, it's normal and reasonable for both parents to make their needs known, but it's not fair to trudge back into ancient history to gain ammunition. Don't bolster your argument with accusations like "You've never been there when he's needed you!" or "You just think your job is more important than mine because you make more money!" If there's that kind of hostility just waiting to be brought into action, this fight isn't about a sick child's care at all, but rather about a deeper resentment you two feel for each other. That's scary stuff; not just for the child, but for the marriage, too.

Before you consider self-flagellation as the appropriate form of punishment, let me rush to tell you that, if you argue as though you are solving a single problem rather than questioning the sanctity of your marriage, you're probably fine.

I have a Girlfriend Nadia who actually had to go into therapy to overcome her parents' image of a perfect marriage. While they were, and still are, madly in love with each other, Nadia's parents took great pains never to snarl or snap at each other in front of the children. When Nadia got married and found that even the most benign disagreements made her worry that the next stop was Divorce Court, it occurred to her that seeing how partners who love each other work out disputes might have been a useful growing experience for her. She had been raised to believe that love meant never having to say, "Are you out of your f-ing mind?"

It took Nadia several years of therapy and an investment equal to the cash purchase of a sporty car to understand that, not only do married couples disagree, but that talking about it is part of the give and take that allows people to move on to some sort of consensus. She hadn't wanted to witness talons extended, names called, loud voiced battle, but she could have used a few examples of how people can vigorously disagree and not ultimately wish each other dead.

Together for the Sake of the Children

When the day comes that one or the other of you marriage mates has had it up to here with all the arguing, fair and appropriate as it may be, you may ask yourself whether life would be less tense and acrimonious if you just divorced. You're fed up with the emotional mayhem, he's working late at the office to avoid another confrontation, and the kids are begging you to stop fighting all the time.

It's fashionable these days for experts to counsel that, when a marriage is consistently filled with strife and unhappiness, the parents are doing their kids a favor to separate, if not divorce. The theory is that any levelheaded child would rather have two happy, unconflicted parents loving him from two different addresses than to spend the rest of his years in the family home being subjected to endless arguing and tension.

I'm gong out very far on this limb, I know, but I totally disagree with the experts on this matter. Nora Ephron, the author-director-goddess, once had one of her characters say something to this effect in one of her movies: "If a child had the choice of hearing his mother weeping of loneliness and unrealized dreams in her room beside his or of lovingly and generously sending her off to her lifelong dream of love and fulfillment on a beautiful tropical island, the child would choose the crying for the rest of his life." I think she's spot on. As a child of divorce, myself, I can honestly tell you that I'd have rather sat through twenty crying Thanksgivings and burned turkeys and thirty tense Christmases, where my dad let off some steam by punching a hole through the closet door with his fist, than have either parent leave our home.

I'm not so retro that I think everyone has to stay married, no matter how miserable or unworkable the marriage, but I don't think a parent alive can honestly say they got the divorce for the sake of the kids, unless, of course, the kids were being brutalized by one of the parents. I've seen so much now, in my mommy adolescence, that underscores my opinion. So often, I find couples splitting because it's the ultimate "F You" to their cheating or ambivalent mate. But I've also seen the icky stuff that comes after: unequal child and spousal support arrangements, visitation schedules that never work out as they were intended to, the awkwardness of reentering the dating world, primarily if you're the one with primary custody of the kids, and children who cry for two hours every night after their daddies have dropped them back at Mom's.

All right, I give it up to the parents who tell me that there is no way on this earth that a marriage can endure under their circumstances. I'm not trying to be any more judgmental than usual here. I'm just saying that this is a bumpy time for all of us. We may not get flowers on our anniversaries without ordering them ourselves, and we may think our mates find us less compelling than a piece of gum on the bottom of their shoe, but I sincerely hope that reading this chapter wakes everyone looking to regain their groove to the fact that it isn't being handed out for free with a purchase over $100 at the supermarket. I'm going to go one step further and suggest, if you and your mate can make it through the ups and downs of this middle part of parenting life, you may be surprisingly rewarded with a new appreciation for each other and a more mature intimacy as your children need less and less of your youth, your breath, and your blood.

Mother of One. Mother of All

An amazing thing happened when I became a mother: I felt maternal about everybody. I no longer considered asking for a refund on my ticket when I saw that a toddler was sitting next to me on my flight, I was willing to wipe nearly anybody's nose on my sleeve and I didn't automatically gag if someone around me vomited. I joined the sorority of moms, and I've worn the secret insignia like a badge of honor.

Here's the problem: It's just a little tumble down the slippery slope of motherhood before you find yourself treating your mate like just one more kid. One more person who wants dinner, one more person who needs clean socks, one more person who wants to tell me about his day—no matter how backed up my e-mail is. Take my Girlfriend Marla, for example. Marla adores her husband, the father of her three kids, but when I asked her how she was holding up, running the household alone while her husband was on a long business trip, she replied, "Are you kidding? It's great! I get to eat microwave popcorn for dinner every night, and I get the whole bed to myself!"

Being a mother, even after the kids are old enough to put their own toothpaste on the brush and to rewind their own videos, leaves most of us Girlfriends feeling, as my father so picturesquely put it, "like a one-legged man in an ass-kicking contest." We wake up in the morning, resist the temptation to pull the blankets over our heads and hide, and then dig into a day defined by other people's needs. Little Jenny needs her retainer tightened, Little Jordan has a Boy Scout cookout, Little Janey has been feeling mopey and neglected for two days and needs some extra Mommy Love, and Little Husband wants everything from a wife who wears matching undergarments to a plate of lasagna like his dear old momma used to make—oh, yeah, and sex, they always seem to want more of that.

The minute we put our kids and our mates in the same "Needs" category is the minute our marriages enter the Twilight Zone. As your Girlfriend, I'm telling you this from personal experience. We raise our kids, we partner our spouses—there's a big difference here. If the gods are smiling on us, we spend about a fourth of our lives actively parenting our kids; if truth be told, they're really only ours for the first twelve years. But if those same gods are still smiling, we can end up spending half to three quarters of our lives with our mates. You do the math. Most important, our marital partners are fully baked by the time they choose us as lifemates. They are who they are, for better or for worse. Sure, we can upgrade their wardrobes and suggest a better haircut, but otherwise it's caveat emptor.

Mum's the Word

Not that you're asking me, but if you were, I would tell you that the most potent tool in my marriage survival kit is my willingness to bite my tongue—often so vigorously that it could bleed. Words can be like serpents leaping from our mouths, and sometimes the kindest act of all is to choke back the snakes. There comes a time in all marriages when Toto pulls back the curtain to reveal that we are married to the regular guy behind it, not the Great and Powerful Oz—and vice versa. One of the things that separates the wives from the ex-wives is our wisdom in knowing when not to pay any attention to the man behind the curtain.

If this advice leaves you feeling all frustrated and unresolved, let me give it to you another way. There also comes a time in every relationship when a man realizes that his mate howls at the moon and gains ten pounds in water weight once a month, that she passes gas after mixing Mexican food and beer, and that she loses her wallet and needs to cancel all the credit cards at least four times a year. Now do you see where I'm going with all this?

One of the most important parts of getting our grooves back is learning to make peace with our own imperfections and embracing them in those we love. Nagging should be the first thing to toss overboard. It signifies a lack of faith in those on the receiving end of that laser pointer. It says that even the person closest to you sees more holes in you than in Jarlsburg Swiss. It leaves the nagg-ee feeling like he has no safe haven that accepts him no matter how vulnerable he feels. Icky, icky, icky.

Sometimes, the most heroic behavior you can hope for is silence. "I told you so" should be permanently barred from your marital conversation. As a matter of fact, kids hate hearing those words, too, so toss them out entirely. "You embarrassed me" is another phrase for the Dumpster, as is "After everything I do for you . . ." (fill in the blank). Like most truisms, this one, too, is true: "If you haven't got anything nice to say, don't say anything at all." Even if you can't come up with encouraging words or words of love, at least you won't do any damage with letting those serpents slither out all over the place.

But this isn't where it ends, because I've observed that those of us stricken with the nagging gene are equally capable of directing the burning lasers on ourselves. The accusations may be silent, but inside our heads is a mosh pit of voices accusing, "You're still too fat," "You are a failure as a mother," "Your boss thinks you're a clock watcher," and "You suck at knowing how to blend your cosmetics." Even after spending more than a year on this book and devoting what's left of my gray matter to the question of "how to get our groove back," I still count my failures instead of sheep at night. I still don't cut myself enough slack, give myself a responsibility "casual Friday," still don't spend enough time celebrating my successes.

My personal goal is to approach my chronic guilt over a job less-than-perfectly performed the way an alcoholic stops drinking, one day at a time. Every time I feel myself contorting to kick myself in the ass, I resolve to find one small success to celebrate instead. Maybe it's just that I haven't raised my voice or whined once all day. Maybe it's that I managed to shower and dress in matching clothes *before* I drove the kids to school. Or maybe it's because I actually had a good answer when my youngest asked me why her big brother had a book with *"condoms"* illustrated inside. Am I a success if I potty train all four kids before they enter preschool? Am I a success if three out of four of my kids get accepted into a college, even if it was one of their "fall back" choices (don't obsess about this; it's material for another book at another time). Or am I a success if, after all four of them leave the nest, they are still willing to come home for Thanksgiving and remember to send me Mother's Day gifts? Since I have no idea where the motherhood marathon finish line lies, or even if there is one, I have decided to break the race up into the bite-sized daily pieces.

Baby, Baby, Who Gets to Be the Baby?

This time around for my Girlfriend Sonia, there were no engraved invitations or guest lists a mile long. She called me two days ago with the date and location of her wedding and told me to come dressed "in anything comfortable and barefoot." Her intended is wearing a Hawaiian shirt, as are her son and his. Jon, her husband-to-be, seems to expect her to show up on the sand at nine A.M. in some simple frock—none of us has ever told him about the beautiful pale cream, corset-waisted silk gown she bought a year ago in a frenzy of optimism and has hidden in a garbage bag at the back of her closet. Even if the blinders of love have been lifted, the bride's desire for fantasy still remains.

Sonia and Jon aren't absolutely sure whether or not they'll add a baby of their combined biology to their newly blended family of her two and his one. Many other couples in their position plan to adhere the various members of their family together with the sticky glue of a new baby right away. After all, if love between two people (and their preexisting kids) is great, then expanding the circle of adoration to include a new baby can only make it transcendental, right? Well, yes and no. If there's one truth that we Girlfriends all accept, it's that morphing from babes into the mothers of babes is a much more fundamental and permanent life change than any of us could ever imagine.

The first body blow that parenthood levels at a marriage is the undeniable physical evidence that neither our husbands nor we get to be the baby of the family anymore. My Girlfriend, Chasen has the best stories about what a shocking experience this turned out to be for her and her mate. She and Gordan were both golden children and the apples of their parents' eyes. Since they were married for several years before they had the first of their kids, the biggest challenge at the beginning of the married life was deciding which set of parents to eat Shabbat dinner with. Other than that, they pursued their careers, took fabulous vacations in the south of France and spent party weekends with their other childless friends on houseboats on Lake Powell. Married life wasn't much different from their single days, except for the fact that their wedding had given them a full set of silver and china, an heirloom hutch for their dining room, and the down payment for their first house. Other than that, the party continued.

Chasen tells stories about how she and Gordon would be lying in bed in the morning and one would turn to the other saying, "I don't feel well today. You're going to have to get up and let the dog out and make us some breakfast." Without missing a beat, the other would roll over to face the ailing partner and reply, "I'm much sicker than you are! *You* have to get up!" You can only imagine how ill-prepared they were for the ensuing years when there was a toddler between them with a diaper so wet that the entire mattress was soaked and the dog had long since been banished to the garage.

Wisdom, the Consolation Prize

I recently carpooled with a fellow I vaguely knew through work and inevitably the conversation moved to his marital and parental status— hey, it's what I'm most interested in! After an hour of intrusive questions from me, he explained that he was the father of a little boy and recently divorced. "What would you say is the biggest lesson you learned from all this?" I pressed.

"That both people in a marriage should have a career," he replied without hesitation.

"Still paying spousal support, I take it?" I indelicately continued. You know how snotty I can be at the mere suggestion of men resenting paying money to spouses who gave up their own careers to stay home with the kids. But no, it wasn't about the money. In fact, this fellow turned out to be more than decent about the cash component. What he'd discovered was that no partnership in which one person looks to the other and says "Complete me" can stand the test of time. Frankly, it stunned me to learn that fathers and husbands can feel as depleted at six and seven as mothers and wives. He just couldn't face walking in the door each evening and facing a wild-eyed woman with a kid under her arm, looking at him for compliments, support, news from the outside world, and a reason to shave her legs each night. If I were him, I'd run for the nearest bathroom with a locking door and sit down for an hour or two.

In fairness to my gender, it can be just as intimidating to be the one standing in the doorway with the kids and a mate entering with the burning need to have your undivided attention while he downloads a day's worth of news and office machinations. If they'd go for it, I'd happily lock the kids and the mate in the bathroom and go running into the garage for some peace and quiet. Clearly, during the foxhole years of parenting, things work a lot more smoothly if both adults come to the battle with their own canteen and flack jacket.

The truth is, however, that everyone is the victim of his or her biorhythms. And in any marriage that endures beyond the perfunctory ten days in the Caribbean or Hawaii, there will be several thousand shifts in who's going to be the one to suck it up and keep the family train on track so that the other can be distracted, working overtime, down with a bug, or otherwise defeated. As stuck in traditional gender roles as many of us may feel, a true partnership depends on knowing when one of you has nothing to give and the other rises to the occasion. That, in my humble opinion, is the most urgent value in having two parents around to raise kids, even if the two parents no longer live under the same roof: Kids don't necessarily need two parents simultaneously fluttering around them, but rather, *parents* can really use knowing that, when they can't flutter, someone else who adores the child can start flapping his wings and keep the family flying.

Is Motherhood a Choice or a Surrender, or a Little of Both?

For about seven years my Girlfriend Margaret was the only single, childless charter member of the original Girlfriends gang. That may have meant that I didn't run into her at the local toddler gym or shopping for diapers in her nightgown at ten o'clock at night, but with eight or ten birthday luncheons a year for the gals, we saw each other with a cozy regularity. One afternoon, I think it was at Corki's and my joint birthday party, Margaret held up her champagne glass and announced that this would be her last Girlfriends' party because she was, frankly, sick and tired of hearing us go on and on about our kids and husbands. She wanted to spend more time with women who read books and knew that Yugoslavia was no longer a republic.

I told her she'd have to post a personal ad in the paper to find girlfriends with those qualifications, unless she was looking for a college dorm mate, but we all were remarkable in our acceptance of her rejection. Sure, a couple of us might have made a mental note to find out exactly where Bosnia was, but not a single one of us thought for a moment that we should expand or alter our world perspective. Most astonishing to me was the way the rest of us gals, usually very prickly about our total devotion to our jobs as mothers, graciously accepted Margaret's retreat. We didn't think she was wrong; simply uninitiated to the miracles we'd experienced. We knew deep down in our hearts that

185

Margaret'd be back in our lives, eagerly chiming in with her fascination with baby poop and extramarital affairs, just as soon as she married and had kids.

She was true to her word; we didn't see much of Margaret again for nearly three more years. Then, about two years ago, I ran into her in the health food store. She was absolutely gorgeous, with full pink lips and cheeks and cascading hair—and a gigantic pregnant belly. I was so joyful at the realization that she had "crossed over" to the narrow-minded world of motherhood that I immediately forgave her for being so damned good at pregnancy. Our darling Margaret was back and she was a poster girl for the inevitability of reproduction. We didn't have to expand to accommodate her; she was folding in to reconnect with us!

A couple of the Girlfriends visited Margaret, her husband, and their beautiful baby several times last year (I'd since moved out of town), and let me tell you, she so embraced her new little world that I felt like Madeleine Albright by comparison. She and her hubby were completely uninhibited about sharing their parenting beliefs, such as how it helped their bonding, as well as facilitated breastfeeding, to spend as much time as the thermostat would allow nearly naked with their baby so that she felt the skin-to-skin connection, or about banning all chemicals from the household so that the precious one's lungs never caught a whiff of anything stronger than white vinegar diluted with warm water.

After every glowing report of how enthusiastically our darling Margaret had taken to marriage and motherhood, the rest of us would smile beatifically and take profound comfort in the fact that we had another convert in our flock. It was always such a relief to hear confirmation of our absolute devotion to the white-hot focus of our own lives. Maybe we were fulfilling our destinies. Maybe we weren't failing to live up to our potential. Maybe our yearning to nest and create families out of chaos was still in fashion. Then again, none of us would be truly satisfied till we got that first call from Margaret in which she wept because her husband wanted to raise the child as a Catholic and she always thought he'd be a Presbyterian and then lapse during adolescence, like the rest of her family.

It's all in the Attitude

I may be annoyingly simplistic here, but I think that the marriages that stay together for the long run are those created like Ann's husband, the Mafia fan, described. I guarantee there will be times of such disharmony and unhappiness that you're more tempted to drown your mate and bury his body under a new brick barbecue in the backyard than to stay in the saddle, sharing a bed and the first pot of coffee in the morning. Murder, not generally accepted as a settlement of domestic disputes, leaves a marriage's survival up to how thoroughly a couple has rejected all other alternatives but staying married. As Billy Joel once wrote, "It's a matter of faith." If we don't allow ourselves the option of walking out, then we must have faith that we'll always be able to some way rediscover the magic of the love that brought us together and created this family.

This staying connected can be a teensy tiny bit less painful if we're careful not to resort to spewing serpents in the midst of a fight. Holding grudges is also terminal. And if I had one single bit of advice to share with you, my Girlfriend, it would be to go to bed tonight accepting that your mate is not your personal work in progress and you must fully understand that your belief in your ability to change him one iota will lead to abject misery for both of you. Love the one you're with, and you'll be loved back in spades. You owe it to your mate to "leave him be" because you chose him and it's deeply disrespectful and insulting to suggest that he was taken into your life conditionally. You owe it to your children because they will model their relationships on yours. If you constantly undermine him and your measurements always come up short, you will raise children who feel free to pick people apart like rotis-

187

serie chickens; you and I both know that only leads to a shortage of dark meat and a fight over the carcass. Icky analogy, but oddly poetic, don't you think?

Just the Two of Us

I feel obliged to keep reminding you (and ME!) that the goal of successful parenting is to prepare these heart-lassoing little angels to have the confidence, passion and skills to leave us one day. Yup, the big "prize" for being a great parent is to find you and your husband standing in your children's empty bedrooms, wondering whether to create a shrine to them or to install a yoga room. Wouldn't it be nice if, as you stand there in the quiet, deserted bedrooms, you make eye contact and realize that you have the promise of a great romance ahead of you? You're looking at twenty, thirty, maybe even forty years of shared toothpaste and pulling each other out of deep chairs, *if you're lucky*, so it doesn't take a genius to realize that it would be nice if you entered that next chapter with one or two mutual interests, besides the kids, not to mention a real and deep affection for each other's companionship.

Trust me, you won't be able to muster this stuff up in the week or two after dropping your youngest off at college. Neither will you be able to "fake" your intimacy for the down times between the beginning of Fall Semester and Thanksgiving Break. You have to stake your claim now, during the groove-reclaiming era, and keep it growing till the end of your life. Think of it a little like making plans for an incredibly fabulous celebration, say, like your wedding. Start picking the luggage, find the dream location, take up golf or tennis or whatever your dream destination has to offer. What the hell, pick a rewedding dress and a going-away-from-motherhood outfit.

Stay likable and interesting. Treat your mate at least as politely as you treat your third grader's science teacher and as lovingly as you hope he will always treat you. Treasure what he brings to enrich your life, but have no expectations for how he can make you bigger, faster, shinier, and one of a kind; that's your job, Girlfriend, no matter how distracting motherhood invariably proves to be. Remember how my husband illustrated his take on what happens to me, the Pie, when more children came along? The one thing he failed to point out, when he said that the kids' pieces of the pie stayed full and equal and his got noticeably smaller, was that my piece disappeared to nothing. Guess what I've learned? I'm not only responsible for shaving a piece off everybody's piece to restore my piece, but, like in Trivial Pursuit, I lose if I don't have all the pieces of my pie in place. Sometimes the greatest act of courage for a mother is to carve out enough attention and nurturing for herself to remain a significant part of that pie. Remember, with your piece missing, the whole thing collapses and leaks in on itself.

The Children You Have vs. the Children You Deserve

I recently had lunch with several women to organize a fund-raiser for my church. All of us were moms and all of us were so incredibly busy (that's kind of redundant, after the "mom" description, I mean), but we were all deeply committed to the cause and had reorganized our lives to accommodate the committee meeting. There were a few women I'd never met before, but since we all shared mutual Girlfriends, I was confident that we'd adore each other. We spent nearly three hours deciding whether it was unethical to have a carnival booth that gave away goldfish, seeing as how most of the fish usually died after being fed a steady diet of Cap'n Crunch and caressed by their tiny owners, and whether a cotton candy cart was tantamount to offering amphetamines to the customers. By the end of the meeting, I got into my car to pick my son up from tennis lessons and noticed how tight my shoulders felt and how out of step I'd felt with a couple of the gals. I was beginning to go into a funk, since I have so little time to spend with my mommy Girlfriends and have grown to expect any such meeting to be as spiritually nourishing as a wedding or a baby shower.

191

Of course, rather than just suck up this feeling of disharmony alone, mild as it was, I called one of my long-term Girlfriends who'd also been in the meeting on her car phone. "What was the matter with that committee?" I demanded of her. "Where was the Girlfriend magic?" Kara knew what I meant immediately and informed me that it was obvious that I just didn't click with one of the other women, Arden. "I don't get it," I obsessed, "we're all smart, fun, happening *mommy* Girlfriends, but I walked out of the meeting feeling like I was the Grinch and Arden was Cindy Lou Who. Where was the chemistry and immediate bonding?" Kara tried to reassure me that sharing ovaries and offspring were not always enough to create lifelong friendships, but I refused to listen to her wisdom and obvious insight. "Wait a minute," I interrupted, "how many kids does that Arden girl have?"

"One, a little boy," Kara replied.

"And how old is he?" I pressed on, totally forgetting that I was supposed to be fetching my son and driving about fifteen blocks past the city tennis courts.

"Ten months, I think," Kara patiently replied, demonstrating that incredible recall other moms have about each other's delivery dates. He wasn't a year old, he wasn't a half a year old, he was precisely ten months on this earth.

"That explains it!" I screamed hands-free into my car phone.

"Wait, you're cutting out," Kara could be heard to say, more or less, as our cells threatened to lose their symbiosis.

"That explains why I felt like Arden was from Saturn and I was from Pluto! She is still a new enough mother that she hasn't had the crap kicked out of her yet!" I hollered.

You might think, like my husband so often does, that I've just taken you on a very long ride to get to a bottom line that could have been stated at the beginning of this chapter, but I just wanted you to understand what an epiphany this was for me. It was as I was doubling back to my waiting son that I realized that, within the sorority of moms, there are differing factions. Sure, we'd all invested our hearts in the beings of little creatures who would roam the earth uncontrollably and kick our coronary organs around with abandon, but some of us had the scars to prove it and some of us still lived in bliss. The latter faction still believes that, if they put all their love, effort, commitment, and devotion into raising their children, they will turn out to be the evolved, intelligent, achieving, ethical, and athletic beings that we envisioned the moment those darlings were placed in their arms; and then there are those of us who've made that investment in our little darlings, and have been enlightened, by about four or five years into our home biology projects, that our children are destined to be *human,* as terrific or as terrifying as that might prove to be.

When my first baby was still in my arms, I used to resent those Girl-friends who would suggest that I "lighten up" about my worries concerning live viruses in infant vaccinations or suppress a laugh when I announced that, one week after a second child had been introduced into our family, our eldest "adored" his little sister and showed no signs of sibling rivalry. They all seemed so darned smug, as if their own unexceptional parenting experience could provide any indication whatsoever of how my superior mothering performance would turn out. Individuality was undeniable, I would reassure myself, no matter how timid I might have been about several hundred of my own childrearing decisions. Just because my Girlfriend Angela's two older kids exhibited such imperfections as bug phobias, asthma, and binkie dependency, that was no indication of how my own kids would turn out.

First of all, there were so many breakthroughs in childrearing techniques, I reasoned. Angela had raised her little children in the dark ages of five or six years ago, when Montessori was still considered the most forward-thinking parenting concept around. I had the benefit of the Rye Method and Organic Intelligence to give my kids an obvious leg up. Second, I had gotten a head start in grooming my gifted children, having recognized the importance of cultivating my childrens' gifts the moment my home pregnancy tests had come up positive. I admit, that nightmarish bout with colic with my first and third babies, which some respected experts maintained was an indication of stress and/or ambivalence in the gestating mother, gave me several weeks of maternal insecurity. But once we'd survived those first three hellish months, I regained my confidence, both in the perfection of my children and in my own well-prepared mothering. We were back on track and I was driving this locomotive.

I lived in that fool's paradise as long as my willing suspension of disbelief allowed me to overlook the millions of times my brazen little offspring demonstrated to me that they had personalities and preferences that varied from my master plan. Yes, one of them almost refused to be Ferberized. In fact, a decade later, she still creeps into our room just to say "Hi!" And yes, one of them was so terrified of having his head shampooed that he turned blue and gasped for air at every bathtime. And yes, one of them was so phobic about hearing people laugh that we couldn't watch sitcoms for almost two years. And your point would be?

For Better or for Worse

Lest you think that I'm obsessed or disappointed with the odd behaviors of my children, let me assure you that I'm even more stunned by their beauty, wisdom, and preciousness. Getting a little mommying experience underneath your belt, while occasionally deflating a Girlfriend's faith in her ability to protect, provide, and propel her children into the stratosphere of perfection, is also certain to humble you by letting you witness their startling talents, insights, and contributions.

Just last night, while I was sitting at my computer and working on this book, my husband corralled the four kids and started a soccer game in the backyard. Athleticism is not our middle name; in fact, by the time our third and fourth kids came along, I'd misplaced the AYSO and Little

League phone numbers in hopes that I'd never spend another season sitting in the bleachers, getting sunburned and making deals with God, if only He'd let my child turn left after touching first base instead of continuing on a straight trajectory toward the dugout of the adjacent game or if she'd stay standing on her own two feet when she saw the cluster of fellow soccer players rushing at her on their way to the goal, rather than curl up into a ball in the dust and scream "Help! They're chasing me!"

Anyway, I heard so much laughter and yelling last night that I hit the "Save" key and ran outside to see if I was missing any fun. It was still light out, but the sun had just disappeared on the horizon. The lawn looked so rich and cushiony. And my five beloved Iovines were running around, tackling each other and having a glorious time chasing that little ball around. Where did they all come from? What had I ever done to deserve a husband who seemed to tolerate, if not adore me, twenty years after our first date? Who could I ever thank for giving me four pregnancies that resulted in four incredibly gorgeous children, all of whom could run and kick and leap and laugh? There weren't enough diet Cokes to forego through my forty months of gestating to make me deserve such a blessing. I felt so insignificant and humble watching those five unique individuals running back and forth—I might have carried four of them in my belly, and convinced the fifth one that marriage and parenthood were his destiny, but I could no more claim credit for their existence and perfection than I could for the sun that had just set. Nearly as amazing as that bucolic vision was the realization that our baby, our fourth child, dribbled the soccer ball like she was Pelé's daughter. After four years outside the realm of team sports, it appeared we had a player on our hands, but I digress . . .

The lesson here is that your best mothering only goes so far. You can give four kids the exact same piano, the exact same teacher, and the exact same nagging about afternoon practice, and you may get one or no musicians. You can read to all of your kids for two hours a night and end up with one early reader, one storyteller, and two kids who absolutely hate Harry Potter and his friends. You can't make them taller, you can't make them thinner or fatter, you can't will them to have straight or curly hair, and you have absolutely no control over when they get breasts or underarm hair. Live long enough as a mother and you are certain to learn one redeeming quality: Humility.

In the Beginning . . .

Think back to the first few days you spent getting to know your precious infants. Now look at them. Isn't it uncanny how "just like themselves" they still are? Scholars can argue till the next millennium the question of nature versus nurture, but we moms know that our kids arrived fully baked. The more kids you have, the more astonishing it is that each one, in spite of dipping into the same gene pool, sharing the same two parents, and living in the same house, is a unique individual and so very different from his siblings.

Our first son astonished me with his unblinking and solemn gaze upon the world. He used to stare at the mobile hanging over his crib as if he were memorizing photos for a police lineup. Our first daughter immediately reached up and grabbed my hair and wouldn't let go. Our second son took a quick, blurry look at me as I tried to nurse him on the delivery table and then quieted when his daddy put his face into his fuzzy orbit. Our second daughter hurried out of my womb and into this world so quickly it was as though she was worried she was missing some party going on without her. Some may insist that I was in no position to analyze my babies' natures, what with the epidural, the post-delivery painkillers and the hormonal hysteria that clouded my judgment for days after each was born, but they would be wrong.

Today, with our oldest son nearly a teenager and our youngest child, our second daughter, six years old, each of those mini humans is simply a bigger version of the unique little creature he or she was at birth.

Jamie (or as he now calls himself, *James*), the big guy, still appraises the world and its inhabitants with a level and intense gaze. Jessica, our ten-year-old, has spent her entire first decade of life trying to climb back into my uterus, or at least into my pocket, and can't be within twenty feet of me without reaching out to hold my hand or rub the softest part of my clothing between her fingers. Jeremy, the cherished little brother, never enters the house without asking, "Is Daddy home yet?" and comes into our bedroom every weekend morning to ask, "Dad, do you want to play a game?" And Jade, the baby, who knows where she is? She learned to dial the phone at age four and has been planning her own elaborate social life ever since. I fully expect to receive a collect call from her someday soon in which she announces, "Mommy, I decided to fly to New York with Carson, and I was wondering if you'd send me a suitcase of clothes."

It's really kind of a relief to learn that Mother Nature didn't entrust us with shapeless lumps of clay to blindly sculpt into fabulous human beings. Considering how much of my mothering has been ad-libbed, I would be deeply concerned if the human race's future depended on whether I managed to potty train my kids before they started school or if I was responsible for giving them a sense of rhythm, since I don't know a downbeat from a deadbeat.

We mothers devote years of our lives wondering whether we are the mothers our precious children really deserve. Nine times out of ten we come to the conclusion that we come up short in most measurements, and the tenth time we think we made the mark through sheer dumb luck. We are too distracted, too tired, too impatient, or too stupid to even care if we remotely resemble those moms who write first-person articles about how they home-schooled all ten of their kids into Ivy League schools and missionary posts. At the end of the day we lay our heads upon our pillows counting failures and shortcomings instead of sheep. "I shouldn't have yelled at him in front of his friends," "I should have been sincerely interested when she recited her 'I Have A Dream'

197

speech in preparation for Martin Luther King, Jr. Day," "I should have nursed all four of them until they were old enough to microwave their own Spaghetti-Os."

For the first few years of our children's lives they have done little to even out the scales of disappointment. Sure, those colicky years were brutal and a little resentment about that dark season of biting all play-mates and pets was justified, but really, just by virtue of being born healthy, adorable, and in love with us meant that our offspring fulfilled their end of the parent-child contract. It would be beyond unthinkable, in fact, sacrilegious to suggest that the loves of our lives disappointed us or let us down in any way.

You Can Nurture Till the Cows Come Home

Even with their adorable little dispositions intact, we enthusiastic parents still are driven by some irresistible force to begin pruning away any leaves that ruin our idea of a perfect little shrub and encourage any shoots that comply. Like a whole generation of bonsai farmers, we start early, especially with our first babies, toiling in the soil of their DNA. Between us Girlfriends, I didn't know Mozart from Mohammed until I saw the movie *Amadeus,* but that didn't stop me from playing classical music full blast during my pregnancy and kneeling on the floor, halfway between the two speakers, so that my little fetus was stereophonically inspired. In my defense, let me add that I never did warm to the idea of speaking French or reading Shakespeare directly to my own belly; feel-ing that letting the child within my womb eavesdrop on my telephone conversations with my Girlfriends was stimulation enough for a human of any age.

The first few months after each baby was born, I was so numbed by the one-two punch of no sleep and utter ineptitude that I pretty much let my babies be. As soon as I was rested and competitive enough, however, I was back at sculpting the wet clay of the child I just knew would be the best of me, the best of my husband, and the fulfillment of several of our unrealized dreams. When my first baby was born, the fashion was to stimulate newborns' literal and vaguely colorblind minds with vivid black-and-white images. Pale pastel nurseries were considered as unenlightened as baby walkers with wheels and wood-slatted playpens. I propped soft cubes adorned with black and white line drawings of people's faces and objects like balls and birds in my darling's bassinet in hopes that sometime during the twenty seconds a day he spent there awake that he might cast his gaze upon them and learn . . . something . . . I can't remember what. Perhaps I was hoping that someday he'd grow up to be able to draw one of those figures in a comic book; that, along with $100, could guarantee his acceptance into a correspondence class in cartooning. Who knows, a guy with talents like that might eventually end up with a career as a courtroom artist.

By the time his sister came along, I'd already invested a small fortune in phonics games, flash cards, and alphabet puzzles. I'd prop her up in her infant seat and bedazzle the two of them with my memorization of the Dr. Seuss ABC's and *One Fish, Two Fish, Red Fish, Blue Fish*. When we'd go for a ride in the car, I'd hand my toddler firstborn a picture book and slip a matching cassette into the car stereo—the kind that told you to turn the page whenever you heard the chime. I can tell you now, eleven years later and with all hopes of personality engineering beaten out of me, that more often than not, by page two, my older child was maiming his infant sister with the book while I screamed from the driver's seat, "Don't make me stop this car!!!" and grabbed inconsequentially at the flying pages as they passed in my peripheral vision.

I kept this baby tutorial up for about four years, until my third child came along and rendered me completely incapable of even speaking in complete sentences, let alone knowing a vowel from a consonant. Go figure, somewhere along the line my third little baby, the one who was nearly deprived of my urging and prodding, the one who just happened to be in the room for the lessons because I was wearing him in a baby sling while I conducted enrichment courses for his older brother and sister, was the one who could read by age three. While they all are, at least as far as I can tell, absolutely brilliant, the first two kids learned as much from crawling away from me or chewing on the corners of the flash cards as they did from anything I intended to teach them. But that's hindsight speaking now. At the time, I still fervently believed that I was the bridge that stood between them and an Ivy League college. I scarcely remember now what special efforts, if any, I took with my fourth baby, who came screaming into this world shortly after her closest sibling's second birthday. I do remember my Girlfriend Linda, who also happened to be a pediatrician, coming over with her two babies for a playdate and a diet Coke and nearly falling out of her lawn chair when she saw the baby teething on Oreos, but that's a whole other chapter. . . .

My mother-in-law always explained perverse behavior in children by saying, "Well, the apple never falls far from the tree." I would nod with a measurable level of smugness, confident that my apples were all falling exactly as I'd groomed them to. Some parents, using my bonsai example, might settle for letting their kids grow up to resprout their weeds or wild branches. I, however, had been tilling their soil since conception. I even had evidence. Not one of my children sucked his thumb or was dependent on a "binkie," let alone threw a wayward root above ground. And, if my own evaluations were biased, I had my bi-monthly pediatrician report cards to prove that they were growing and blooming according to specifications. Not too tall, not too heavy, with head circumferences right in the median range—they were perfect. Sure, not a single one of them rolled over or walked a moment before they were scheduled to, but still, they were holding up their end of the agricultural agreement.

Nature Prevails

Imagine our shock when my husband and I realized that one of our kids had developed the habit of perpetually rubbing his right eye when stressed, and another was traumatized by costumed characters at birthday parties and theme parks, or still another became unglued whenever her hair was shampooed. I'll never forget the first time it really came home to me that a child of my loins might have a special sensitivity or inclination: I was very pregnant and I'd signed my older child up for swimming lessons. Although the pool was comfortably heated, it was no longer summer and every time I slipped out of my muu muu, I was struck by how blue the veins in my pregnant breasts were in the cool morning air. Five other three- and four-year-olds eagerly listened to the swimming instructor as they sat on the second step of the pool. My child, the offspring of a Certified Water Safety Instructor, was wrapped around my neck and trying to climb to the top of my head to avoid the water. All the other mothers would drop their little grunions into the pool and head off to Starbucks for forty-five minutes, and there I was, extremely rotund, sitting in the Jacuzzi with a hysterical toddler.

The Jacuzzi years could have been dismissed, if it hadn't been for the ensuing years of witnessing countless other episodes of my biological offspring, or those of my Girlfriends, picking their noses through the entire preschool Christmas play, lying down in right field during a T-ball game and going to sleep, and grinding their teeth nearly flat when a puzzle piece didn't fit properly. All of this was BEFORE we even hit the trials of kindergarten. Where did they come from, these tiny phobics, compulsives, and anal retentives? I could write an entire chapter about the child who so resisted our efforts at potty training that he/she (they won't be able to point me out to their therapists here!) didn't go poo poo for five consecutive days, but that's ancient history now, and I'm over it . . . well, pretty much. What's a little poop among Girlfriends when there are indications of stammering, "lovey" obsession or chronic eyebrow plucking among the offspring of my dearest Girlfriends?

Nature Prevails

It turns out that those little apples my mother-in-law referred to fell much closer to the tree than we would have wished. Here's the good news: Our kids are fully-formed, exceptional individuals when they are entrusted to our care. Here's the bad news: Our kids are fully-formed amalgams of our best and worst traits when they are entrusted to our care. This never fails to be a rude awakening. The day you discover your gorgeous little angel can't even be trusted to sing "Happy Birthday to You" in full voice without wrecking the party, when you'd been dreaming of a Motown contract and already invested in a karaoke machine and violin lessons, can be a tad disappointing. The day your mate has to come to terms with the fact that his little Dodger can't even put his "athletic cup" on properly, let alone refrain from crying when called out at first base, even though he "ran as fast as he could," will certainly be worse.

As tough as it may be to deal with the behavioral traumas of your children, things get pretty horrible when you learn that one of them has inherited your asthma, your mate's nearsightedness, or your shared attention deficit disorder. I sincerely wish that I could tell you that watching your beloved children revisit all your demons and deficits would ease up as time went on, but, judging from my own parenting experience, for every fly ball caught there are two missed, for every remembered "thank you" there are three take-and-runs, and for every Super Speller award, there are four tests that suggest your child has never even seen the English language in print. You may have Girlfriends, and I used that title casually here, who maintain that their own children love school, thrive on competitive sports, and have never uttered the word *crap* once in their lives, but I'm telling you they're lying or providing shelter to a sociopath. Hey, it may just be me, but I don't think so.

Call it maternal insight or chalk it up to our loving familiarity with their weaknesses, but most of my Girlfriends and I are much more adept at recognizing the mutual foibles of our children and their fathers than we are at noting their resemblances to us. I saw the way our kids cleared their throats compulsively like their father, their fear of change in routine, like their father, and their need to close cabinet doors three times, not twice, not once, but three times, like their father, every time they took out their toothbrushes or clean socks ages before I happened to notice their chronic nose rubbing, frequent headaches, and their need to sleep with one leg outside of the covers, habits which were reminiscent of their mother.

The Expository Years

As challenging as acknowledging my children's personal challenges was, it was nearly as trying when they turned out to have their own appraisals of me and my life. For example, our second son, a nearly perfect eight-year-old, was named President of the School last week. Although he was most certainly deserving of this honor, if not for his scholarly achievement then because he is certainly one of the cutest kids in the the school, I must confess that his honor was bestowed weekly on every second grader, since they were studying citizenship and the democratic process. Still, when my baby's week came, the whole family rose early and participated in the inauguration. The most thrilling aspect the first day was the fact that he wore a suit to school. All four of my kids attend a school where they must wear uniforms, so this was a big deal.

There we all were at six-thirty in the morning, Daddy, the three other kids and me, fussing over his navy blue double-breasted, gelling his hair and buttoning down his collar. My husband, a true rock and roller of the seventies and eighties, couldn't remember how to tie a necktie, so we called in Uncle Gregg (he's our neighbor) and, still dressed in his bathrobe, he saved the day. Finally, as I was putting the pleat in the tie that my second grader told me was how "Regis on the Millionaire show" did his ties, he looked right into my adoring face and asked, "Why does your breath always smell like that in the morning?"

Okay, so I hadn't brushed my teeth yet, but still, I didn't think I was offensive. No one has ever mentioned it before. I hate mornings! I hate pressure for school! Yet there I was, not only punching his tie in to achieve the right drape, but I had taken nearly half a roll of photos of him, too. What did I get for gratitude? A very pointed suggestion that I had halitosis. Did I smack him? Did I remind him of how insensitive and ungrateful he was? Of course not! I actually droned on about how people swallow to rinse their mouths two hundred times during the day but only about twenty times while they're sleeping and how that, combined with the fact that I, a woman who has met forty head-on, wear a retainer at night, and I hadn't remembered my predawn Altoid. It was pathetic. Even worse, odds are at least even that he showed up to lead flag salute and announced that his mother had poor dental hygiene. God forbid that I should get plastic surgery or go on a diet—they are certain to be grist for "Show and Tell" in all four of my kids' classes.

I once sat through a kindergarten orientation (who remembers which child it was at this point?) during which the teacher said, "If you promise not to believe everything your child says about me, I promise not to believe everything he says about you." All us parents chuckled in that self-deluded way that the inexperienced have. Let me tell you, Girlfriend, you'd better live and die by that motto because your little ambassador is absolutely guaranteed to relate everything from how you take a little pill every night to make sure heaven knows you're not ready for another baby to how much back hair your husband has. No wonder the teachers look at you with such familiarity when you drive through the carpool line.

Don't Hold Your Breath for the Gratitude

I think it's safe to tell you that it's completely normal for your child to assume that you were put on this earth to ensure her comfort, health, and happiness. In fact, it's safe to assume that you won't get anything resembling a thank you, at least not spontaneously, until your child has had a child of her own and it finally dawns on her the sacrifice you've made. My kids are sweet and polite, and they don't intend to take advantage of me, but still these are the same people who, until recently, acted like they were hugging me when really they were wiping their nose on my shirt. They still feel completely entitled to spit their chewed gum into my hand, vomit in my bed, and invite me to join them in the bathroom to inspect their toilet deposits.

I don't begrudge them any of his familiarity; in fact I secretly love it, but I do confess that I thought motherhood would be a tad more, well, *sacred* than it's turned out to be. I guess I'd always imagined that I would be a teacher, a spiritual guide, a kind of Rose Kennedy of my brood. Instead I often feel like a very large Kleenex. Lots of the technical child development books about infants explain that babies don't even *know* that they are separate human beings from their mommies for the first several months of life. I'm here to suggest that they don't really fully fathom the separateness until they go off to an out-of-state college.

This Person Can't Be Related to Me!

I call this chapter "The Children You Have vs. the Children You Deserve" because there are going to be many times when you ask yourself, "How did our DNA recombine to create this creature?" Sure, having your entire personal life exposed to people you might never even invite to meet you for a quick coffee is tough enough, but it gets even stickier as time goes on. You would think that "the apple doesn't fall far from the tree," but you might be wrong. Take my Girlfriend Naomi, for example. Naomi was one of those girls in school to whom an overhand throw and the 50-yard dash were second nature. She grew up intending to be a physicist and achieved it. Not only that, but she was a Betty Friedan feminist from the day she was conceived. She may have gotten a manicure for her wedding, but she certainly hasn't had her hands held by another woman since then. She dressed her daughter in greens, oranges, even blues, but never pinks and never, ever florals. All books and toys were gender neutral, as was her interaction with her little sweetie.

Now, at age five, her mini-me is addicted to feather boas, high-heel mules, and a tutu left over from an old Halloween costume. Naomi is frantic. Where did she go wrong? What forces outside her home conspired to corrupt her little human? What will the two of them ever have in common as the years go by. Naomi doesn't even own a tube of mascara, and already her daughter is asking about lip liner.

Or consider my own dilemma: I have recently discovered that my beloved firstborn loves nothing more on this planet than professional wrestling. What button doesn't this push for me? I can't stand long hours spent before a television, I loathe violence, and I detest the greasy-haired guys who devote themselves and their grown children to the sick mythology of good fat guys prevailing against bad fat guys. Where does this fanaticism fit into the thousands of hours I spent reading Caldecott Medal–winning books to my boy? What about the hours of piano and violin lessons? Why did I kill myself to keep our home free of all toys that could be construed as weapons? How did all my pointed remarks about the lowbrow entertainment value of people who decorated their cars with more than three rock band stickers and nasty vanity license plates go unappreciated?

Mother Nature must have a really perverse sense of humor. The one thing we parents thought we could depend on is that our offspring would be miniatures of our own personalities, talents and points of view. Yeah, right. I'm a writer; wouldn't you think that my kids would appreciate the written word as I do? Forget it! If it's not a part of e-mail gossip, my daughter won't read it. Worse still, she couldn't care less about how any of it's spelled. My husband, devoted Daddy that he is, wakes up every Saturday morning wanting to play catch with someone. My six-year-old daughter is willing to accommodate him, mostly because she knows there will be the reward of a frozen yogurt after, but the other three hide under their beds when their dad reaches for a ball. Both of us would gladly cut back on our jobs and commit ourselves to being weekend sports parents, but, as my oldest son explained, "I hate it when they want you to run around and get all hot and possibly injured." You can't argue with that. But then again, we *do* have that budding soccer star that could save the day and justify our purchase of portable folding lawn chairs!

I Can't Live Through That All Over Again!

As hard as it may be to acknowledge that the fruit of your womb doesn't share your world outlook, it can be worse when you discover that they are just like you were at their age. Very few of us are so evolved that we can lovingly embrace our childhoods and adolescent years in all their permutations, but get ready, Girlfriends, because you may eventually have to do that very thing. Ultimately, genetics and environment will influence your offspring, and the results can often be more staggering than their moments of strangeness. I never shared with my own kids my phobia about undressing and showering with the rest of my team, and sure enough, my older son, after about two weeks of middle school communal bathing, expressed a phobia that the peoples' water might spill over onto his feet on its way to the common drain, thus contaminating his own little paws. My very young and statistically much shorter than their classmates children also adopted "enchanting" little habits of exploiting their tininess by begging the manly coaches to carry them on their shoulders so that they could watch a scrimmage from a position of safety and the best possible view.

Well, it turned out that during a parent/teacher conference we discovered that one of our little homespun geniuses had a little trouble concentrating on the task at hand, as well as sitting alertly at his desk. Just the suggestion that our baby was engaging in interplanetary travel while the majority of his class was concentrating on the addition of three-and four-digit numbers inspired me to sweat all around my hairline and my resting heart rate to go up at least twenty beats a minute. Desperately, I turned to my mate, the co-parent of this child. He was horizontal in the little chair, swinging his legs back and forth and reading the presidential biographies that were displayed on the bulletin boards. I didn't say a word. I just shared a glance with the teacher and all was understood. Yes, I could have taken an eraser and bashed my husband in the head at that moment, but there was no need. In an instant, she and I both recognized the immutable fact that biology was at play here, too, in spades.

All apples tumbling from the Vicki-heavy tree have the inability to stop talking once starting; their favorite mode of conversation is a series of "what if" inquisitions; "If my mouth was put by God on the side of my face rather than where it belongs, would you think I was funny or would you ask a doctor to put it back where it belongs . . . even if it involved massive surgery?" My little offshoots also raise their hands to answer questions, ask questions, or interrupt questions with the ferocity of those contestants on *Jeopardy*. I recommend herbal teas for those fortunate educators who meet the produce off my family tree.

Baby, Come Back!

My Girlfriend Marla is in the middle of experiencing the same biological imperative with her first-born daughter, but on a physical level. Simply put, Marla was a babe by the time she was twelve. She had the breasts, she had the legs, and she had the blossoming sexuality before she hit the teen years that I didn't know till I was about eighteen. Somehow, Marla had amnesia about those years of her own life. Boy, oh, boy, does she ever remember now! She'd have to be blind not to notice that her oldest baby has begun a stunning metamorphosis into becoming a woman that several thousand early adolescents would give a limb to call their "Baby." Not a day passes that she doesn't have to confront a living example of what it's like to have at least one Lolita live under your roof. She's damned because she's not only regaining total recall of her own physical growth; she's remembering how sexy and alluring she felt at the time. Talk about life's scariest moment!

We're unanimous in wanting our discerning children to pick among the very best of their gene pool and become all that is smart, kind, brave, coordinated, hardworking, and great fun at a party. Concommitant to that is the need to play down any behavioral embarrassments and tendencies to enjoy the more antisocial behaviors of excessive masturbation, nervous ticks and performance anxiety.

No Refund, No Exchanges

One afternoon, while I was hiding in my bedroom and removing my toenail polish with the television on for grown-up companionship, the movie *Parenthood* came on. If you haven't seen it, go to your local video store and rent it. It stars Steve Martin and a whole bunch of other great actors and follows several related families as they struggle with raising children of all ages. I stayed in my hiding place long after I'd changed my polish and moved on to tweezing my eyebrows, completely invested in the story, in spite of the fact that my husband had offered to make us sandwiches for a lunch on the patio over an hour ago and my son's drum teacher had come and gone without so much as a howdy-do from me. There was a scene in which Steve Martin and his movie wife, Mary Steenburgen, were in some filthy and dark alley behind a Chuck E. Cheese–kind of restaurant, frantically rummaging through greasy garbage cans in hopes of finding their son's retainer. At one point, Mary turns to Steve and asks something like, "Did you really think that if you coached 'Bobby's' (I'm very bad with names) baseball team and did magic tricks at his birthday party, he would turn out to be different, *better,* than you?"

**The truth about parenting, Girlfriend, is this:
Our children are not us.**

Not only that, but they have absolutely no responsibility to repair our own childhoods or give us a free ride for a rerun of our cherished memories. Just because you wet the bed on your first sleepover doesn't mean that it's up to your son or daughter to become the Slumber Party king or queen. Just because your entire childhood can be reduced to that one fabulous summer you had at camp, where you learned to water-ski and make S'mores, doesn't mean that you deserve a child who willingly boards a bus to experience a couple of weeks in the wilderness. Just because you were so tone deaf that you learned to lip-synch "Happy Birthday to You" by fourth grade, doesn't mean that your child shouldn't be encouraged to try out for the lead in the school's production of *Annie.*

Home Is Where the Acceptance Must Live

They may share your cowlick, you nail-biting or your mate's pointy chin, but they are precious new creations who are entitled to discover their own destinies. I know that a certain degree of pain and pride will color the experience of watching your little babies reveal themselves to you, but it's out job to trust that Mother Nature has a grander plan in mind. The world can be severely judgmental and inhospitable to anyone who is "different," and it's our job as moms to provide the single place where there is total acceptance. My sister-in-law once told me that her father convinced her as a child that she was the main attraction of every Christmas pageant, dance recital, and baton-twirling demonstration in which she participated. No matter how many other kids were performing alongside her, her daddy made her believe that the other parents might occasionally glance at their own kids, but they were really there to see her because she was the true star.

Before I had kids, I would join her in that little jaunt down Memory Lane with a certain level of disbelief and disapproval. Her story was charming but so delusional and so fawning by her father. It was his responsibility, I secretly maintained, to give her a realistic appreciation for her place in the world; more special than some and less special than others. Now I know that the universe is just sitting out there, waiting for the chance to tell each and every person that she's prettier than the other kids or slower to read than most. What a gift to bestow upon our perfect little babies, to let them know that, no matter what the SAT graders or the coaches of the All-Star team may think, *their mothers* know that they are the greatest little humans to land on this planet?

Never lose sight of the Girlfriend Truism; that you never know how well your kids are really coping until they go off to find their own careers, fall in love and perhaps marry, have a couple of kids of their own to drill into their own psyches an eventual awareness that we weren't nearly as misguided and dictatorial as it had seemed to them ten years earlier. Setting up successes and failures for children depends on the parent believing that each particular development race has been completed. Hey, if we moms still consider ourselves a work-in-progress, the least we can do is extend the same kind of acceptance and freedom to the little loves of our lives. Remember, Girlfriends: Our children's job in this life is not to right the wrongs of our own youth, but to figure it out themselves while the parents stand below them, holding a safety net that will catch them if they fall too far.

This is Your Life, So Get Used to It

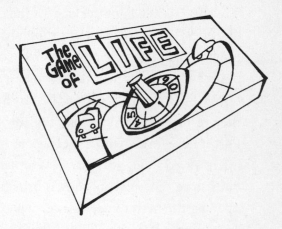

I have this idea for a movie. It's about how I envision my family living if, God forbid, something should ever take me away from them. The inspiration for this screenplay came to me during the darkest two weeks of my existence when my youngest child was about five months old and I was told I had breast cancer. Let me rush to assure you that the diagnosis proved incorrect, a blessing I acknowledge every day, so don't worry, this chapter will be devoted to a peevish diatribe about my elusive groove and getting it back, nothing more earth-shattering than that.

Anyway, between the night I discovered a lump on the side of my breast and the morning ten days later when I awoke from anesthesia to the good news that I was all right, I had quietly excused myself from this world and devoted all my waking hours to making plans for how my children would be cared for if I weren't there to do it myself. Stick with me: I promise the story gets funny soon. So after I'd extracted a promise from my sister-in-law and her family to sell their home in New York and move into our house in California so that my kids wouldn't have to change neighborhoods, and after making my husband drive carpool with me three days in a row to imprint in his memory exactly where it was they went to school, I spent several hours a day keeping my terror at bay by cleaning every closet and drawer in the house.

This is when I got the idea for the opening scene of my movie. Lots of people are standing and sitting around in my house making polite funeral small talk, obviously at some sort of reception after I've been fittingly laid to rest. The camera avoids everyone's face and focuses instead on the busy hands of my Girlfriends heating and serving the casseroles they've brought. One opens the microwave door and finds a yellow Post-it note inside with a message in my handwriting saying "Cover all microwaved foods with Saran Wrap and rotate them every fifteen seconds since the revolving tray is broken." Cut to another pair of hands opening the velvet-lined drawer where my wedding silverware is kept and lifting out another Post-it with the directions "Hand-wash all the Reed and Barton!"

Cut away again to another faceless Girlfriend opening the refrigerator to get some condiment or other and finding a little yellow note with the instructions "Move old eggs to the front holes in the rack and put the new eggs behind them to be used in order of freshness." In the fourth shot a Girlfriend reaches toward the sink and sees my note explaining "Clean the garbage disposal once a week with a mixture of ice cubes and baking soda—and remember, no celery, EVER!" At this point the camera pulls back to show my beloved Girlfriends giving each other looks as if to say, "Good riddance!" and they would all march out of the kitchen with glasses of my best wine in their hands and casseroles left neglected and cold on the counter.

I share this story with you not to reveal my dark, disturbingly compulsive side, but to illustrate a truth we all know: We mothers are the heartbeat and the operating manual of our families' survival. Of course, the Post-it thing never really happened, but that doesn't mean it wouldn't have, especially if my surgery hadn't turned out so well. I sincerely believe that, no matter how much our mates insist that all family responsibilities are split 50/50 between the spouses, the psychic commitment alone that we women make to our families puts us at 75/25, and that's before we even start with the discussion of who takes the kids for their vaccinations or who is in charge of addressing the family Christmas cards. I may not be speaking for the entire universe, but in my little world, I know this to be true: Whenever the shit hits the fan, the first cleanup call goes to me.

His Life Is His Life, My Life Is Everyone's

My husband and I both have careers outside the home. We are both absolutely crazy about our kids and each other. That is where the similarities end, at least from where I'm sitting. You devoted dads are free to send me all the poison pen letters you want; I still believe that most men would diagram their life commitments by drawing three big, separate circles. Inside one would be Work, inside another, Family, and in the third, Myself. Women, however, would diagram their lives by drawing one big circle, in which they would write Family, Work, and Whatever Else I Can Fit In. That's a very significant distinction. Once a child is added to the geometry, women undergo a stunning change in their world views: Their babies are put at the center and everything else radiates out from there. Men, too, are changed by parenthood. They may feel the added responsibility and shift in priorities, not to mention a lifelong love affair, but they, unlike most women, are biologically capable of forgetting for several consecutive minutes (if not days) that they have a higher calling to preserve the species.

If you're not convinced, ask yourself this question: If your darling child were to fall off the monkey bars at school (heaven forbid) and walk off to the nurse, cradling her arm against her body, who would that nurse call? Would she frantically reach for your family's emergency response file and dial you or would she dial your mate first?

Assuming your role as chief boo-boo kisser is undisputed, as it is in my family and those of most of my Girlfriends, that call is coming to you, my dear. The moment a child needs aid, unless she's stuck in a traffic jam in some forsaken place where her cell phone doesn't work, the mother is rounded up. This is the way we want it, I admit. Mothers create and inhabit a world in which we are perpetually ready to rush in and rescue our children. We are the first line of defense between the outside world and our beloved families. Sure, daddies may look bigger, stronger, and more powerful, but are *they* the ones who carry the kids' hospital emergency cards in their wallets or who've memorized the entire family's blood types? And who drives the car that has the first-aid kit, several bottles of water, and enough trail mix to sustain a forest of squirrels, should there be an earthquake or typhoon?

Getting back to the arm scare, an alarming but not life-threatening situation: Let's assume the school nurse has reached you; can you even imagine a situation in which you'd reply, "I'm really tied up here at the office, so would you mind calling my husband at his work to ask him to take Little Jenny in for X rays?" I didn't think so. If your family functions anything like mine, you will call your husband to share the crisis, at least right after you've speed dialed the pediatrician for further instructions, but it'll be *you* who calls him from the hospital if it turns out to be a break. Argue with me all you want; I just cannot imagine the tables turned and your mate happening to get the news first, and even if he does, if you stand there and maintain that you'd stay at work until he called you from the radiologist's office, I would have to call you a pathological liar.

Perhaps the injured arm example is too serious to make my point. Let's consider, instead, what happens when you and your husband both have early-morning presentations or travel plans for the next day and the night before, one of your little darlings comes into your room crying because he has an earache. Is there a chance in hell that your husband, the child's father, will quietly get up and find the Children's Tylenol and the baby Benadryl and then read to the poor miserable child until the medication takes effect? If the answer is "yes," then I congratulate you on your good fortune and excuse you from the rest of this chapter. But, even if your mate is magical around sick kids and completely competent, which is not the case in my house, he would still wake you up to take commemorative pictures and join in the fun.

Girlfriends, however, have been known to do this entire Florence Nightingale routine so efficiently and quietly that their mates only hear about the crisis the next morning when they can't rouse us to get up and make the coffee. There seems to be a genetic disposition in fathers that makes them crave an audience for their best parenting moments. So, even if your mate could handle the earache with greater artistry than you, he will almost always need to awaken you to let you witness his miracle working.

You're Not Alone

I'm not saying that all parenting dynamics are like those in my own home, but I share our particular "style" with you just in case you have ever worried that you're the only mother on the planet who faces most stitching and bone-setting decisions in a vacuum. First of all, even if we were relaxing over a board game of Iovine Family Trivial Pursuit and my husband got a card asking him to name the kids' pediatrician, his general location in town and a way to access his phone number, he would definitely lose the piece of the pie. Ask him to recall the same urgent information when one of his cherished children is hurting and needs medical attention immediately, and he can't even remember the difference between our pediatrician and my ob/gyn. If, through some sort of nervous breakdown, I'd left my cell phone and pager at home and was blithely appearing on some live TV show, talking about what to do when kids tell fibs and my husband had to leap to action, there's a very real chance that he would deposit the injured tyke at a doctor's office better equipped to give it an IUD than stitch up its forehead. Thank heavens I've never put the care of our three dogs, two birds and fifteen fish in my husband's hands, or our child could end up spayed and neutered before anyone knew that he'd come to the wrong doctor.

Let me take a breath here before I continue on this rant, which could easily get out of control. First of all, it makes some obvious sense that mommies are called into the fray when a child has an emergency. Most of us spend more hours in a day with our kids than their daddies do, so statistically, it makes sense that we have greater chance of being within grabbing distance of a child who is going to fall while running beside the pool or who really believed that a bed mattress laid below his second story window would break his fall like those big air bags do for stuntmen. Unless the mother has some compromising circumstance, like no car or the inability to drive while simultaneously splinting an elbow that seems to be bending in the wrong direction, she will scream for all the kids in the house to get into the car, "and I mean NOW!!!" and off they will all go to the doctor's office or local emergency room. It wouldn't make sense or be fair to the hurt kid to wait until the father could be reached so that he could come home and take over.

Let's also not forget that mommies are instinctive fixers of all "boo boos," starting with circumcision pain, progressing through teething soreness and diaper rash and who it is who offers breast or bottle to a baby who is howling from a DPT shot, no matter how cute the Peanuts Gang character Band-Aid. Once we become mothers, we seem to live our lives for this stuff, and we get a tremendous sense of strength and power from our heretofore unknown healing abilities. Even the queasiest among us can carry the day when our kids are suffering.

We mothers are as surprised as anyone at our newfound bravery in the face of all sorts of upset and injury. I will never, ever forget the morning not too long ago when my Girlfriend Maggie, the mother of a three-year-old son and a still-nursing baby boy who works as a writer and editor from her home office, left the boys in the kitchen with her mother's helper so that she could check her voice mail in her office upstairs. Before she even got to the top of the stairs, she heard the scream of the older boy, followed quickly by the louder scream of the mother's helper.

She leaped from the top landing to the ground floor without a thought to discover blood everywhere and her weeping son holding a bloody sleeve up to her, as though she had a magic wand to make it disappear. Maggie fought an urge to vomit right then and there, took a gasp of air, and rolled the cuff up to discover that her son hand put his hand in a juicer and turned it on! She directed the helper to call 911 while she talked to her baby, the fruit of her womb, in singsongy voice about how Mommy was going to get him to a nice doctor who would make everything all right. She noticed that the tip of one of the fingers was missing and had the temerity to empty the blender to find the missing piece, in case it could be reattached. Finding nothing but undifferentiated juice, she set the jar aside and climbed into an ambulance with little Thomas and rocked him and his bloody hand all the way to the hospital.

She sang Barney songs, she sang Raffi songs, she even remembered baby songs that she'd learned in preschool. She just never stopped singing and rocking, even though in her mind she was thinking, "He will never learn to write properly. He can never grow up to be a pianist. He won't be a quarterback in college. And, worst of all, he might grow up feeling deformed." If ever a mother needed a little hit of that oxygen bottle those emergency vehicles carry, it was Maggie, but she never thought to ask for herself.

If anyone had asked darling Maggie what she would do if one of her children should get hurt, she would have sworn that she'd pass out and rely on the kindness of strangers. Her husband was in town and could have rescued them all within minutes, but Maggie faced the crisis like a ninja; no vapors or hysteria, at least not until Thomas was stitched up and in a deep sleep. She realized at that moment that Mommy Magic is as potent as the best medical care when a baby needs help.

Home Is Where the Mommy Is

One day when I wasn't feeling too well, my husband got up early to keep the kids occupied while I slept feverishly for a couple more hours. He was a real champ. He taught our youngest to ride a bike, he played two full rounds of "Who Wants to Be a Millionaire" on the computer with our thirdborn and his sleepover buddy, and he made plans to take our oldest to a music supply store to buy him a metronome for his weekly drum lessons. All this must have been accomplished by about ten A.M.; either that, or he felt that he deserved a break to return some calls and check out the stock quotes on television.

All I know is, I, still feeling pink-cheeked and sweaty, awoke at about 10:05 to find five children in my bedroom. My two girls, who are always exploring ways to reattach themselves to my body, had already dived under the covers beside me. Jamie, the oldest, stood near the foot of the bed with a vague sense of decorum holding him a respectful distance back, and Jeremy, the eight-year-old, and his sleepover buddy were sitting on the edge of my bed, looking cautiously into my face. Jamie maintained that he was only disturbing me because he desperately needed to know, at that very minute, where I'd hidden the extra-long shorts I'd just bought him (They were folded in his drawer, of course, but that's another book), but the little ones stood there entirely without pretense. They simply needed to reconnect with the person who knows where the circuit breaker switches are hidden, who knows how to use the satellite dish, and whose permission is needed before anyone in the house even thinks of watching World Wrestling Federation reruns.

As you all have heard countless times, my sleeping attire on sleep-over nights is such that I am prepared for guests at all intimate hours, so I had on roughly what a local fireman would wear. Leggings, a couple of muscle T's (since my daughters maintain that one shirt alone does not adequately cover my nipples) my hair controlled in a ponytail, and my glasses beside my bed. They were looking for something ethereal, something only a person in touch with the Mother Occult could offer: reassurance that life was proceeding in its natural state, that I would make sure they got a good breakfast, and that all of them were in my thoughts constantly, even if fever threatened to push them from my frontal lobe.

I was miserable, I was tired, I wanted to move to a hospital at that very minute, but I was even more joyous that they had come to me as their emotional compass. I think that when the day comes that they have their own compasses, or worse, start relying on the compasses of others, I will want to dissolve into a puddle on the floor like the Wicked Witch of the West when she got doused with a bucket of water. After about twenty minutes of sharing my sick bay with five kids, my husband ran upstairs to report that he'd lost all the children. The relief on his face was tremendous when he saw that they were all accounted for, but I couldn't help noticing a bit of chagrin that my Mommy Magnet proved still strong, even when I was sick, asleep, and hiding.

Job? What Job?

I love my career and take it very seriously. I cannot, however, say that I take it as seriously as my husband takes his. Who knows? Perhaps it's a throwback to caveman times when men derived their sense of self from the number of bison they were able to throw on the campfire. Speaking for myself, I must confess that becoming responsible for the propagation of the species has made every one of my other endeavors pale by comparison, even if it's not noticeable to anyone but me. Of course, I'd never mention that to my boss, but I think it's safe to share that among us Girlfriends.

The keen concentration that it takes to convince your colleagues and superiors at work that you'd rip out your uterus for the firm while still spending valuable company computer time tuning into the nanny-cam Web site that your child's daycare has so thoughtfully installed has most of us moms so schizophrenic that I'm thinking of buying stock in the company that manufactures Prozac.

It all started out innocently enough. As I've said before, in high school and college we girls were allowed to take the same courses as the boys—sitting right beside them as the teachers shared the secrets of macro economics or the negotiations that led up the division of North and South Viet Nam. No one took the girls aside after class for a private tutorial on what to do if you couldn't find your laptop computer with your accounting records ever since your toddler stole it to play "Putt Putt the Magic Car" or how to respond when your electric breast pump threatens your office power supply. In fact, it would have been *illegal* if they'd done so. That's why home economics eventually went the way of "Fortran, the Computer Language of the Future."

I'm willing to bet that your education never included a teacher who would explain how your career would collide with the "Mommy Ceiling" or had a course on the art of composing a white lie so that you could sneak out of work to attend the Moms and Muffins party at your daughter's fourth-grade class.

Assuming you didn't become a mother in high school, you probably spent your formative years thinking that you were just like the guys in your class, except that you shaved your underarms and carried tampons in your backpack. You competed against males for grades and then you competed against males for jobs. And once you got the job, you competed against males for promotions. Even if having a husband and kids were always part of your long-term plan, I'll bet dollars to diaphragms that you never thought you might lose an account because your let-down reflex kicked in during your presentation.

When Do Things Go Back to Normal?

Pregnancy, itself, while physically obvious, was still fairly easy to ignore at work. Most of us are so worried about losing seniority or medical benefits that we feel safe talking about our coming babies only around the nice grandmotherly types who come through the office selling bagels and croissant sandwiches. But when we're around our coworkers, we are over-amped cheerleaders for the cause of working until we're five centimeters dilated and coming back to work in time to return our phone calls before they've gotten stale.

While you were gestating, particularly for the first time, I think it's safe to assume that you, like my Girlfriends and I, took that six-week maternity leave as a mathematically accurate measure of the time it would take for us to recover our footing after the free-fall of pregnancy and new motherhood. And if *we* could pull it together in a month and a half, it was completely reasonable to assume that our mates, even those who shared our pregnancies so enthusiastically that they got morning sickness and put on the requisite maternal weight of fifteen to fifty pounds, give or take an ounce or two, would be back to normal even sooner. It certainly wouldn't be too much to ask during those critical first few months, when our episiotomy stitches were still dissolving and postpartum depression hovering on the horizon, for the guys who'd put us in the family way in the first place to step in and pick up the slack, right? Well, let's take a closer look into that little question, shall we?

It All Starts in the Bathroom

I will never forget the first time I was alone in the house with my first infant and could no longer ignore the cloud of dust and foul aroma that enveloped me like the *Peanuts* character Pigpen. No new mother in her right mind would even dream of taking a shower while her precious baby napped—how would she ever hear it cry or notice if it stopped breathing if she was reveling in the hot stream of water on her aching shoulders and greasy hair? After two or three days of consideration, I deduced that I could only reclaim my former hygiene and still qualify for Mother of the Decade if I could do both simultaneously. Ingeniously, I strapped the tiny creature, wide awake, into his infant seat and placed him on the floor outside the shower door, facing me. Lest the door steam up or the water drown out the sounds of his wails, I had the tremendous inspiration of leaving the shower door partway open. That way I could scrub and shampoo myself and talk to him the entire time. Of course, by the end of my creative cleansing routine, my cooperative little baby was splattered from head to bootied foot with water and flecks of suds.

I bring this up, not to give you more grist for your suspicions that I'm downright loopy, but to make the point that NEVER in my own fabulous husband's bathing life has he made any adjustments to accommodate another living creature, at least not one past the age of consent who offered to scrub his back. Even now, when you'd think that I'd overcome my irrational fears about potential kidnapping or feelings of abandonment in my children while I entered the showering chamber alone, I still hold the world land-speed record for the quickest personal cleansing time since the advent of indoor plumbing. I can soap up, shampoo, condition, exfoliate, and shave pits, legs, and bikini region all within four minutes.

My husband, my equal copartner in the parent-hood, spends up to twenty or thirty minutes a day in the shower. "What the hell is he doing in there?" you may ask; I've asked it myself. Sure, he has his own shampooing and sudsing to accomplish, but there's not a lick of shaving or exfoliating going on, nor has he hung a diagram in his shower demonstrating the proper way to do a self breast exam like I have. By his completely guilt-free descriptions, he's *thinking* and *preparing for his day* under the soothing massage of gallons of hot water. Rarely, if ever, is his reverie interrupted by interlopers, particularly seeing as how he locks the bathroom door before he even turns on the water. Out of profound frustration and resentment, I've occasionally used the skeleton key to let one of our sons in to to ask him where the Ping-Pong paddles are or if he would take them to the video store after he dried off, but for the most part, he's left in peace.

Here's how my showering experience goes: One or two of my kids is guaranteed to be standing in my closet with me as I take off my clothes. At least five times out of ten I will climb into the stall and turn around to close the door, only to discover that one of the kids and a family pet has entered right behind me. Sometimes I just surrender and pull off their respective clothes and collars and share my higher-priced hair care products on their wispy hair and shaggy coat. What the hell, I'm a sucker for multitasking, so why not get at least one kid and one dog clean, as well as me, in one fell swoop? Other times, however, I scoot the visitors out and pull the door closed so tightly that it sounds like an airlock separating us.

Look, you're a mom; you know that this is never the end of story. The dog and the child will stand right outside the shower's glass door and stare at me. Occasionally, I will wipe some of the steam off the glass to see the child moving her mouth energetically as she silently informs me of anything from the fact that her brother is the meanest boy in the sixth grade to her insistence that she smells smoke emanating from downstairs. I have no self-control, and I repeatedly open the door and engulf her and her pet in steam to ask, "What did you say?" Then I usually follow up with a wet lecture about how Mommy is entitled to at least five minutes of peace, for Heaven's sake, and a plea to them to leave me alone.

Not only don't they leave, they form a sort of welcoming committee that stands between me and the two towels I need; one for modesty and one to wrap my hair in. "Mommy, why is the hair on your head red and the hair down there brown?" my bystander is sure to ask, while her annoying pet is licking the water rivulets that are running down my legs. Even *I* don't want such front-row seats for this spectacle, and the prospect of having to explain the origin of stretchmarks is too intimate a lesson in abject humiliation. My mind reels with the potential questions our inquisitive sons could ask their father, should they happen to be there waiting for him as he came out of his shower reverie. I'd give them a nickel to ask why he has hair on his back or growing out of his nose. But, as I said, my husband is safely drip-drying behind locked doors.

On a regular day my emergence from the shower and donning of my towels rings a silent alarm through the rest of the house that I am, again, open for business. In come my other impatient offspring, followed brazenly and with a faith in my unfailing hospitality by whichever of their friends happen to be visiting. I put lotion on my face and legs, and three or four other little hands reach out for a squirt. I sit down at my vanity to scrutinize my eyebrows, and I'm immediately encircled in my round magnifying mirror by five or six keenly interested sets of eyes. Evidently, whatever magic I intend to perform will not be denied their prying intellect.

Just to take the focus off me, and to thin the crowd out a bit, I usually reach into my vanity drawer to find my nail clippers and announce, "All fingers and toes in this room must be cut!" One or two of the boys will usually sprint out of the room in self-defense, but the rest all stay as I clip away, sending stray nails flying all over the bathroom. I don't want to beat a dead horse here, Girlfriends, but I don't think my husband has ever once allowed his own showering experience to climax with the cutting of nails—he can barely stand the sensation of cutting his own nails.

But getting back to my little beauty parlor, don't think for a minute that the little customers who are awaiting their turn for a trim are sitting quietly, reading back issues of *Glamour* or *Redbook*. Oh no, they are sampling all my lipsticks and polishes, performing rudimentary examinations of the blue mole on my shoulder, and asking me to put some refreshing eye drops into their already-refreshed eyes. By far, the most popular pastime is taking each other's temperature (orally, thank God!). I'm only called into action here to clean the thermometer with alcohol swabs between mouths and to determine if anyone is sick enough to get to sleep in my bed that night. My husband doesn't even *have* a thermometer in his drawer, let alone the ability to read the mercury indication. In fact, if truth be told, he, too, comes to me to get his temperature taken.

By the way, we have an entire bathroom devoted to our kids that is outfitted with all the kiddie products they might need. Do you think they use it? Not if they can come up with a good excuse not to. You see, they like nothing more than to soak in my tub while I dress to go out or even just for bed. Sitting beside me as I scrutinize my pores in the magnifying mirror provides endless opportunities for tattling on their siblings. In fact, that's one of the reasons I've continued to be such a pushover—I've learned about my oldest son's first kiss, how a classmate of my fourth grader pulled his pants down on the playground to show his manliness, and the unexpurgated lyrics to the popular Eminem song I've only heard in its bleeped version on the radio. You'll agree, I'm sure, that this intelligence is just too valuable to forego.

The same comfort and entitlement that inspires my kids and their friends to join me during and after my shower or bath extends, naturally enough, to the personal business of the toilet. This, however, is where I try to draw the line, especially since all my kids are potty trained now and no longer in need of firsthand demonstrations of the art. Here's how it goes in my household and in those of all my Girlfriends. Not a one of us is physiologically capable of getting out of the car after several hours shuttling our kids around the universe and stopping at the one-hour photo place in September to pick up the kindergarten graduation rolls of film we dropped off in June and *not* sprinting directly to the bathroom. Like running a sort of gauntlet through yelping kids, our bladder-taxed bodies become deaf to the cries of "Mommy, I left my backpack on the playground," "Mommy, can you show me how to turn the computer on?," "Mommy, I think the kitty is going to barf up a fur ball." No matter how many Kegels we've done, there are certain urges that are simply irresistible.

I finally make it to the potty and relax into a sort of relieved unconsciousness. But when I venture to open my eyes again, I usually find one or two kids and one or two dogs brazenly pushing the door open. Sure, I've locked the door! I'm not a total idiot, but it's hardly worth it when you eventually come out to find your dependents weeping and piled in a huddle that you have to step over to get to the sink to wash your hands. I've become so efficient at relieving myself that I can actually stop the flow once the urgency has passed and save the rest for a quieter moment.

As soon as I've met the most essential calls of nature and am able to rejoin my family, which takes less than ninety seconds, I return immediately to the hubbub in the kitchen or family room. I may have kicked off my heels and pantyhose on the way back to the fray, but the rest of my uniform is intact as I empty backpacks, check spelling and math test grades, and hear tearful accounts about which Junior Girlfriend has decided to be the best friend of someone other than my precious daughters. I collect all the mail and school bulletins and set them on the staircase to remind me to take them up to the table beside my toilet for later concentrated reading. Magazines are placed on the coffee table, as if to suggest they will eventually be read in a moment of leisure, and all phone messages are jammed into my pockets—perhaps to be replied to before bed and equally in danger of going straight to the dry cleaners, untouched.

So, What's in This for Me?

I would no sooner dream of telling my kids to give me an hour of private decompression time at this point than I would tell them that I had decided to get a studio apartment of my own that they could visit on alternating weekends. That's the essence of my mothering dilemma: I think I "vant to be alone," but if I am, I go searching for somebody who needs me. After thirteen years of defining my day by the rhythms of my little baby, I confess, the prospect of coming in from work and finding no one except the dogs waiting in the driveway isn't as seductive as I thought it would be. Thankfully, I'm not yet there, so my obsolescence is still held at bay.

You may ask me, in the gentle way of my revered editor, why I still haven't managed to get the upperhand in my house and claim a meager few moments of depressurization for myself. This same editor, my Girlfriend Chris, the *really* working mother of two little girls, a toddler and a kindergartner, has reclaimed the sanctity of her marital bed, too, so I'm sure she's scratching her head from time to time, wondering where the Girlfriends' philosophies have failed me.

The truth is; they haven't. As much as I moan to my Girlfriends (and even more to my mate) about the superhuman efforts required to be all things to all people, including a pillow to curl up against after a scary dream, there's just something about the pride and gratitude I feel when I, little old me, can become Mommy the Monster Killer, Mommy Who Instinctively Knows When an Application of Ice is Better than Heat, Mommy Who Can Be Trusted to Sit Down and Listen to the Story of the Mean Referee, and Mommy Who Thinks That My Children Are Angels (albeit occasionally unrecognized in the outside world) Who Are Blessings Among the Ordinary and Unremarkable.

I cannot recall a time in my life when I heard my calling so clearly stated by the universe and was willing to heed the call. Silly as it may seem, I'm pretty proud (not to mention surprised) that I can make a sleepless, anxious child doze off in under thirty minutes. I love the way I can promise a four-year-old that his tummy ache will disappear if he takes a seat on the potty and relaxes there long enough to give me the rundown of the shows he'll be allowed to watch after dinner. Go ahead and call me delusional, but I so treasure my ability to see a temperature or headache coming on in one of my lambs before such "cheats" as thermometers can catch it.

There are few experiences besides mothering that simultaneously bestow a life purpose of unassailable significance in the world AND give us the cockpit seat from which to steer this interplanetary traveling machine. Even when I'm feeling inadequate to the job at hand, like potty training a toddler in a weekend with nothing more than eagle-eyed supervision, forcefeeding liquids and a stash of M&M's for rewards, there is an inevitability that keeps the world a spinning that we mothers will eventually rise to the occasion and triumph. If we moms didn't think it was our divine calling to handle such life milestones, we'd send our toddlers to behavior academies like we do our dogs; insisting that we wouldn't come back to pick them up from the kennels until they were completely housebroken.

While this isn't necessarily a horrible idea in theory, none of us is willing to miss witnessing our child struggle with a new learned behavior, work to understand it, and eventually succeed at it. We want to be there to comfort during the struggle, marvel at the learned behavior and celebrate like crazy at the local ice cream parlor the eventual success.

From my humble vantage point, the privilege of experiencing my children accomplishing "ordinary" skills and confidences is the sublime payoff for being a mother. I recall once, when I was backpacking alone through Europe as a high school graduate, my endlessly wise father wrote me a note that I should make an effort to make lasting friends among the other vagabonds because seeing the Eiffel Tower and sharing it with someone else also seeing it for the first time was more than doubly wonderful. I would be experiencing my own discovery and watching someone else get overcome and moved by its majesty at the same time. "All good and irretrievable moments are best shared with someone," he sagely told me.

So, I guess that's my feeble explanation for why I want to be there, to bear witness if you will, with each of my kids as they explore the completely fresh and new world that awaits them. The Grand Canyon is more phenomenal when you're showing it to your kids, the White House is more grand and sacred when you see it with a group of fifth graders studying civics, and the wisdom and courage required to cross a street alone are ten times more magical and miraculous when you watch your little innocent succeed for the first time. If this weren't true, then how could you explain all the eager beaver parents at the dinosaur exhibit at the Natural History Museum, Disney World, or Stars on Ice shows? We not only delight in the discoveries our children make, but we can, for that moment, see it through their eyes and be moved to tears or rapture over anything from the theatrical version of *Beauty and the Beast* to touching a dolphin's smooth skin at the Oceanaquarium.

In fact, the creeping sense I've been getting lately that more and more of these life delights will be discovered by my kids *without* me is a major inspiration for writing this groove book. It won't be long before I will have to find my own miracles to witness, or at least have to back off and let my children experience them with their peers, and the prospect breaks my heart.

Please be kind and indulge me in saying what Girlfriend Mothers have been saying to us all along: This joy all passes in the wink of an eye, so you'd better get all you can out of it while it lasts. By the time your baby reaches middle school, you will have to settle for second-hand accounts of fantabulous experiences, all divulged after a lot of prodding and in a language that is best compared to that of Cro-Magnon Man's.

Surviving the "Witching Hours"

So I guess that is my defense for some wussie mothering with my kids. But no matter how precious I find the world through their eyes, I can forget the magic for days, if not weeks on end, as I nobly struggle to nag them into finishing their homework, clean up the rooms they were too busy to attend to in the morning, feeding them a little something from at least two or three of the four major food groups, and providing clean gym clothes on two hour's notice. Whatever enlightenment and Zen I might have found at Sea World is quickly lost when my son is in the bathtub, next stop bed, and he tells me he needs two cardboard egg cartons to take to school in the morning. I don't generally save such things, and if I did, the teacher would discover our dark little secret that our eggs come in ecologically offensive foam containers.

But none of this daily loss of Mommy Zen is strange or new to you moms: From about five P.M. till the kids' bedtimes around nine P.M., most mothers' lives are devoted to pouring a quarter teaspoon of water and some milk-soaked crumbs of bread into the ant farm condominium their kindergartner built, wishing they could sustain their own kids as simply, settling every one down for homework (which, in case you've been in a coma, is much harder than anything we had to do at their ages), peeling off one or two kids at a time for baths and the removal of henna tattoos surrounding their belly buttons, and then trying to concentrate when their spouse comes home with his own daily news. These are the "witching hours." These are the hours when we lose sight of the lovely sail across the sea on the ark that is our family and see only shark-infested waters. Here's the bottom line: Swimming in the sea of the full-time job that begins as the sun goes down is about enjoying the sensation of floating, not about making it to the shore. If I could give you a navigational map to set a true course through these mundane distractions of motherhood, I think I would confidently raise the price of this book. But then again, you know what they say about advice: It costs nothing and it's worth the price, so I will suppress my greedy desire.

Share the Load (And I Don't Just Mean for the Washer)

Parents who are interested in getting their groove back are generally parents of children who are old enough to pick simple locks, find our hidden condoms, and orchestrate social lives as complicated as those of the characters on *Friends*. **The first word of advice I give you is to delegate** some of your chores to those mini Henry Kissingers you've got living under your roof. This always has a slow start, since teaching a skill is ten times harder than just going ahead and doing it yourself, but you have two higher callings to satisfy here: First, you owe it to your kids to teach them rudimentary homemaking skills now so that someday the mysteries of dishwashing detergent and completely closing and locking the dishwasher door are made clear, and second, now is the time to make it known in your home that it takes a village to get a clean linoleum floor and nonsticky kitchen counters.

Even if your children are very young, they should begin by being encouraged, if not outright forced, to stand in the kitchen and watch you prepare the evening meal. Imagine their awe and amazement when they discover that carrots don't come out of the ground in clean, peeled cubes! If nothing else, they will get a sense of how much time and planning goes into even the most humble repast.

After this, when the kids are about seven or eight, they can become truly helpful and responsible for certain aspects of helping the family not only survive, but enjoy, the "witching hours." They can set tables, they can pick flowers for centerpieces, they can pour the other kids' milk, provided you've got a lower table for them to work at and you don't fiendishly hand them a half gallon bottle from which to pour.

Eight- to twelve-year-olds are as good as indentured servants, if

you've got a little Simon Legree in you. If not, teach them to prepare sal-
ads, add condiments to the table, AND expect to stay around till the end
of the meal so that they can load the dishes into the dishwasher. Unless
they have a genetic disposition toward a Mr. Clean–type fetish for
grease- and streak-free surfaces, most kids will not grasp the final
niceties of finishing up the kitchen until the age of twelve or thirteen.
Until then, you'll have to come in for the once-over after the little kids
have done their best.

Experts know it, the Girlfriends know it (but don't always wish it
was true), and you know it: **The most important event of the day is
the time a family spends over dinner.** Truly, the food isn't that important. In fact, if the kids have already eaten before Dad comes home,
serve them dessert or a bowl of popcorn to keep them involved during
this mealtime gathering. What is critical is for the family to get together
and plan to stay together in a televisionless room for somewhere
between twenty minutes and an hour. If you don't have time to cook
AND to sit down and enjoy the camaraderie, you have the Girlfriends'
permission to order in a pizza and serve it with all the pomp and circumstance of a Thanksgiving meal.

The dinner table in our home has a tendency to become more rau-
cous and filibustering than a Senate hearing. That's fun if you have all
night, but, since we are on a tight timeline, we have **the Wooden
Spoon Rule: The only person allowed to talk is the one holding the
wooden spoon.** And I have total and unquestioned authority to determine when one person has held the spoon too long and must pass it on
to the next sibling or parent. That utensil has extraordinary powers; for
example, very few fights have the chance to get traction because each
person is allowed to finish his or her thought before the inevitable
rejoinders and ridiculing start. My husband says it makes him feel like a
goon, but he's willing to put up with the indignity because of the amazing announcements and judgments that come out of these crudely
ordered conversations.

This gathering of the family, short and sweet though it may be, is the highlight of our evening. It's the event around which we plan all our other activities. **Homework must be finished before dinner,** unless excused because soccer practice or dance rehearsals ran long. **The phone is allowed to ring into oblivion** for that private party, too. Now that the kids are all old enough to know their own numbers, plus those of three or four close friends, our phone rings about twenty times during the "witching hour." Since I'm the Head Witch, I say, "Off with their heads!" and they'll just have to chat with our voice mail until the kitchen is sort of clean. And, hey, if the skillet is just too much work to clean after a vigorous dinner conversation, then shake some Bon Ami and water into it and let it set until Scarlett O'Hara comes to clean it tomorrow, which *is* another day.

Here's another bit of controversial news that pertains to the "mommy witching hours:" **Kids are supposed to do their own homework to the best of their ability** and turn to Mom and Dad for final correction or when they need direction in finding an answer for themselves. "Oh, yeah, right!" you'll scoff. "And that's how come the winner of the science fair made her own thermonuclear reactor." Trust me, the Girlfriends and I have entered and even won several elementary school science fairs. We've also researched Alfred Nobel and the Nobel Peace Prize so deeply that we know exactly how many sticks of dynamite caused the greatest catastrophes in World War I. Without exception, however, I've learned that we've pulled the wool over exactly zero teacher's eyes. "But the kids whose parents get really involved get better grades, even if the teacher knows the student didn't do all the work!" This is when **it's up to us as adults to say, "Fine, my child will do all the work and get a C, and that will be just peachy with me."**

It's absolutely beastly to leap up from the dinner table to move on to fixing the sump pump in the laundry room, ironing six or seven dress shirts, and scooping the cat litter. **Even the most primitive people understand the need for an hour of peaceful digestion.** This can be an ideal time to slowly and calmly move the process to the bathroom. Kids can play in the sudsy warmth and you can touch base with the outside world. After the age of six, your children certainly know how to bathe themselves, even if you have to occasionally rinse soap out of an eye or scrub a back. Your biggest responsibility is to govern the bathwater temperature to prevent scalding or chilling. After that, you should be free to sit down on your vanity stool or on the edge of the tub and return phone calls or take a look at the day's mail. Every once in a while you can interrupt to bark out a reminder like "Wash your privates and underarms, too!" and then get back to your self-centered, but much-deserved, business at hand.

Once again, this is a perfect opportunity for the bigger kids to pitch in and help. I once traveled to Nepal, where I saw six-year-old girls and boys carrying baby slings with their infant siblings in them. They were astonishingly competent and would laugh to see how many of us American moms would still be carrying our six-year-olds in the sling if our slipped disks didn't prohibit it. Look, you're there if there's an accident and to supervise the older kids bathing and rinsing their siblings, so what's the worst that can happen? The hand-held shower soaks the surrounding curtains, carpet, and you? No big deal to Wash-and-Wear Mommy

Last, but not least, **average the bedtimes of your kids and deduct an hour. That should be the universal bedtime in your house until your older kids can be depended upon to turn off the TV and lights and go to sleep.** Until that grand day, gather all the kids in your bed or on the couch for the group read. I've been sticking with Harry Potter for the past four months because the older kids love it and the younger kids are droned to sleep by all the sophisticted language and situations. It's no mean attribute that *I* love the books too, and often keep reading after the kids have all fallen asleep. Once they're all in the Land of Nod, my husband and I urge or carry them to the boys' room or the girls' room for the rest of their night's sleep.

It should be about nine P.M. by now, and you may have an hour or two of productivity still screaming to be noticed and set free. Knock yourself out, Girlfriend. If you can't sleep until you get two loads of laundry washed, dried, folded, and put away, you go, girl. **Remember, however, that these extrafamiliar obsessions are yours and not necessarily your life mates.** In other words, it's completely inappropriate and statistically ridiculous to believe that you can nag and guilt him into wanting to defrost the refrigerator at midnight simply because you have a hankering to do it.

From the kids' bedtime, which may drag on for an hour or two, until you both surrender to bed, you and your husband are on separate and distinct military missions. His may be watching yet another A&E special about Al Capone (considered in this house as critical to American development as the presidential terms of Abraham Lincoln), and yours may be e-mailing your best friend from high school to commiserate about her daughter getting a driver's license in the next seven days. Either way, this is the adult version of "free play."

This is not only condoned but recommended because of the next bit of been-there-done-that advice from my Girlfriend Donna. According to Donna, a happy wife of thirty years and the mother of a sophomore at college in Ithaca, **the evening should end with both partners going to bed at the same time.** This is the time for all sorts of marital communing, whether it's hot monkey sex (As if! After a day like you've both had! But I don't want to be accused of having a narrow scope), a massage party, or some alluring pillow talk in the comfort of the darkened bedroom. This simultaneous lunar landing can only occur if both of you clear your dockets and commit to it. No fair promising to join him there after you've finished placing your J.Crew orders for spring.

Everybody's Living for the Weekends

The secret to getting our grooves back is to maintain realistic expectations. If you and your mate have delusions of spending the weekend sleeping late, hitting a flea market, going out to lunch, taking a long nap, and then exercising at the gym, you're gonna hate what the Girlfriends and I have to tell you now. Are the words *weekend school projects, AYSO soccer competitions* (including setting up and breaking down the field), *shopping for kids' cleats that fit this week, washing the cars, attending one birthday party for each of your children's age groups,* and *showing up at your place of worship* strange and foreign notions to you? If they are, you have serious delusional problems and need professional help immediately.

The ideal situation is to stretch and pull your weekend obligations so that they are bunched up on either Saturday or Sunday. This can be nearly impossible, I know. In fact, there have been many Saturdays when I've wished we were Jewish or Seventh Day Adventists just so that I could get all our obligations concluded and still look forward to Sunday as a literal day of rest. **Any activity that comes within your purvue should be carefully and intentionally on one or the other of the weekend days.**

A relatively calm Sunday, for example, not only allows for a relaxed reading of the paper, but will provide you with recovery time, should **you and your mate actually ascribe to that chestnut of successful marriages and have a "date night" on Saturday.** Any date worth the maitre 'd's tip should include a glass or two of wine and lead to some sexy "homework" to complete in the comfort of your own bed, and who needs to have a six-thirty wake-up call to get your alter boy to the church for the early service? Maybe further religious instruction will just have to wait until team sports are over and you can change "date night" to Fridays. This is when you're in the driver's seat, Girlfriend, not the Director of Youth Services, so don't be timid.

238

Golf, or the Invention of the Anti-Parent

Having done my level best to pass on to you the wisdom of the Girl-friends who've passed through these doors ahead of you, I have one last expression of astonishment to get off my chest. It's about the game of golf, a sport I hold nothing against personally, but one which I find a little counterproductive for parents who are struggling to get their groove back.

Parents, especially those of the male persuasion, who have looked around and noticed that their kids have started creating lives of their own, filled with playdates, Little League games, and endless birthday parties, are coming to one unanimous conclusion: After three or four years of parental sacrifice, they are ready and deserving of pursuing one tiny little hobby of their own to relieve the stress. The game of golf seems to be the indulgence of choice in my social circle. The same guys whom I've known since the days when they'd club until the sun brightened the sky and then sleep as long as their wives would resentfully allow are now emerging from the mole life of parents to find themselves drawn like lemmings to the still-dark golf courses and clubs that sing siren-like to them in the night.

My husband is in the music business, which is like saying he's the sheriff in a gold rush town. The only rules that applied, at least until about eight years ago, were a vow of silence and condoms provided in every hospitality goody bag. Forget the condoms now, they all dig right into the bags for personalized fingertip towels or those gadgets that personally engrave their balls—their golf balls, I mean. This is, without a doubt, an improvement in the level of entertainment offered at the two or three music conventions that occur over a year. Fresh air, athleticism, and male bonding are pretty hard to find fault with. I just have one teeny tiny problem with the golf epidemic among the daddy ranks: Do you realize that it takes a minimum of five hours to finish playing eighteen holes?

It's as if an entire generation of responsible fathers got a doctor's note to sneak out of the house long before the breakfast rush and hide out on the rolling links throughout those weekend hours that were once devoted to getting the car washed, getting the dog spayed, changing the refrigerator filters, and checking to see if the relief map of the continents that your daughter is making has finally dehydrated enough to keep Asia from bleeding into Europe. Most infuriating of all, those guys look pretty darn cute in their Gap pants and Tommy Bahama shirts at an hour when most of us moms still look like we've spent the night sleeping upside down like bats.

Yeah, yeah, they all maintain that they're reachable by cell phone all day, but have you ever tried to get an answer from a guy who swears he sees Tiger Woods teeing off right in front of him? There must be something potent in the grass they grow on those courses, because I've never met a man yet who remembered that he even had children, let alone was married as he blissfully went from sand trap to the green. Not only do they spend half their days chasing those dimply balls around, but as soon as they finish, they immediately begin to speculate whether they can fit in another eighteen holes without their mates driving to the club and dumping all their kids on the seventh hole, and perhaps the family dog, too.

Granted, I wouldn't know a five iron from a steam iron, but it's not my lack of sophistication about the allure of the Sport of Kings (mind you, not a queen mentioned once) that gets my dander up. It's the sublime entitlement that the fathers of America feel in devoting so much of their time to mastering the game. Just between us Wife/Mommy/Girlfriends, we can be open with each other about the extraordinary kind of self-delusion that keeps these duffers coming back for more. I'll never forget a dinner party recently when one of the over-forty aficionados tried to reign in his pride as he shared with us the appraisal his *paid-for* professional instructor told him that he could have been on the pro tour if he'd started a little earlier—like, say, age nine? This golf thing has taken over family time, has challenged family budgets as the guys join clubs, pay greens fees and invest in whole video libraries about the value of the Big Bertha in their training program.

How do you think this comparable scenario might fly at your house? You rise at five A.M. and slip out of the house, hair done and sporty makeup in place, and join a group of climbers to attack El Capitan. Sure, the cell phone reception up there in Yosemite, not to mention the difficulty of pulling out the phone while rappelling down the face of the mountain, keeps you in constant touch for "emergencies," but a couple of hours after your escape, your children start filing into the master bedroom dressed in their Little League catcher's gear, the brand-new toe shoes that need lacing properly, two groggy preteens who want to know, "What are we going to do today?" and a preschooler who has awakened to mortifyingly discover that she has wet her pajamas in her sleep. And in unison, they announce that they're starving and want everything from toaster waffles to oatmeal to a hard-boiled egg sliced onto white bread and dolloped with mayonnaise.

If that were to happen just once in my family, I would fully expect to see my husband hovering over Half Dome in a chartered helicopter, dropping a rope for me to climb aboard and come home where I belonged.

All right, I admit it: I'm jealous. If I could only recall what it was I had a passion for doing before I became a mother, this would be the time to pull it out and dust it off. But that's part of my problem; I don't clearly remember anything I did with the single-mindedness and self-righteousness of motherhood. And now, when needlepoint, ladies' soccer leagues, and book clubs are so common you can't meet a woman who's not trying them, I am having a hard time letting go of being the chief boo-boo kisser. Still, you can't blame me for a little resentment, here, can you?

Most Dads Live on a "Need to Know" Security Clearance

In spite of my jokes to the contrary, my mate really commits his brain capacity to information that he absolutely must know. Yes, he can find our kids' school, even if he can be relied upon to piss off all the other carpool moms by making an illegal right-hand turn into the school driveway and thereby cutting in front of the twenty or thirty cars that have patiently snaked through the neighborhood side streets, pursuant to the school's Conditional Use Traffic Regulations. Heaven help us, however, should he be asked to pick up the ferrying slack to such exotic destinations as the orthodontist, our daughter's horseback riding lessons, the dance studio, or the "Young Einstein" summer program.

For the sake of marital harmony, I have long ago stopped asking my husband to remember the names of his kids' teachers, and this is before our oldest has begun middle school, where he will have several teachers to call his own. If this can be found to provide some sort of justification or tolerance, let me hasten to remind you that this same fabulous daddy can't remember his or my mother's maiden names, which has led to a couple of times in which his credit card was confiscated when a conscientious store sought further identification.

Yeah, I know, my husband is spoiled and not really representative of all fathers. He was given to me that way from his own mother and adoring older sister, and I willingly kept up the cocooning until God gave me real live children of my own to fuss over. I confess, I'm totally babying my co-parent, at least until the day when all four of our kids have flown the coop, but I accepted this duty when I came on board. Of course, at that critical time, I had no idea what curveballs motherhood would throw me.

Selective Deafness

I drive one of those gigantic SUVs. Trust me, I'm not living out some repressed need to appear more powerful than my slight chick frame connotes. I really need all the seats. A simple family outing includes six of us, and, if you haven't already discovered this truism, we parents are often reduced to abject bribery to get our preteeners to deign to join in our family expedition, usually in the form of a buddy to tag along and be willing to whisper preteen stuff in the farthest back-seats. It's traditional in our car travels for me to do all the driving, since, as a California native, I seem to have been born knowing how to parallel park.

Being in the music business, my husband immediately begins amusing himself by slipping demo CDs into the stereo and calling his colleagues on the car phone to discuss their relative merits. From the minute I take the car out of park and roll out of the driveway, a chorus starts from the two rows of backseats behind me. "Mommy, I can't find my seat belt clasp," "Mommy, I need to sit next to a window or I'll get carsick," "Mommy, I hate this song, can you change it?" or "Mommy, can I use your phone to call Amelia to ask her if she wants to meet up with us so that I don't have to sit with all boys?"

I answer every darn question as if it's my higher maternal duty. Funny, though, how almost none of the questions being ricocheted from the backseat start with the identifying address of "Daddy." It's my theory that he's trained them into ignoring him by his selective deafness in the car. He gets to ride like the boy in the bubble while I function as the chief researcher at the Library of Congress. He's certainly at least as smart and full of information as I am, but his deafness seems to suggest that all serious inquiries should be sent to him in writing.

These car rides are what inspired me to the epiphany that Home is Where the Mommy Is. Sure, you can think it's the kitchen or the family room that provides the sense of safety and belonging that foster confi-

243

dence for our family, but if you fail to show up there on a daily basis, you're just as apt to learn that the Heart of Rock 'N' Roll is Still Beatin', even if that heart is in bed with you with the flu. As cranky as I may sound about this realization, I want to go on record right now saying that I'd give my eyeteeth in exchange for having this ineffable attractiveness to my kids no matter how luscious the sixteen-year-old girlfriend proves to be or how thrilling the nineteen-year-old's convertible will predictably be.

Sure, I may have to revert to using guilt or bribery to keep these beautiful creatures hovering outside my shower door. Maybe a condo in Hawaii or a time-shared ski chalet will do the trick. All I know is that I thank my Higher Power every day that we live in a world of cell phones, and the speed dial is programmed to Mom. I will gladly ride to the rescue for the rest of my life. It was the first real "calling" I ever experienced, and, so far, nothing else has encroached on my devotion to it.

The Ten Commandments of Grooving

10. Be humble and grateful for every day.

9. Keep up with your children's innoculations.

8. Get a pap test and mammogram once a year.

7. Give your kids a sense of family and heritage.

6. Tell your kids how much you love them, at least twice a day.

5. Tell your mate how much you love him at least three times a day.

4. Laugh and cry in front of your kids.

3. Be the grown-up.

2. Read for pleasure.

1. Laugh out loud with your family.

Guilt-Free Grooving

*T*he most common emotion experienced by mothers who are trying to meet all their masters, family, work, community and themselves, is GUILT. We're running as fast as we can, and yet we all seem to be a day late and a dollar short. In those brief moments before we fall asleep, we're more inclined to obsess about our failure to help our third grader write his campaign speech for student council, the load of clothes wrinkling overnight in the dryer instead of folded and put away, or our lack of choices in clothing for tomorrow because we're retaining too much water to close the zipper.

As demoralizing and confidence-eroding as guilt is, we never seem to try to eradicate it by lowering the bar and expecting a little less perfection from ourselves. Instead, we just clutter up the picture more by adding more timesaving "systems," more electronic appliances and more caffeine, and mastering that most popular mothering circus act: multitasking. I see my Girlfriends all over the city streets in the hours after school and work; driving minivans or SUVs, talking on the phone, listening to their kids, jotting down notes on a pad mounted on the windshield, consulting their Palm Pilots, and reading school bulletins on their way to orthodontist appointments, violin lessons, and Brownie meetings.

I recently saw one of the more poignant and amusing examples of compulsive multitasking on the morning show *The View*. The ladies were discussing the relative merits of certain beauty care products, and Barbara Walters was giving her personal testimonial for a new, *quiet* blow-dryer. She explained that this was a dream come true for her, because she talks on the phone while her hair is being done for the show and has always had a hard time hearing the other party. With this miraculous invention, however, she could carry on a normal conversation and become groomed at the same time. Let's be real here; I think Barbara Waltersness is next to godliness, but can't the hardest-working woman in show business just sit and stare at herself in the mirror while an appliance that's louder than a leafblower is three inches from her eardrums?

Even during those precious few minutes when our children's retainers are being adjusted, do we just sit there, thumbing through old issues of *Working Mother*? Of course not. We're urging our other kids to begin their homework in the waiting room while we call to see if our antibiotic prescription has been filled yet. And if we're really at the top of our games, we're kegeling the entire time. When did it become illegal, or at least socially unacceptable, to just sit and stare at the waiting room aquarium during this brief respite?

Where Does This Guilt Come From?

All I know is that I wasn't born this way. Sure, I was bossy and an obvious Type A personality, but so are all firstborns, right? But really, I was dedicated to perpetuating my constant groove, even though, once I reached puberty, most of those peaks and valleys (and I'm not referring to my breasts) were romantic in nature. Even after I graduated college and got a job, I still lived for me and my happiness. My marriage was to another obvious self-serving child; kind, sexy, generous, and endlessly committed to his career ambitions, but still childlike in putting his needs first, like me. I think that all that sex we delighted in during the first couple of years distracted us from the compromises and unnerring respect that would be called into play further down the line.

Thinking back, I guess that my first twinges of guilt came when I found out I was pregnant. It doesn't make much sense, really, since I'd been trying to get pregnant for so long. I had taken folic acid supplements religiously during that time in training, I still couldn't fathom a meal in a restaurant with more than a modest glass of good wine, and I had built up a huge list of my bargains with God, should She allow me to get pregnant. I would embrace morning sickness at any time of the day or night, I swore. I would sacrifice coffee, diet sodas, artificial sweeteners, and foods with preservatives or hormones. I would give birth at home in my bed with nothing more than a wooden spoon to bite on when the pain racked my body. I would live each day in a state of gratitude and jubilation, no matter how bad the hemorrhoids or burping fits.

You all know me well enough by now to predict with confidence that I was never up to any of those oaths (except the total ban on drinking and smoking, which is absolutely required). In fact, the first time I barfed at work, I wanted to lie down on the cool tile floor and sleep until it was time to go home. And from the moment my ob/gyn detected a healthy heartbeat, I felt free to start kvetching about my sciatica, my heartburn, and my fashion crises. I did all that, but I was starting to feel guilty.

It wasn't until I found out I had placenta previa that I really kicked into guilt overdrive. I figured this just had to be my fault and it was up to me to find my culpability in the matter. This situation, which resulted in the very successful delivery of a strapping baby boy, provided me a bouquet of guilt flowers from which to pick, day or night.

First of all, I was lying on my ample ass 24/7. Every book I'd read on pregnancy had endorsed maintaining all physical activity the mother-to-be had been doing before she got pregnant. I truly believed, if I was worth my salt as a New-Age mom, I would be playing tennis until I was at least four centimeters dilated, the only allowance being that I could resort to doubles during transition labor. Clearly I had blown that image and I'd certainly spend the rest of my life lying around like a queen bee, munching on the larvae of my worker bees. I felt kind of like Jabba the Hut stuffing toads down his gullet. After about two days of crying in self-pity, I read every book and article I could find about placenta previa to prepare myself for this special challenge.

Every single publication stated that the most commonly known cause of my condition, aside from pure dumb luck, was chain-smoking. I didn't even smoke, and yet took this information into my guilt file. Perhaps I'd spent too much time around second-hand smoke. Hey, everyone knows how much smoke there is in a rock music club, not to mention that I'd smoked like a chimney in my junior year of high school. Plus, I'd followed my husband to Europe two times since our marriage, and absolutely everyone smokes on you there.

Although I felt wrongly accused of my condition, having done nothing that could be medically identified as its source, I bucked up and committed to taking the lemons of my bedrest edict and making lemonade, sour as it might be. Heaven forbid that I should claim those last few precious weeks of aimlessness as a gift from above. As I recall, my first pregnancy coincided with the 200th anniversary of the Bill of Rights and the Supreme Court. Having been a lawyer in my previous life, I vowed to commit these twenty weeks of confinement to brushing up on legal philosophy.

I dispatched my trustworthy lawyer-Girlfriend Mandy to buy me five or six books on constitutional law. She dutifully piled all of them on my bedside table, but I never personally touched them. Instead, I quickly learned the story lines of all the ABC soaps and never missed a single episode once through that restful period. Those shows, *Vogue* magazine, and pregnancy books kept me satisfied for the endless time I spent eating the recommended protein for the mother of twins or an Olympic decathlete. One more evidence of guilt-inducing behavior.

Motherhood Is Even More Rife with Guilt

This self-flagellation only became more pronounced early on in my parenting life. As my Girlfriend Sonia told me one weepy morning after two full days of wild toddlers ganging up on her, "When I went to bed last night, all I could think about was the fact that I hadn't said a single thing to the kids beside "NO!" for two days. I was so tired and frustrated that I never once told them I loved them or even played a single game with them." It was all she could do to restrain herself from going into their room and waking them both up to hug and kiss them and offer them hot fudge and ice cream.

By the time my third and fourth babies were born and my career was hitting its stride, I was a certifiable masochist. I'd lie there in the presleep darkness and calculate how much attention I'd devoted to each child once I finished my work for the day: Let's see, I had an entire hour alone with my oldest son when we got stuck in a traffic jam on the way to his tutor, and we'd talked about why he hates team sports and why he likes a certain girl more than the rest in his class. I'd sat by my younger daughter as she half-recited and half-read a kindergarten book about a missing goose. I'd put my older daughter's dance bag together for her and combed her hair into a regulation ballet bun and sent her to class with a classmate's mom. That wasn't really a joyous interaction, since my daughter has a head of glass and I comb her like she's a show horse, but, hey, I was trying my very best. And my third oldest, I'd totally neglected him right up to his good-night kiss. He might as well have been a boarder here in our house for all the attention he got from the mother, and I felt like shit.

The dynamics would change from night to night, sometimes getting so bad that I'd work late and show up just in time to turn off their bedside lamps, eventually finding a guilty pleasure in drawing a bath and reading the school bulletins from amongst the bubbles. It was clear as the crow's feet around my eyes that I'd flunked parenting completely, and the only way to make peace with it was to play up the fact that I'd put in my time during the "witching hours." That's all that stood between me and turning in my membership card to the Sorority of Mothers. After all, don't all those parenting experts constantly point to the family dinner as the great separator of maternal wheat from chaff? Sure, we might not all be actually *eating* at the time, but we did manage to sit down as a group around sunset from time to time.

Guilt is Like Radioactivity; It's Out There Even If You Can't See It

Kids are pretty rich sources of guilt, but they are by no means the only ones. In fact, one of the most alarming characteristics is how deeply contagious it is. How many times have you been in a gathering of mothers, feeling pretty okay about yourself and minding your own business, when one of them stands up to announce that she wants to recommend a "swell" idea for a family holiday. She and her husband took their six- and eight-year-old kids to the American Southwest to work on an archeology dig.

Oh, for heaven's sake, weren't there any mothers out there who fessed up to shipping off all children over the age of six to sleepaway camp for the summer or sending them to Grandma's condo in Palm Springs for a month? The school year was hard enough; wasn't there anyone who could assure me that my mate and I were entitled to three or four weeks that weren't devoted to the entertainment and enrichment of our offspring, especially with the hot weather and humidity and all? Evidently not.

I beat myself up with extra ferocity when some well-meaning mother explained that she thought her daughter was a math wizard in sixth grade because of all the piano training she's had since she was four. First of all, how was I supposed to know that scientists have detected a link between understanding and reading music and doing well in math? I barely have the time to check out the "What People Are Wearing" section of the *National Enquirer* while standing in the grocery checkout line—perhaps if they provided copies of the *American Medical Association Review* beside *People*, I'd have had a chance to learn this. And second, my kids hated piano lessons. What was I supposed to do, handcuff them to the Steinway in the family room?

Another sure kick in the behind to get my guilt mojo working was to notice how many women in carpool are dressed in their workout clothes, clearly intending to head off to yoga or Pilates or weight training. I drive the kids to school in one of two ensembles; either I go in my pajamas with a long sweater over them and a baseball cap hiding a fearsome case of bedhead, and dark glasses, or I go in full makeup because I've just finished doing a five A.M. satellite feed to some New York–based television show. No matter what the outfit, my recurring fantasy is to drop the sweater and/or makeup and go right back to bed after the kids have been dropped off.

I promise to recommit to reclaiming fitness as part of getting my groove back, but even if it's not my workout day, seeing other people going makes my stomach turn over and flop all cold and heavy. Have you ever felt my pain?

Just between us Girlfriends, since I'd never like my colleagues or collaborators to think that I'm anything less that totally devoted to my career, I confess here and now that I often give short shrift to my work outside the house. Nonetheless, I am completely capable of feeling those pangs, too, when I feel that I've given my work the glossing over, usually so that I can be there for a child's vaccination, the fourth-grade breakfast, or drive to school a social studies book that was left in the driveway in the madness of getting four kids loaded into the car in the morning. When people ask me why I don't write more books, appear in more television shows, or join the lecture circuit, my only answer is "Well, I think I've just about filled my dance card already." Sounds pretty glib, I know, but who really wants to hear how painfully I have peeled off the layers of my personal dreams that included becoming the Martha Stewart of Mothers, the Erma Bombeck of our generation, the West Coast Anna Quindlen? While the choices were valid and unassailable to devote myself to my family first, I still suffered tremendous guilt for failing to achieve everything my college adviser had in mind for me. Not to mention the looks of disappointment from the people who have the nerve to ask me what I've done to actualize my "talents."

Is Mommy Guilt a Product of the New Millennium?

Not too long ago, I was chatting on the phone with my editor and Girlfriend Chris when it occurred to me that chronic guilt might be the by-product of modern women having too many choices. Think about it; if we were still devoting our lives to the very real threat of dying in childbirth, losing a child in infancy, having the entire family get the bubonic plague, and finding food when the potato crop failed, would we still be beating ourselves up wondering whether we'd done enough to inspire the "little artist" within our children and the Fabio within our mates? It doesn't take much more than a Sunday afternoon of TV shows devoted to saving the children or hunger relief to notice that our preoccupation with public versus private schools is a tad privileged.

Don't get me wrong. I'm as immersed in my own world as the next mom, but occasionally I wonder whether all this guilt and failing to measure up isn't really just the twenty-first century equivalent to navel gazing. If you've had a crisis like the loss of one of your parents or a health crisis in your family, you know how easy it really is to clear the deck of all bullshit and focus on the only thing that matters: keeping your family pod healthy and intact. Unfortunately, the resiliency of the human mind allows us to eventually let go of the urgent need to survive, and within a few months we're back to worrying about whether leather pants are as politically incorrect as fur coats.

I'm certainly no historian or sociologist, but I'm gonna guess that mommy guilt as we know it came into being around 1950. The men were home from the war, women like Rosie the Riveter put away their drills and put their aprons back on, and the burgeoning national economy (not to mention the G. I. Bill) created a groovy world in which one income was enough to buy a house and sustain a family. At about the same time, such modern marvels as antibiotics and the polio vaccine, not to mention washing machines and vacuum cleaners, were getting moms out of the sickroom and the kitchen in record time.

It didn't happen overnight, the guilt thing I mean. My own mother might disagree with me, but my recollection of her early years of wifing and mothering seem blessedly unconflicted and uninspected. She knew her turf. It was the same as her mother's, only better because she had a car and stores that offered layaway plans. The image that keeps running through my head is *I Love Lucy*. Like so many of her generation, Lucy seemed to sense that there were other ways to invest her time and talents besides caring for Ricky and Little Ricky, like dancing at the Copacabana, but she never seriously considered taking her apron off for good.

No, I think the first moms who felt the conflict of devoting themselves to hearth and home and trying out their wings in the world outside the home became epidemic in the sixties. My mentor-Girlfriend Phyllis has worked in the publishing business since before her three kids were born, and her husband has consistently maintained a well-respected medical practice. "But she's married to a DOCTOR!" disapproving people would say. "Why does she need to work?" Whenever I beat myself up for missing a back-to-school night or a Brownie meeting, I ask Phyllis to tell me *again* how it was for her when she'd rush in late to a PTA meeting, looking way too chic and sophisticated for most of the other moms' liking. "They hated me!" she chuckles. "They wouldn't talk to me and they would have given anything for me to have three hapless, helpless children. Unfortunately for them, my kids were superstars, so they couldn't pop a hole in my boat."

My own mother's harmonious universe hit a sour chord after ten years of marriage when my parents divorced. Her role as keeper of the home fires was unceremoniously taken from her and her agenda was painfully simple: She had to get a job for money to help support her babies. Evolution being as slow as it is, I feel safe in speculating that my mom would have given up her job in a New York minute if she had remarried someone who could afford us, but I think she was the last of an era.

Sophie's Choice

Nowadays, most women work before they have babies and resume their careers after the babies have been safely deposited with a sitter or daycare center. Most families need two incomes even to hope to achieve the American dream of owning their own house and putting their kids through at least the first year of college. Vacation? Schmacation! We're talking fundamentals here. Let's not forget that we're dealing with two or three generations of women who have been raised and educated to believe that they have skills and talents to contribute in the workplace, too, and who take tremendous pride and a sense of being essential in their chosen field.

You don't have to remind me that not all work is equally inspiring and contributing to the betterment of the world. Work for women is a mixed bag, and boy do I know it. Some of us spend our days trying to maintain a good humor at our checkout counter while a shopper allows her child to open up and spill a 3-liter bottle of Pepsi while she searches for her clipped coupons. Others of us take our lives in our hands when we deign to put a parking ticket on a Mercedes while the owner is sprinting out of the nearby chi-chi restaurant while screaming that he's going to turn our little cart over or report us to his close personal friend, the mayor. And let's never give short shrift to the huge percentage of working women who are devoted to some aspect of the teaching profession: inspiring job, frustrating conditions, appalling pay.

Of course, this picture is incomplete until we factor in the statistics about divorce in this country, not to mention the high percentage of deadbeat dads. What we're left with is a couple of generations of working moms who are as devoted to their kids as June Cleaver, but who have to work harder than Ward to keep the food coming to the table. It's almost a relief for some women to be able to point to their jobs as time-consumers that offer little more spiritual and intellectual fulfillment than the satisfaction of knowing the utilities won't be turned off this month. That means that they haven't placed their jobs ahead of their children voluntarily.

While other women are fortunate enough to discover their passion at their work, there aren't a lot of people applauding their blessing. After all, since nobody gets it all, her family must be suffering to pay the price for her success. All it takes is some old guy with misty memories of his dear old mum to suggest that she's thrown out the babies with the cooler water to get those of us who work for fulfillment, to make a contribution and, hey, *because we really like it*, to start stuttering and striving to sell ourselves as women who have never, ever, disappointed anyone at home or at work. We may be disappointed with ourselves five days out of seven, but that's a sacred Girlfriend secret, not to be shared with the enemy. We must stay silent, or else we will be devoured by the Monster of Mommy Guilt.

If Guilt Is Like a Hammer, Why Do I Keep Hitting Myself in the Head With It?

What do you suppose would happen if we moms resolved to take half as good care of ourselves as we do of our mates, kids, and coworkers? Would we just have a whole new category of guilt with which to beat ourselves up? For example, when we noticed that we hadn't had a professional pedicure since last summer began, would we add that to our list of frustrations and disappointments? I don't think so, Girlfriend. Being as intimately familiar as we are with the discomfort of chronic guilt hanging off of us like fifty-pound bandoliers, we'd never wish it on the people we love. So it just follows that, when the day comes when we decide to treat ourselves with a full measure of love, guilt would have to be the first thing to throw overboard. Part of getting our groove back, I'm convinced, is learning to extend the same tolerance to ourselves that we so willingly share with our other loved ones.

What if I spent an entire day playing and indulging whatever mood inspired me? Would I thank my lucky stars for a day spent in such unmitigated joy, or would I have a some huge "obligation debt" that I'd spend the rest of my life paying back? Would my whole family fall apart?

I'm not talking about lounging around beside some hotel pool and drinking daiquiris, although that sounds really nice right now. How would I feel about myself, no matter how great my indulgent day had been, in those brief moments between putting my head on my pillow and falling into my nightly coma? Would I go to sleep with a sense of peace or with those regrets that one feels when she has drunk too much and danced with every guy at the company Christmas party?

We recently took the kids to visit my Girlfriend Lili and her family who live on the beach. It was a hot summer day, but Lili, being a true Girlfriend, had put up several strategic umbrellas to protect my freckled Irish skin. It was a fabulous day, exceptional for many reasons, but at the top of the list was the miracle that all four of my kids can now swim like fish and I only needed to sit near the surf in a beach chair while they boogie-boarded and swam to a speedboat anchored nearby. No one was going to drown unless he was first cold-cocked by a Frisbee. I didn't even have to put on my bathing suit, and that in itself is a sublime gift.

It was a reunion of the "core" Girlfriends and all our kids, one of whom just completed his first year at Brown University, another who would be heading off to Berkeley in the fall, several of whom were sprouting body hair and hormones, and all the way down to my Girl-friend Stacy's eighteen-month-old who had a little girl/big girl crush on my six-year-old. It was heavenly.

As we made the long drive home, I was glowing with the satisfaction of the day. My kids were asleep in the back of the car, all as brown as berries from a day on the beach, my husband was mellow and sweet, and I was absolutely delirious from achieving one of those truly great days when all six of us had had a good time. It took me several hours, however, to understand why that afternoon was exceptional. I went to bed thinking that I was happy because my kids and spouse were happy. They'd all seen friends they were crazy about, they'd all exhausted their energies, and the day had lasted long enough that no one left feeling that some bit of fun had gone undiscovered.

It wasn't until the next morning that I had the "Duhhhh!!!" moment when I discovered that part of the magic of that day was that I—yes me, the Mother—had piggybacked a great time on top of my family's pleas-ure. I'd inhaled the lazy, unstructured time with my friends as deeply as I'd breathed the clean ocean air, not to mention the guacamole dip. My Girlfriends and I sat and talked, sat and not talked, checked on each other's kids, talked some more, gossiped about our husbands (or

259

boyfriends, in Corki's case), and even just dozed off or read fashion magazines. It all left me wondering, when did my world view change so radically that I put myself so far down the list of People Needing to Be Pleased By Vicki?

It's All Smoke and Mirrors

I don't know about you, but I used to gauge a day's success by the barometers of my kids. If they were happy, I was happy. If they weren't, it was somehow my failure. Beautiful as it was, the day at the beach example is really only a preparatory lesson in giving up guilt as our personal companions. The more advanced course is trickier because it would involve allowing yourself to *still* have a great day, even if your kids got too much sand up their behinds or hated the food or got into a fight with another chum. Learning to embrace and separate your joy from that of your family is much harder to do, but it's critical for us grooving moms. Think of it this way. The day has come and gone. You're in the car driving home and one of your kids is moaning about getting stung by jellyfish or your mate is complaining because he doesn't eat red meat, and steaks and burgers were the only things served.

If you're anything like me, you'll be tempted to totally discount your grand time and join the team of the dissatisfied. Makes sense, right? What self-respecting mother can judge a beach party a success if one of her kids or her mate didn't feel the same magic she felt? The correct answer, my dearest Girlfriend, is to hold on to your happiness and bind it up in bubble wrap for protection. You did your very best to make sure that everyone had a good time, you let *yourself* have a great time, and it's all over now but the cheering, or lack thereof. We have to learn that we are entitled to cherish the memory of a day pleasantly spent, just as the rest of the family is free to resent it as a close encounter of the jellyfish or red meat kind.

260

Rule Number One: Never Judge Fairness on a Daily Basis

Okay, so we've discussed the importance of quarantining your own pleasure from the guilt-inducing disappointments and indignities "suffered" by your loved ones. It's too much, I know, just to let their complaints slide off your back like water off a duck, but it is possible to lend a sympathetic ear to their whining and still hold your own enjoyment safe in your pocket. You deserve it; it's not your fault that everyone else didn't feel the magic like you did, you're willing to offer commiseration and comfort for those who've been so disappointed, but more important, you're groovy enough to know better than to toss away your own fun memories and end up with empty pockets again.

The next lesson I learned about getting the guilt monkey off my back is to explain to my children that there will be no measuring of fair treatment among the four of them on a daily basis. After nearly eleven years of trying to make sure that no sibling was gifted with a trinket, a privilege, or a bath with Mommy that the others didn't get, I've thrown in the towel for good. The way I see it, the kid who gets the short end of the stick, like having to go to math club when the other three are going to Toys R Us to help me pick out birthday gifts for the three or four parties they go to each weekend, is not allowed to bitch and moan about that sacrifice until our family dinner on Sunday night. Even though I'm reasonably trusting that everyone's chimes will have been rung in the course of a week, I admit, I do kind of keep track so that Sunday dinner turns out to be yet another pleasure for little ol' me to slip into my pocket.

This is also a perfect opportunity for us moms to begin teaching our older kids that "equally loving treatment" can come in seemingly different packaging. For example, if I were to pick up a Make Up Mindy doll for Jade during the birthday gift shopping foray into Toys R Us, things don't have to be made even Steven by my oldest son getting a Mindy, too, or any toy for that matter. His special gift may be getting to invite two of his friends to a movie and then over to spend the night. You and I both know that kids can be very literal, so this is a good educational opportunity for you to teach your offspring that fairness is an elusive and attitudinal concept. Trust me, this will free you up in ways you can't even imagine yet.

Rule Number Two: Kill the Guilt Monster at Work

I maintain that one of the reasons we mothers feel guilty about appearing to put our family first and our careers in the backseat is the Girlfriends' uncontrollable need to give way too many details to our superiors and coworkers. It's like when people tell lies and can't help but embellish them with long, detailed and slightly deranged explanations. A simple declaratory statement like "I won't be able to meet with you at four o'clock tomorrow because I have another commitment," really is sufficient under most circumstances.

Same thing with excusing yourself from work to delight your child with your devotion, reassure them with your presence when they're afraid or insecure, or simply drive them to an appointment that they could never otherwise get to. If you are a conscientious worker, as I know you are, and are not regularly asking other coworkers to pick up the slack for you, a concise and simple statement like "I'm going to be out of the office for two hours on Thursday morning" should be enough.

If you still feel compelled to share every detail about which mode of transportation you'll be taking, how uncooperative your pediatrician is about adjusting his office hours to accommodate working parents, how green the mucus is that's leaking from your child's nose and eyes, and how frantic and guilty you feel about having to leave the company in a lurch while you cover for your lazy-ass co-parent who promised he'd handle the next doctor's visit, but can't be reached at his office, on his cell, or at his new girlfriend's house, you're just begging to get one of *those* looks from the unlucky recipient of the story. If you've shared this play-by-play with a man, heaven help us, you're bound to get a petulant look as if to say, "That is far more information that I ever hoped to have" combined with, "Why can't these crazy women get their childcare handled and out of the workplace?"

I will tell you right now that I'm not totally above the little white lie for these situations. If you must get some time off and you don't think your supervisor will be particularly sympathetic, feel free to try out this old chestnut, "Sorry, Tom, but I think I've broken a molar and if I don't get nitrous oxide within fifteen minutes. I may become violent." Most men are so squeamish about drills and Novocaine needles that they'll just lose their coloring for a moment and tell you, "Good luck." Make sure, however, that you never try this excuse out on a dentist, for obvious reasons.

Rule Number Three: Look for the Gift That's There

If you ever find a free moment to leave the parenting and children's sections of the bookstore and wander into the gigantic self-help displays, you're sure to find one or two hundred books that tell you essentially the same thing: You only get one go-round in this life, and it's up to you to dig it while you live it. I must have half of those books stacked beside my bed and on the little toilet side table in my bathroom. I guess I "get it" intellectually, but I've yet to integrate such wisdom into my everyday life.

But just a moment ago it was all spelled out for me. I just took a break from writing to make sure all my kids were in the Land of Nod and at least partially covered with blankets. I think I've already told you that my two girls share a room and the two boys share the other. Anyway, after I turned my eight-year-old right side up so that his head, rather than his fanny, was on the pillow and put a fresh sports bottle of water beside the big brother's bed, I continued on to the girls' lair. They sleep side-by-side in matching twin beds, and when I walked in and waited for my eyes to adjust to the darkness, I noticed that the "baby's" bed was empty.

Before the panic moved past my throat and into my loud mouth, I caught sight of her silhouette spooning her big sister in her bed. Relief immediately relaxed all my muscles, and I could barely walk up closer for a better look, but once I got to the head of the bed, my eyes had grown familiar enough with the dark to see, in perfect detail and relief, the most beautiful vision imaginable. Their heads were sharing a single pillow, with their waist-length manes of taupey blond and deep brown all mixed up and intertwined. Jade had her arm over her big sister's body and was breathing deeply into her jammie-clad back. In the halflight I could see the similarities in their chins and cheekbones. Their comfortable intimacy was stunning and miraculous to me, their mother. Then I started to weep.

This is what won't last forever. They won't always sleep comfortably in such a small bed, nor will they want to when the disputes over borrowed clothes and borrowed boyfriends begin in earnest. But for now, they looked like a pile of kittens, wrapping their bodies around each other with no inhibition or territorial claims. Their combined body heat warmed my face as I bent down to kiss their hair-slashed faces. I swear, I could have passed into the next world if God could promise me that theirs was the image I'd see for eternity.

Hey, we're only human. By morning I will be back to yelling at them to get up and ready for school. One of them will spill a bowl of cereal and milk on my work notes, and they will be arguing about who *really* owns the pink scrunchie. But I'm going to hold on to that peek at perfection till the day I die. I think it was Mother Nature's divine intervention to remind me that, in spite of my distraction during dinner and my impatience with the report about presidential candidates, I'd been blessed with healthy, loving little kittens who love each other as much as they love me. And, best of all, I was there to witness the miracle. Admit it, Girlfriends, that's a legacy worth dreaming of.

My Best-Laid Plans

With that precious image in my heart, as well as a couple equally poignant glimpses of my younger son's hero worship of his big brother and the bigger boy's gruff, but protective demonstrations toward the little guy, I know I'm on the path to getting my groove back. Quite simply put, I want to devote as much of my life as I can to doing everything I can to encourage my children to love, trust, and cherish each other above all others. Think about it: Siblings generally have longer relationships with each other than any of them will have with my husband and me and even longer than the most successful marriages I can arrange for them before I get too senile to recognize any of them.

My pledge to myself in getting my groove back, at least for this season of my life, is to fight mightily for my front-row seat in the drama of their lives. When I'm not too distracted to notice, it's obvious to me that going through childhood and adolescence with a wiser and more appreciative point of view is the best ride life offers—at least to a Girlfriend of my sensibilities.

Look, I still have a feeble grasp on my maternal reality, and I'm certainly not going to devote the next ten years to watching my son's facial hair grow or calling the mother of a cute young thing who's broken my innocent's heart. I am, however, going to be firm about putting aside the expectations and superfluous commitments that define my life to make room for creating a home in which we all feel essential, adored, and connected. Who cares if I'm not featured in a single family photo from Easter morning to graduation? I'm right there, behind the zoom lens, watching this miraculous creation that almost never came to be: my perfect family.

Okay, so it may mean that I'll continue to be hit-and-miss with my own cultivation as a person. It may mean, as it did tonight, that I will brazenly shake my beddy-bye husband awake so that he can come in and see the kitten pile for himself, and then put him back to bed before visions of sugar mommas start dancing in his head. My most sincere wish is to collect as many of those vignettes as possible before the kids start locking their doors and running for cover the moment they catch sight of me. This is my gift from heaven; better than a gallery of Monets, better than a wall full of honors, degrees and achievements. I will always be willing to throw all the parchment away for one more sight of brown and blond strands of silk floating across each other on the pillow.

Include Your Family in Your Dreams

Unless you're honest about your dreams and aspirations with even your youngest kids, they are bound to see your career, hobby, or continued education as the bogeyman who stands between you and their endless needs. Here's your chance to accomplish two incredible mothering feats: You can share with them the joy and identity, not to mention the money, you derive from being Mommy. Do your best never to set up a conflict between work and kids. If you must miss a field trip, don't say, "I wish I could go with you all to the post office, but my mean boss insists that I work." Own up to your choice to spend a certain amount of time away from the family. Even if you're stuck in a job you absolutely can't lose because of the great benefits program and overtime policy, that should remain your little secret. No kid takes kindly to a boss who browbeats his beloved mommy.

Remember, too, that you are modeling life choices for your children, especially your daughters, every day. I have never yet met a mother who wanted to pass on to her little girls the message that it's ludicrous to hope for a career that makes them proud, in control of their lives, and is commensurate with their skills and abilities. We've already paid for that right, Girlfriends, and our daughters deserve to believe that our efforts bought them a glorious future.

At this still cooperative and adoring age, you will discover that your kids are willing to do anything, from ordering in Chinese food to allowing you to sleep an hour later on Sunday morning to assist you in getting your "chores" done so that more fun can take place later. Not only are they physically and mentally ready to pick up some laundry-folding slack, but they are usually bursting with pride over their particular contribution toward freeing up the favorite gal from her household duties so that she can participate in their thrilling lives.

It's not an impossible dream, especially if you begin teaching your family early on that your freedom to applaud each other at sports, devote a lunch hour to hear your big brother get his chops as the campus disc jockey, and teach your little sister a dance routine that's guaranteed to get her on the prestigious dance team is the direct result of each member chipping in to provide the details of household life. Sometimes, if we're really blessed, we work for its intrinsic joy. Other times, we work to clear a space for the fun that will come after. Please, never set an example for your kids that fun must be curtailed until we've beaten the lime deposits in our shower, 'cause there's always more lime where that came from.

And for you Girlfriends who suffer from my own mental illness of not deserving time that is no more productive than scooping up stray dog doo from your son's soccer field—our challenge is to use the scooping as a sort of decompression from our normal frenzy to achieve the Mommy Zen of being on the field with our future and sensing gratitude for the opportunity.

Perhaps this is what the real difference is between quality and quantity time. All our kids want from us, aside from a ride and a cold bottle of Gatorade, is for us to bear witness to their lives. They need to know that we see who they are, how they rise, and how much they need us when things get all bolluxed up. As my Girlfriend Linda said at the last soccer game, "I figure that if I've got an icepack, a Band-Aid, and some open arms, I can meet just about any emotional emergency."

We already know that none of us is available, or even motivated, to bear witness to every single thing our kids do. That's so okay, Girlfriends. The most important lesson in this chapter is to adjust your way of thinking to recognizing that the special times you spend with your family are even better gifts to you from you than that infamous bubble bath. You have plenty of bubbles in your future, but the rest of this drama is playing itself out in supersonic speed. We deserve to reprioritize our lives to make sure that we participate in the high drama of the lives of our progeny. Trust me, there will come a time when those recollections, videos and photos are all you have left.

The drama may be pretty undramatic at times, filled with a shared drive-through meal here and there, a joke exchanged in the car, and a longer-than-usual bedtime cuddle where you compare feet with your kids and point out that their little pork chops are a genetic gift from Grandma Gladys. And more often than not, as casual as it seems, it will have to be achieved with more planning than the docking of the Space Shuttle with the Space Station. Don't let this lessen your resolve. Turn off the cell phone, march out of the office as soon as your virtual presence is enough, and when you finally reunite with the family, make it the only show in town, then wrap it up with our own private decompression.

They Like Us, They Really Like Us

Sure, the kids will remember these moments for the rest of their lives, but we parents will chew them over and over like magic lotus leaves, reminding us of a time when our purpose was clear and true. So if it seems like the rest of your grooving is on ice for a while, keep the faith—the thaw will come before you know it. These years, my treasured Girlfriends, are among the few promised us by Mother Nature to be so obviously vital and our contributions so irrefutably essential that we are free to dive right in headfirst and enjoy the cool, clear waters. Best of all, these are the years when our kids still want nothing more than to welcome us into their pools. As the mother of a budding teenager, I'm here to prepare you for the years right around the corner when they won't even want to tell us where the pool's located, let alone invite you in. (But more about that in *The Girlfriends' Guide to Teenagers,* the next book in this series.)

We're still the luckiest ones. We have children who can feed themselves, handle their toileting completely alone, know all the U.S. Presidents in chronological order, and can make their own Ramen noodles in the microwave. But they are also incredibly communicative (meaning they can tattle on their siblings), they still think that they want to marry Mommy and Daddy when they grow up, and will give you a gentle heads-up if you are leaving the house with lipstick on your teeth. They're right up there with Girlfriends with the understanding loyalty, and they're almost always happy to see you.

Take your cues from your very generous mate, if he's still in the picture, and your kids and involve them in making your choices between their needs and your own. I swear, it's a lot easier to divide up the Mommy Pie if the rest of the family feels their concerns have been taken into account. Yes, you may only be able to make one soccer practice a week, no Brownies meetings, and one dinner out with your husband's clients, but the whole family will be aware of how you struggled to allocate your time and that each person's needs were factored in equally.

Your Piece of the Pie

After all the best Girlfriend advice we can come up with, you will probably still notice that no one has swooped in at the last minute to stand up for the preservation of your personal time. The first revelation here is that it's up to each of us to act as our own advocates. We are the only ones who know how much soul-sustaining time we need to keep functioning as the locomotives that pull the family train. Go ahead and claim three predawn sessions on the treadmill if you're up to it, but if you discover that your fitness program can be no more organized than taking a couple of laps around the soccer field during your child's practice, taking stairs rather than elevators whenever possible, and lifting some light weights while you're watching *Will and Grace*, then that's got to be enough for now.

Never forget that this stage of mommy adolescence is as fleeting as the nursing or the toddler years. It won't be long before your children are driving themselves to school and spending the rest of the afternoon "doing homework" with their buds. At that point, you will be able to do anything from prepare for a full marathon to golfing eighteen holes a day, assuming you get out of the office before the sun goes down. In case you haven't noticed it yet, this book is intended to transition you from being the lifeblood of your kids to being the one who gives them a Band-Aid when they've shaved too closely and their own life blood is spewing out. It's about a four- or five-year adolescence for us moms, but it passes in the time it takes for a twelve-year molar to pop through your preteen's gum. And those underarm and pubic hairs, well, suffice it to say that they appear as rapidly as a rampant case of chicken pox.

They certainly don't *look* like they need us as urgently as before, but they do, so hang on, Girlfriends. Parental legend has it that our kids are our own until the age of thirteen, upon which point they belong to their peers. So, as tempting as it may be to assume they're ready to function without us, freeing us up to learn the piano and read all of Oprah's Book Club picks, we still have a few years to go. Go ahead and start preparing for our next life, but accept that it isn't really here yet. Whatever you do, don't rush this stage of "middling" kids and "adolescent" parents, because it doesn't get any more fun than this—at least not as far as I can see.

Postscript

R ight before school started again in the fall, my husband and I took the family, which included our four kids plus our oldest son's best friend, Bennett (if you don't know it already, preteens and teens seem to be biologically unable to spend long periods of time away from people who are like-minded and equally disdainful of the "kiddie" activities that parents are infamous for planning on vacation). Take my word for it, there will come a time in your family planning when you realize it's actually *easier* on the parents when they bring a soul mate for their adolescent than to actually *listen* to all the reasons they don't want to go down to the pool with you and would rather stay up in the room, sleeping late and watching old Three Stooges movies on the inroom-movies. Actually, it turns out that the biggest payoff of going on vacation with a "bud" is most undeniable when the two of them ooze out of bed and walk down to the beach or the rec room or wherever else kids their age congregate.

Mind you, while I had a couple of pretty big kids in my possession, I was still the only one with the driver's license and the credit card. That meant, no matter how independent and disconnected to our family pod they considered themselves, they relied on my husband and me for trips to town, for bowling outings, and to organize their scuba dives and surfing lessons. I have no pride—I was willing to do anything as long as I was invited to play with them from time to time. I just love seventh graders (which Jamie now is) and am mystified by how they talk and whether they've kissed a girl on the lips yet.

One night, as I was rubbing aloe vera into my burned shoulders and popping the sand blisters that had been scorched into my feet after a surfing lesson, in which my primary task was finding the instructor and tipping him, then hiding about twenty-five yards down the beach with the other four little kids, I wondered aloud to my husband, who takes to water as enthusiastically as a cat, why I was more tired and busy on this vacation than I'd been at home.

"Because this isn't a vacation," he replied sagely. "This is travel with children. You're not going to have another vacation again until the two of us can go away alone together without leaving a child behind who is taking the PSAT test."

"Then why the hell do we go to this much trouble and spend this much money, considering we're going to want to take to our beds for a week when we finally get home?" I whined.

"Because you're making their memories and we should consider ourselves lucky just to be able to watch, even if it means standing on hot sand and holding their towels and snorkels. They're all finally old enough to remember every family trip we take, and they'll cherish it as much as I cherished going to Wilkes-Barre, Pennsylvania, to stay at a motel near a trotter horse track when I was their age. I can still feel the thrill of staying someplace with an in-the-ground pool and a Jacuzzi. I guess the only way my parents could stand it was because they could gamble every afternoon. There were six guys in one motel room and six women in the other, and I remember being held down by two of my brother-in-law's friends so that they could fart on me. *It was wonderful!*"

273

What more can I add to that insight into one of life's truths? We're living in that precious part of life when the fun part is not to be found in the spa, lounging around the pool, or sleeping late without interruption. It's still too early for all six (or seven) of us to want to hit the links at the same time. We're not ready to go out as a family to sample local cuisine and really like it, and moonlight cruises as a group are rushed to us and boring to them. We may not be there, but we're somewhere I suspect is even more wonderful and rare.

I spent our "un-vacation" teaching our six-year-old to breathe through a snorkel. I scuba-dived with my bigger kids and took underwater pictures as they had their first (harmless) shark encounter and felt braver than Crocodile Dundee. I watched the girls get their hair cornrowed beside the pool and the boys flirt with preteen girls in the Jacuzzi. Best of all, I had the privilege of watching them all lose themselves in the carefree life of looking for sea turtles and dolphins, hike to waterfalls, and dream about what it must have been like for the stalwart American missionaries to sail from Boston to Maui on very small and fragile ships. I would have given anything to be them, but being *with* them was almost as good.

I've been to Hawaii before this last visit, but I don't think I ever saw it as clearly or tasted it so succulently as I did this last time. Seeing the world's beauty is a thrill any time, but it's ten times more wonderful when you get to show it off to the eager children to whom you'd give the entire universe without hesitation. A sunset is a lovely thing, but it takes on a heart-piercing poignancy when you see all the colors reflected on the smooth faces of your kids. I'm so grateful for the front-row seat I have in their discoveries that I'll gladly give up days of suntan and piña coladas for as long as they'll let me watch. This is, perhaps, the "grooviest" part of being a mother. They're launched now and ready to play with us.

Index